THE WORLD OF
JAPANESE
BUSINESS

BY THE SAME AUTHORS:

Japanese Securities Markets (T.F.M.A.)
A Financial History of Modern Japan (T.F.M.A.)
The English Law of Quasi-Contract (N.K.)
Joint Ventures in Japan (N.K.)

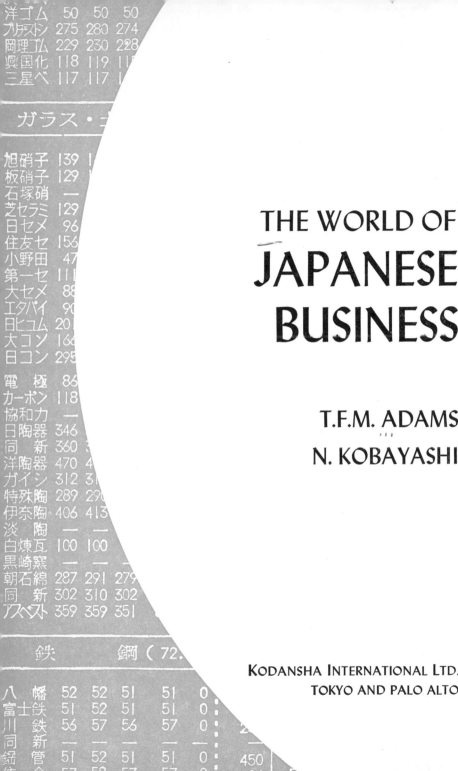

THE WORLD OF
JAPANESE
BUSINESS

T.F.M. ADAMS

N. KOBAYASHI

KODANSHA INTERNATIONAL LTD.
TOKYO AND PALO ALTO

Distributed in the British Commonwealth (excluding Canada) by Ward Lock & Company Ltd., London and Sydney; in Continental Europe by Boxerbooks Inc., Zurich; and in the Far East by Japan Publications Trading Co., C. P. O. Box 722, Tokyo.

Published by Kodansha International Ltd., 2–12–21, Otowa, Bunkyo-ku, Tokyo, Japan and Kodansha International/ USA Ltd., 577 College Avenue, Palo Alto, California 94306.

Library of Congress Catalog Card No. 71–82661
SBN 87011–091–8
First edition, 1969.

Contents

Foreword

Dr. David Riesman, in his book *Conversations in Japan*, remarks: "We returned, naturally enough, more puzzled by Japan than when we came." If so skilled and acute an observer as Dr. Riesman admits to being puzzled, then surely a mere businessman ought to refrain from attempting to explain what Dr. Riesman calls the "mysteries and discontinuities" of Japan. Yet perhaps I have an advantage or two that Dr. Riesman lacked, for I have been actively concerned with things Japanese for over three decades, and for nearly a quarter of a century have had daily dealings with Japan's businessmen. Acting as a go-between, what the Japanese call a *baishakunin*, I have, I believe, made East and West understand each other a little better (if not meet); I have put together more successful joint ventures, license agreements, and trade arrangements in Japan than, I modestly assert, any other person; I have acted mainly for foreign companies but also for Japanese corporations, and I have sat on the boards of directors of several joint venture companies; also, over the years I built up a successful and stimulating business. Thus, I have acquired—if not wisdom—at least experience. So I acceded to the requests of many foreign business friends to put the results of that experience into a book. What they want, of course, is help in understanding Japan, her people and her business structure so that they themselves will find it easier to live and work here and achieve the success they came out for. So, "For my fellowmen," in Goethe's phrase, "I would like to say a few *sensible* words," (the italics are mine) in the hope that they will help to such understanding.

It is important for the foreign businessman to realize that the horror stories he has heard about Japan are not all true. How could they be, since there are now over seven hundred joint ventures and four thousand American license agreements operating in Japan? Some of the companies doing business successfully in Japan are among *Fortune's* first five hundred. It is only a question of learning how. *Kiku wa ittoki no haji, kikanu wa issho no haji,* say the Japanese: "To ask may be a momentary shame, but not to ask and remain ignorant is a lifelong shame." In a book published by the Smithsonian Institute in 1943, Mr. John F. Embree wrote: "The people of Japan have suddenly forced themselves upon the attention of a nation whose citizens have known little or nothing of them in the past, or have regarded them as quaint Gilbert and Sullivan folk in *kimono* who could never really learn how to fly an airplane. We have learned to our cost the error of this attitude." If international marketing men from Detroit or Birmingham don't also learn that their way of doing things is not necessarily right and the Japanese way not necessarily wrong, one of these days there will be very few problems of international marketing for the boys from Detroit or Birmingham to worry about. The Japanese—in the Far East, at least—will have solved them all.

To present as unbiased a picture as possible of the world of Japanese business, the publishers and I felt it would be useful to have the opinions of a knowledgeable Japanese. In this we have been fortunate to secure the collaboration of Dr. Noritake Kobayashi, who has contributed three highly illuminating chapters to the book. Although I am not in complete agreement with certain of Dr. Kobayashi's opinions, they are here given as he wrote them. A difference of opinion is never unhealthy, and I have no doubt that many of my readers will find themselves differing from me. I admit that I am prejudiced (a man without prejudices is like a snake with legs); undoubtedly I am prejudiced in favor of certain

8

methods the Japanese have evolved for solving problems in their own way. The proof that these methods are successful is the success of the Japanese economy. The complaints of many Western businessmen, such as those about the managerial gap in Japan or her archaic marketing system, may in fact be no more than differences in national ways of doing things. If Japan, as many Westerners insist, does everything wrong, how has she achieved her almost incredible post-war success? Cheap labor? It's no cheaper in Japan than it is in the United Kingdom or Italy, and wages are higher here than in many other countries.

The fact is, of course, that Japan has an extremely tight society of the kind that Dr. Kobayashi calls "relationistic," and as a result of the nature of the Japanese society, there is very little of the famed "mobility" that we in the West find so highly desirable. It may be right for us, but quite obviously—as performance indicates—it would not be right for Japan. I would like to suggest that foreign businessmen, when they come to Japan, spend less time complaining about the muddle of Japanese business and more time examining its obvious advantages. They might then find at least a partial answer to the apparently unanswerable question of how this "diligent and disciplined people" has been able not only to recover from a disastrous defeat but also to build in a few short years what is now the third largest industrial complex in the world—a complex that will probably give rise within the next couple of decades to the world's second post-industrial state.

This book could not have been written without the valuable help of many people. I would particularly like to thank Dr. Iwao Hoshii; Mr. K. Hoketsu; Mr. Y. Nohagi; the Misses Hotta, Koike and Tanaka, and then, my wife of long years whose patience passeth all understanding.

T.F.M. ADAMS

Tokyo, 1969

THROUGH

WESTERN

EYES

ACKNOWLEDGEMENTS:
Acknowledgements are due to those publications from which I have quoted; they are listed at the end of the book. Also to Carl Boehringer and the American Chamber of Commerce in Japan; to Handel Evans and Richard Rabinowitz, both of whom I have quoted. In particular I must thank Yusuke Kashiwagi, Vice Minister of Finance for International Affairs and Aritoshi Soejima, Counsellor of the Ministry of Finance, who were so helpful and generous with their time. (T.F.M.A.)

A World of Differences ▍

*"Life cannot subsist in Society but
by Reciprocal Concessions."*
—*Samuel Johnson*

The year 1968, the centenary of the Meiji Restoration, saw the close of a hundred years of growth in the Japanese economy which has been called miraculous—a *wirtschaftswunder*, to use the German phrase. It has been both the admiration and the envy of other countries of the world. From an economically feudal – nation in 1868, Japan has become one of the world's foremost industrial states and the chief producer of several heavy industrial products, such as ships. Today Japan owns more tankers than any other country apart from the United States; it is third in merchant shipping and in steel production, following the two great giants, the United States and the Soviet Union. In the manufacture of automobiles it has recently risen to second place, surpassing both the United Kingdom and West Germany. A formidable accomplishment, indeed, for a nation that, when it wanted to travel a hundred years ago, walked or was carried in palanquins or rode horseback; and when it went to sea to fish, used sail!

Of the top hundred firms in the world today, seventeen are Japanese, while twenty-six Japanese firms figure in the second hundred, making a total of nearly a quarter of the world's chief two hundred businesses, although Japan's population is only a hundred million and its total area is about equivalent to that of California. Further, as the four main islands are extremely mountainous, only a small proportion of land (approximately 16 percent) is available for either agriculture or industry. Yet Japan today is the third most productive industrial state in the world. And it boasts, perhaps to the chagrin of General de Gaulle, a tower taller than the Eiffel Tower.

One consequence of this economic expansion has been, of course, expanded contact with the West. Hundreds of millions of dollars in trade arrangements have been negotiated between Japanese and American businessmen. Import and export trade alone totals some five billion dollars annually. Japan is, after Canada, America's best customer, as America is hers. There are now in existence over seven hundred Japanese-American joint-venture companies. In 1967, eighty-nine new joint ventures were established, and there were 169 cases of acquisition of Japanese corporate stocks (not including individual or institutional purchases through the stock market).

In 1959, only about a hundred technological agreements were concluded; in the period between 1960 and 1962, the figure leapt to over three hundred a year; and in the following two years, to over five hundred a year. In fiscal 1966, the number of cases of induction of technical knowledge reached 1,153. About 66 percent of such techniques came from the United States, followed by West Germany, Switzerland, Britain, France, and the Netherlands. The value of such contracts during the period 1950–1966 amounted to over 1.2 billion dollars, the United States again being the heaviest contributor.

During the occupation that followed the end of the Pacific War, there lived in Japan up to half a million or more foreign soldiers, civilians, and their dependents. The United States armed forces supported at one time over a million Japanese, directly or indirectly. It may be supposed that unmarried troops supported even more, but such statistics are not available. In any case, there were a very great number of service men and their families in Japan, all of whom communicated in one way or another with the people amongst whom they lived.

Since that time the picture has broadened considerably. There are innumerable solely owned foreign businesses, both large and small, in Japan today, and there are over fifteen hundred branches of foreign firms, mainly American. There are bankers, lawyers, certified public accountants, surveyors, engineers, airline and shipping men, advertising and public relations men, designers, entertainers, restauranteurs, newsmen, salesmen, consultants, and other pedlars of every commodity and service. There is an inevitable and constant flow between the West and Japan of executives and of management, marketing, legal, fiscal, and technical personnel. The jetliner has so shrunk the world in recent years that the dialogue between Japan and the West is never still.

Nor, of course, is the dialogue within Japan itself between Japanese businessmen and their Western counterparts—here again, largely American. In attempts to negotiate and finalize agreements, they spend thousands of tedious hours at conference tables, consuming thousands of cups of tea and coffee and thousands of glasses of soft drinks. Much of this time is spent in attempting to overcome the formidable barrier of language and the even more rugged one arising from two differing ways of life and thought.

The language barrier is serious in itself, as the Japanese language is both very complex and very vague. Few foreigners ever master it, and sometimes the Japanese themselves have difficulty in understanding each other. Confucius, who said many things, said, "Clarity in language is everything," but it is doubtful that the Japanese, however much they admire the Chinese sage, have accepted his dictum. Sometimes, in listening to Japanese, I am reminded of what Scaliger is reported to have remarked of the Basques: "They are said to understand one another, but I don't believe a word of it."

At the same time, while many thousands of Japanese have worked for Americans and so have acquired a little English, and while the force of Western ideas and technology burst with stunning force on post-war Japanese youth, the actual impact of Westernization upon the Japanese people remains superficial and has had little or no effect upon their fundamental thought processes. Thus, the foreign businessman, while he may understand what is being said or what is being conveyed to him by an interpreter (which is not necessarily the same thing), is continually astonished, baffled, or frustrated by what appears to be the motivation behind the words.

If he is a resident executive who has daily dealings with Japanese businessmen and bureaucrats, or with his own partners or employees and their labor unions, his nerves will inevitably fray and his temper grow short. Yet, despite his confusion and his despair, he must persevere in his attempts to fathom the processes of Japanese thought. I do not believe that he will ever be altogether successful, but if he is sufficiently resilient, tolerant, and sensitive, he will acquire a kind of intuitive feeling; he will adapt to Japanese life, develop an empathy, and his own life in consequence will become easier. He will come to realize that we must consider mankind, to paraphrase Dr. Johnson, not as we wish them to be, but as we find them.

Another source of irritation will, of course, be the resident executive's dealings with his head office back in that "other country," and sometimes those dealings are a source of greater irritation than the problems he encounters in handling his Japanese associates, since the ability he may eventually acquire (to live and work amicably and fruitfully with the Japanese) may be largely intuitive and hence incommunicable to those back home. He will not be able to explain to them, in a rational "Western" way why his method is the right one and theirs is wrong. But that, as I say, is "another country"—and not one to be dealt with here.

There are innumerable and interminable studies of the problems and the difficulties that confront a Westerner who comes to do business in Japan. Self-proclaimed "experts" on the subject burst forth and fall like cherry blossoms (although in perhaps even greater abundance). Many years ago, a certain Mr. Gifford Palgrave suggested that eight weeks' residence is the exact period necessary in order to become an expert on Japan.[1] Many of the "experts" write books on how to conduct business in Japan, do-it-yourself manuals that have a certain credence among the ill-informed. The fact remains, however, that there is no serious work in English that adequately investigates and explains the world of Japanese management, the people who become managers and how they succeed in doing so, and then relates the manager to his place in his enterprise and the place of that enterprise in the overall industrial society of Japan. The first thing that must be considered is the basic thought processes of the people themselves; then one must look into the pressures that influence them, that dictate certain of their actions, and that affect their decisions—if it can truthfully be said that a Japanese manager makes decisions. It is my intention in this book to provide a clue or two that may possibly lead to some tentative answers to the thorny question of how to do business in Japan or at least to cause our readers to think.

I use the word "clue" advisedly—for I doubt that there can ever be any definitive answer. No matter what the "experts" say, the subject is in itself too complex for any Westerner to fathom completely—at least in a single lifetime. And most of the experts have spent very little of their time in Japan living among the Japanese; they have limited themselves mainly to academic study. Ruth Benedict, for instance, wrote her book *The Chrysanthemum and the Sword*, I believe, entirely in the United States. Others who have written articles explaining the Japanese have lived in Japan for only short periods. Most of the "experts" on Japan's economy and sociology do not live here; they *visit*. There is a vast difference. "Experience," Carlyle said, "is the only teacher, but the school fees come high." Or, to quote an Asiatic on the subject of the Japanese, Sun Yat Sen remarked of them that "to act [with them] is easy, but to know [them] is difficult."

Yet, to know is to understand! That is why—although it may be impossible for any Westerner to *know* the life of Japan truly and wholly—the businessman who wants to live in Japan and do business with the Japanese must make continuing efforts. To understand at least something of Japanese social psychology and of the many pressures and influences which play upon the Japanese worker and manager alike would not only improve communications but would also facilitate international trade and trade relations.

Perhaps, in the circumstances, it is remarkable that so much has already been done, for many billions of dollars have been traded, many factories built, many plants and processes developed, many new sources of materials found and exploited, many new products discovered and marketed—all through some form of cooperation, inadequate though it may be. Obviously, some Japanese and some Americans have learned to live and work together in their ventures, but a great deal more could be done, and done more smoothly, if there were better understanding between the two groups.

An even greater need for better understanding may lie with the bureaucrats, for the truth is that our businessmen seem to have done better in that direction than our government officials—a fact, I believe, George Kennan realized. Quite simply, the successful American businessman who has lived long years in Japan finds it essential to learn to be adaptable. He makes many Japanese acquaintances and perhaps one or two good friends, who give him their affection and loyalty. His age and experience entitle him to a certain respect. In other words, he will have found a niche in which he can profitably live and work; he will not only have won the respect of his Japanese friends and acquaintances but he will also have achieved one of man's greatest goals—a sympathetic awareness of the human situation and a feeling of empathy with humanity at large.

One of the first things that the perceptive foreigner learns is that the Japanese and the Westerner think differently because they *are* different. Very different indeed! Once he realizes this fact, he must learn to accept it and not fight it. Those who fail to do so invent quite astonishing explanations for their inability to get on with the Japanese; they will claim that the Japanese are dishonest, unethical, immoral, devious, inscrutable, or downright stupid. General MacArthur, in his messianic wisdom, stated that the average Japanese man had a mental age of twelve! It is saddening to realize how prejudiced an extremely competent man can be—but that, perhaps, is the path that great generals are doomed to travel.

The American in Japan, if he is to be successful, cannot afford himself the luxury of such prejudices. He must not only admit and accept the fact that Westerners and Japanese think differently because they are different, but must make the next and far more difficult admission that the existence of this difference does not necessarily mean the Westerner is right and the Japanese wrong. Perhaps to acquire sufficient dispassion to deny ingrained prejudice is one of the most difficult things a man who lives outside his own country is called upon to do. But do it he must, if he is to live successfully in a country like Japan. Presumably the Japanese businessman experiences the same difficulty in coming to a decision that he is wrong where the Westerner may be right—but the Japanese businessman, after all, is doing business in his own country. He is only behaving as all other Japanese behave; he can hardly be expected to conform to ways and means that have been found successful in Peoria, Illinois.

Mr. M. Kanno, vice-president of the highly influential Japan Business and Industry Advisory Committee, in answering criticism voiced by a visiting American "expert" on the progress on liberalization, stated: "I ask you to be patient and not to goad us. If you do, I'm afraid you will be courting danger—you have no doubt heard of 'oriental emotionalism.' We may deserve criticism but touching a sore point won't help you, or anybody else."[2] The warning, it seems to me, is clear—and so is the justification for the warning.

Few Western scholars, so called, seem to understand this "oriental emotionalism" and the intense pride that is innate in the Japanese character. The Westerner who has accepted the fact that neither he nor the Japanese is necessarily right or wrong, but only *different*, is on the path to understanding. If, through daily contact, he learns tolerance, patience, and sensitivity to Japanese reaction, he can become a first-rate ambassador, not only for his company but for his country as well. If, on the other hand, as all too many hurried visitors do, he adopts a dictatorial or supercilious attitude, if he speaks down to the Japanese as though they are students in school, or treats them as uneducated and stupid inferiors, he will invariably call forth the reaction of "oriental emotionalism"—at which point all useful communication ceases.

This, certainly, was a contributing factor in the attack on Pearl Harbor!

Why, indeed, did Japan take the fatal step of declaring war on America when so many influential Japanese wished only to avoid it? The debate on that question could go on forever. Truly the jingoists and militarists played their role, inflaming public sentiment against foreigners who had "humiliated" the country. The pro-war party went all the way back to the "Black Ships" and the "unequal" treaties forced on Japan by the United States; they ranted about the "sell-out" of Japan by Theodore Roosevelt at Portsmouth after the war with Russia in 1905 (though wiser heads realized that Japan had come well out of an impossible situation); they described the treatment of the Japanese as inferiors at the Washington Naval Conference; they execrated the insulting Oriental Exclusion Act; they condemned what they called improper interference in Japan's "legitimate aspirations" in Manchuria and consequent American support of the enemy in the China Incident. There were many old wounds to be re-opened.

Then came belligerent warnings from Franklin Roosevelt, which were followed by an embargo and a virtual ultimatum. The Japanese reaction was that the United States was attempting to force them to accept American-dictated terms, leaving no door open for further negotiation. Yet the Japanese continued to look for some suggestion that the door was, in fact, still open, that communication was still possible, and at the last moment sent Mr. Kurusu to Washington in the hope of obtaining such a suggestion. The impasse that resulted, the failure in communication, made the decision to go to war irreversible. To take the grave decision to accept the ultimatum was not within the Japanese character: war therefore became inevitable, even if it was destined to mean national suicide.

No one, in fact, was strong enough to reverse a decision that had already been made; like a snowball running downhill, the movement irresistibly gathered momentum until it became disaster—despite the clear desire of many highly influential men to avoid the war. This snowball quality is inherent in the Japanese character and affects all decision-making, or lack of it, from high government policy down to daily business operations. This will be discussed at some length later.

I should not like to give the impression that I believe adaptation to Japanese life is beyond the power of the average businessman. What is remarkable, considering the diversity of background and prejudice, is how many have succeeded. In this, let me say at once, they have had the wise and frequent assistance of their Japanese counterparts. Those who fail to make adequate use of this assistance usually must leave after a short time. They are rarely missed.

Even those who are destined to success often spend their first months complaining, as do their wives, that the Japanese do everything wrong. But is it only a one-way street? Many Japanese, I have no doubt, are convinced that *we* do everything wrong— although they are too polite to tell us so to our faces.

Yet they certainly dissect us among themselves as we dissect them. Not being Japanese, I cannot say with any assurance what they think about us, but after some twenty-three years of almost daily communication, I may perhaps be allowed to have an idea or two, and I would like here, at the risk of earning a few opprobrious epithets, to suggest what I imagine Japanese think and say about us.

In order to do that, I shall invent a situation, but one which is not unusual. An American company and a Japanese company have undertaken a joint venture, which is now in operation. The American company, having the right to appoint a director of the joint company, has announced that Mr. John Smith, an expert on management and marketing, is being sent to sit on the Board of Directors and act as the Director from the Western side. His arrival is imminent. The President of the joint venture company, seconded from the Japanese parent company, calls a meeting of his chief officers and immediate subordinates. The time of year is a muggy Japanese summer. Any summer . . .

The President speaks:

"*Minasan*. In this extremely hot, sultry weather I must apologize deeply for asking you to come here today, since I know you are all extremely busy in advancing the affairs of our company. An occasion, however, has arisen which requires the mutual understanding and cooperation of all of us.

"I refer to the imminent arrival of the officer, Mr. Smith, designated by our esteemed Western partner. Unlike the technicians, with whom we are usually able to work quite amicably, Mr. Smith will concern himself with our management and marketing methods, our productivity and sales, and our business customs! And unlike other officers who have come and gone in the past, Mr. Smith is scheduled to remain for a considerable time. Perhaps for several years!

"We must all, therefore, endeavor to understand him and to cooperate with him. But that may not be easy! Since only a few of you have been to the United States, I shall try to tell you something about the Americans, and how they think and act in ways that are altogether different from our ways. This will, I hope, enable you to understand Mr. Smith better if by his actions he attempts to disrupt our harmony, which must be maintained.

"Let me first give a few examples of ways in which the Americans act differently from us. Although some of these examples may seem insignificant, when taken together they indicate a profound difference. All, Americans and Japanese, share the same need for a home, a shelter, but observe how unlike us the Americans are in providing that shelter. When a Japanese carpenter saws a piece of wood, he cuts it on the upswing, but an American carpenter cuts it on the downswing! He smoothes the wood by pushing the plane away from him, while our carpenters pull the plane toward them. How could two ways be more different?

"Or consider another basic need, that for a toilet. The American sits on a high toilet, facing outward, away from the wall, whereas our toilets are low and we sit in a natural position, facing the wall.

"There are many other opposites, such as the way Americans knock on a door or beckon to people or count on their fingers. They may even whistle at people! We whistle only at dogs. Americans read and write backwards, and their books are printed backwards and in horizontal rather than vertical lines. They even reply 'yes' when they should logically say 'no.' What then is one to expect of their thinking but that it, like their reading and writing, also moves backward as a crab does?

"I do not have the time to give the many other examples that leap to mind, but I think those I have given demonstrate how profoundly different Americans are from us, and in ways that are not easily changed.

"Bear in mind also that there is no concept of an American people to be compared with our own. Nor has the American a homogeneous culture like ours, but instead he has a hundred sub-cultures. Thus he is unable to understand his own culture—how then can he understand ours, which is two thousand years old?

"The invaders of North America killed off ninety percent or more of those who might truly be called natives. We have never committed a similar wickedness! Instead, we have preserved the purity of our Yamato race by the enclosure of our country, cutting it off from the rest of the world. It was only the brashness and the might of the Westerners that forced us, reluctantly, to admit them to our land. The bamboo, however, though it bends in the typhoon, springs back afterwards. That is something for you to keep in mind.

"Perhaps the most difficult problem of all arises from the American approach to business and to what the Americans term 'values.' Mr. Smith, in other words, will be coming to Japan for his own personal benefit—to impress his company back home so that he may earn more money and gain more power and, incidentally, keep from being 'fired,' a strange term. But it is an American preoccupation that we do not share in Japan.

"We do not have to worry about advancement or about suddenly finding that we have no job. We know that advancement comes naturally with age and experience; we know that as a result of our spiritual harmony we win material goals. We do not have the horrible daily fear of insecurity that plagues the American employee, and even the manager and executive. The constant struggle to advance, to gain position and wealth, is termed by the Americans themselves 'the executive jungle' or 'the rat-race.' What a sad state of affairs! We should feel pity for the Americans, who must go into this jungle or this rat-race in order to survive—particularly since many of them are very likable.

"The American, furthermore, is convinced that he knows how to do things better than we, and so he will try to force us to work according to formulae he learned at a school or in his company. He will find it difficult, if not impossible, to understand that here in Japan we work as a group, not as individuals. Therefore we do not fit Mr. Smith's formulae. Nor do the Japanese people respond to the same inducements as Americans, although this, too, Mr. Smith will probably not believe. He will try to push you into various types of embarrassing and aggressive sales maneuvers and ways of advertising that we would describe as 'very dry.'* This tactic must of course be resisted, but courteously, with smiles and ostensible agreement. Then we will do, as we have always done, what is best for the company. Perhaps, if he is the right type of person, he will ultimately come to understand.

"I should like to mention two other characteristically American qualities, a knowledge of which may help you to get on with Mr. Smith. Americans appear to be convinced that almost everything of value was invented or discovered in America; they do not look deeply enough to see their error. Take Kleenex, for example: Americans naturally suppose it to be an American invention. But we Japanese, as you know, have been using disposable tissues, which we call *hanagami*, for over seven hundred years! Or consider, prefabricated houses, which Americans think they invented. The fact is, every Japanese house that was ever built is prefabricated. Generations ago we worked out standardized measurements, and materials have always been made or cut to size before they reach the house site. If this is not prefabrication, what is it?

"Another observation about the Americans is that they are highly sentimental, while they think of us as being inscrutable.

---

*"Dry," as opposed to "not dry," is an adjective almost impossible to explain. It has the connotation of "harsh, unfeeling, cruel, insensitive to the feelings, position, pride, and rights of other."

They have no knowledge of our Oriental emotionalism, which is not aimed, as their sentimentality is, at 'love,' but rather seeks to protect the family, the clan, the company, and the nation. Mr. Smith will arrive, convinced that the American conception of democracy is the best in the world, and he will not for a moment imagine that it is not necessarily a good export item.

"One area in which we will have to instruct Mr. Smith—unobtrusively but definitely—is that of decision-making. He will want our important decisions to be made, as the Americans say, yesterday. He will not understand that important matters require long deliberation and the thoughts of many people. But if he is capable of learning, then our task will be to instruct him, so that our association prospers. If he cannot be taught, then we must arrange matters so that he is sent home, meanwhile thinking of him as a typhoon, not arguing with him; one doesn't argue with a typhoon, but bends with the wind like a bamboo and then springs back afterwards.

"In any case we will act with courtesy; we know that 'even in killing one's enemies, it is necessary to remember the proprieties.' At the same time we will remember that we also can learn and that Mr. Smith may have much to teach us. It is in the best interest of our company and our country to learn as much as we can from him. We will of course do our best to keep him happy in mind and body, and if possible to distract him with any non-company matters to which he may seem especially receptive and uncritical.

"The last matter I want to mention to you today is that we and the builders have decided upon the twenty-eighth as the day to dedicate our new building. You will note that it is *taian*, a day of good luck.

"I thank you all for coming."

Is it all nonsense, the speech that I have invented? Is it mere fanciful distortion? Some people will say so, but I ask them to remember that I have attempted to see ourselves as the Japanese do, and as we so often, in reverse, see the Japanese—as strange and sometimes incomprehensible figures. But in Japan it is we who are the strange ones, not the Japanese. We are *mezurashii*, not they.

Nor, incidentally, is the President's remark on choosing a lucky day for the dedication of the new building either nonsensical or pointless. The Japanese well know that there exist in the universe far greater forces than mere man and that the power of such forces must be acknowledged. Ever present in the Japanese mind is the possibility, or rather the probability, of unforeseen and unpredictable natural events and pressures from indefinable sources. This awareness colors the thinking of the Japanese and their decision.

When, for example, an American friend of mine died suddenly in Japan, it devolved upon me to arrange for the details of his funeral. The Japanese undertaker, when he was told the day set for the cremation, became extremely disturbed because, under the old Japanese calendar, the date chosen was a very bad one and the undertaker did not wish to send another human being, even a foreigner, on his way to eternity on such a day. I immediately agreed to change it, despite the objections of other so-called friends and the certainty of condemnation by the Church. It seemed to me that, although the day perhaps had no effect on my deceased friend, it was nonetheless of importance to living Japanese.

As a director of a real estate company, I know that the Japanese consider it only natural, *atarimae* as they say, to consult the calendar when choosing a day for ground-breaking or other ceremonies in order to be certain that it is an auspicious day. I doubt, frankly, that tenants would choose to live or work in a building if the owners and builders had neglected to take these precautions.*

The basic differences which I have suggested in this chapter are obvious, but they are further compounded by custom, habit, and tradition stemming from the remote past. Since these traditions have survived Japan's modern economic development, they continue to affect the thoughts and the actions of most members of the modern business community. A human being, after all, is an untidy bundle of the traits, habits, forces, prejudices, customs, and pressures that he has inherited from the past or recently acquired.

---

*The Australian Government decided upon an auspicious day and had the Shinto priests dedicate and purify the ground for the Australian Pavilion in EXPO '70.

Industrial Foundations 2

"Continuity with the past is a
necessity, not a duty."
—O. W. Holmes, Jr.

It is impossible to understand contemporary Japanese enterprise and management without taking a look, however cursory, at the origins of the industrial society in Japan, since many of the conditions that prevailed a hundred years ago prevail today and many of the factors that accounted for the beginning of Japanese industrialism and its rapid growth are still to be reckoned with.

The miracle, as so often happens, turns out—when clearly examined—not to have been a miracle after all: it is the result of what I call, in my role as devil's advocate, "valuable inheritances" acting upon the kind of people who were in a position to receive them at a time of "fortuitous circumstances." Even the extraordinary growth after the devastation of the war, which economists applying classical dicta find so difficult to explain, is explicable in terms of earlier Japanese history. During the remarkable period since 1950, the Japanese, it seems, did everything wrong—and yet it turned out right. Galbraith and others have used the analogy of the bumblebee which, according to the laws of aerodynamics, cannot fly, but the bumblebee, being ignorant of the laws of aerodynamics, does fly—and gathers a bit of honey as well.

First, then, the people. They are, by their very nature, hard-working, curious, dexterous, eager to learn, and ready both to adopt and to adapt. Their remarkable adaptability, which has resulted in an equally remarkable resilience to adversity, has been demonstrated almost yearly in their acceptance of and recovery from such acts of the gods as earthquakes and typhoons, tidal waves, floods, and fires. The latter were of so frequent occurrence in Tokyo that they were known, during the Tokugawa period, as "the flowers of Edo" (Edo being the former name for the present-day capital). Nor can there be omitted from any listing of the qualities that compose the character of the Japanese, their strong, occasionally headstrong, nationalism. It existed a hundred years ago, and it exists today; and it has played a crucial role in the growth of the economy, particularly where it has been acted on by external stimuli, which were sometimes disastrous but more often beneficial, by the recurrence of "fortuitous circumstances"—the recurrence, that is to say, of opportunity without excessive risk.

By the other factor—"valuable inheritances"—I do not mean inheritances of property, goods, and money (although these were important) but rather traditions of literacy and skill, of work habits and thought processes. The availability of skilled artisans and other manpower and the fact of fortuitous preconditioning enabled Japan to use and develop her "valuable inheritances" from the Tokugawa period and employ them, when circumstances dictated, toward the rapid building of an industrial society. The foundations of a vigorous nation were already laid when what appeared to be an unprecedented calamity overtook the still feudal islands. Admiral Perry appeared off Tokyo Bay.

For some two hundred years before the arrival of his "Black Ships" in 1853, Japan had maintained a state of feudal isolation, repelling all Western attempts to establish commercial or cultural relations. But with the arrival of Perry in 1853 and his return in 1854, the shogunate realized at last that the barbarian was too powerful to be repelled any longer. (Originally, I believe, the term "barbarian," meaning "foreign, strange, or different," was not in itself particularly derogatory—except in the sense that the Japanese considered all foreigners to be inferior.) The national temper at the time was to fight, to "repel the barbarian," but the shogunate accepted the fact that the barbarian was a numerous and powerful tribe and that to attempt to repel him forever would ensure defeat and humiliation. Hence the wiser decision was made to allow limited intercourse, so that the Japanese might learn all that the foreigner had to teach, thus making the country powerful enough to deal with the intruders effectively some day in the future.

It was not an easy decision for the shogunate to make or for the Japanese to accept. Anti-foreign demonstrations continued, despite the conclusion of "forced" treaties with the United States and Great Britain in 1854, and with Russia and Holland in 1855. Recalcitrant samurai, in a kind of dying exuberance, assassinated a certain number of resident foreigners—including Henry C. J. Heusken, who was secretary and translator for the first American minister, Townsend Harris—yet the process continued, slowly but inexorably. The end in view was termed *fukoku kyohei*, "a rich country and a strong army," and to this end the Japanese began to borrow and adapt all aspects of Western technology that were made available to them. Their intention was to build and modernize the economic, industrial, and particularly the military strength of the country—so that some day it would be on equal terms with the great powers of the world and so rid itself of the inferior status to which it had been relegated. This process, once it got truly under way, was found to be admirably suited to the national temperament.

When, in 1857, Townsend Harris at last forced an audience with the Shogun—the date, ironically enough, was December 7—he prepared for this momentous visit by having an artificer from a visiting American frigate make metal shoes for his horses. Apparently this was a new idea in Japan, and the Shogun arranged to borrow one of Harris' animals and soon his own horses were similarly shod—an early example of transfer of technology, and this time unpaid for.

This failure to expel the barbarian, coupled with the sad state of the national economy, the impoverishment of the people, and the moral decay of the samurai, was sufficient to bring about the collapse of the shogunate and the restoration, so-called, of the emperor. Some historians object to the word "restoration," saying that there was nothing for an emperor to be restored to, since he had had no power for hundreds of years. Yet whatever word one uses, what happened in those years was a remarkable accomplishment, as was the even more remarkable recovery after the end of the Second World War. Both situations arose out of seemingly adverse but ultimately fortunate circumstances, and both took directions that had been neither intended nor foreseen. Yet they resulted in success, success so phenomenal that the world still wonders at it.

History, after all, is made by people. Or, as Richard Aldington put it, "the true wealth of a country lies in its men and women." Japan has been unusually fortunate in that the right people have appeared when they were most crucially needed—save for the disastrous period of twentieth century jingoism. Yet just as "miracle men," to use Ralph Hewins' phrase,[3] appeared after the war to lead in the rebuilding of Japan and to help bring it to its present worldwide industrial status, so men of similar stature gathered around Emperor Meiji, possessing the vision, the courage, and the ability to foresee new directions, to formulate new policies, to reorganize virtually the entire national life, and—what would formerly have been inconceivable—to accept, in the name of the Emperor, the intrusion of the West, and its technological guidance.

Many foreigners who are not particularly well acquainted with Japanese history believe that the Emperor himself was responsible for the industrialization of the nation and point to the Meiji Constitution as evidence that the Emperor was by conviction democratic. But the fact is that here—as in all events relating to the Japanese emperor between the Restoration of 1868 and the surrender in 1945—it is difficult to determine precisely what role he played. But one may suppose, since Meiji was only a boy of fifteen when he succeeded his father in 1867, that he could not have wielded a decisive influence in the formulation of the new policies.

To unravel the myriad factors and the sometimes byzantine intrigues that resulted in the collapse of the shogunate and the "restoration" of the Emperor is beyond the scope of this book, but perhaps a word of background might be useful in understanding the "industrial revolution" after the accession of the young monarch.

Already, under his father, Emperor Komei, the foundation of power in the country was beginning to shift. For long years, the Japanese emperor had been little more than a kind of chief high priest, living in the traditional, intrigue-ridden court at Kyoto, while true power was vested in the shogun, who always governed, however, in principle at least, in the name of the emperor. The inevitable rift between these two forces, the Imperial court and the shogunate, widened with the obvious inability of the shogunate to deal effectively with the intrusive barbarians. The strong anti-foreign feeling in the country centered around the powerless but age-old symbol of Japan, the emperor. "*Sonno Joi!*" became the clarion call of the most xenophobic of the clans: "Revere the Emperor and expel the barbarians!"

It is ironic that with the accession of the new Emperor, the most bitterly anti-foreign of the provincial daimyo threw in their lot with the court nobles and effected the overthrow of the shogunate: ironic because the end result of the "restoration" of the Emperor was the firm intrusion of foreign influence in Japan and the building of a Westernized industrial state. According to Jean Lequiller,[4] this momentous shift in power was accomplished by only a score of men using what Roy Miller[5] called the "newly discovered charismatic powers of the Emperor." Everything that was done was done in his name. However, as the years passed, it seems that Meiji himself played an ever more active role in the political life of the country. There is sufficient evidence that despite his upbringing in the stultifying antiquity of the Kyoto court, he was a man of vision and intelligence. Certainly, even if only through his advisers, he served as a catalyst for the new ideas and the new adventures of the new Meiji men.

However, since he was in reality only the "charismatic power" behind the actual rulers, no moral obligation was laid upon him for final performance. (This situation reflects the typical Japanese method of decision making—i.e., a concensus decision behind the name of the legitimizing authority, in this case the Emperor.) Nonetheless, by use of this charismatic power, almost anything could be accomplished, and much was. Certainly the development of the industrial complex was an astonishing performance; Japan was fortunate, as I remarked earlier, in that the men were there to effect it.

Meiji's advisers were drawn largely from the Satsuma and Choshu clans: it was they who founded the Dajokan, the body of advisers to the Emperor, and they were the men who sparked and speeded the development and modernization of industry as well as the innumerable necessary readjustments in the whole life of the nation. This was not, as we know, an altogether new process. The shogunate, though on its last legs, had attempted much the same thing; and Japan had, in fact, as long ago as the seventh century, borrowed technology from the Chinese. But never had the process been undertaken with quite the impetus the new men gave it. Daniel L. Spencer, in a very perceptive article, writes: "A nation or people as a whole have a kind of cultural personality which makes them more or less prone to a certain line of conduct. In borrowing cultural traits from other countries [and technology is but one type, albeit a vital one, of cultural traits], a nation may show marked willingness or marked reluctance to borrow. In the case of Japan this propensity [to borrow] was quite high." He continues, a bit later: "Japan had an existing accumulated stock of technical knowledge which ante-dated western contact and enabled them to absorb foreign high-level technology."[6] Although Mr. Spencer is speaking of contemporary, post-war Japan, his comments apply equally pertinently to the Meiji period.

As early as 1871, a deputation of three was sent abroad to investigate military preparedness in both the United States and Europe, for the government had taken as its motto *fukoku kyohei*: "a wealthy country and a strong army." In America, the three Japanese inspected arms-manufacturing and the training of cavalry; in Queen Victoria's London, they admired the guards in front of Buckingham Palace; they investigated the French national arsenal; and they travelled through other advanced countries of Europe, looking at battlefields and studying recent military history. They were amazed by the state of military preparedness in the various countries. One of the three favored the adoption of the German army system, but Japan eventually was forced to accept French military advisers as a condition for the withdrawal of French warships then off the Japanese coast. Thus, the Imperial Japanese Army was modelled in its inception after the French.

A national conscription law was enforced in 1872, calling to the draft commoners as well as members of the samurai class. This was the first time non-samurai were officially required to bear arms, and the samurai were bitterly resentful of the fact that they were being treated the same as peasants and merchants. Their discontent became one of the causes of the Saigo rebellion of 1877, which was put down by government forces after a few months.

The government's defense of national conscription was based on the belief that all Japanese should share the obligation to defend Japan. The single loophole in the law—that anyone could avoid military service by paying ¥270 (roughly equivalent then to US$270.00)—was severely criticized and was soon abolished. Finally, in 1885, the government invited German military instructors to Japan, and the Imperial Army was reorganized after the German system.

The new Meiji government realized, of course, that a country, no matter how good its army, could not be militarily strong unless it was also sound economically. There was, however, not much of an economic base to build upon, although in some places, where the clans had developed certain skills, it was surprisingly good. On the whole, though, such enterprises as there were were scattered and small. In the past there had been no system for the accumulation of capital; the new government, therefore, had to supply it. Entrepreneurs, as we use the word today, did not exist in private industry; therefore, the first industrial organizations had to be government enterprises (kangyo). This supremely important fact has affected the development of all Japanese enterprises from their Meiji beginnings to the present day.

Chief emphasis was laid initially on transport and communication, engineering industries, and the production of military equipment. The government provided large sums for the construction of harbors and shipyards, roads and railroads; it opened new mines and developed existing ones; it established a communications system. It also built factories to manufacture cement, bricks, glass, chemicals, and silk filatures; it built mills for both cotton and wool; it erected sugar refineries and breweries. It bought foreign machinery and brought in foreign engineers and other specialists. This phenomenal activity—all performed by the government with borrowed Western techniques—became the basis for Japan's later astonishing technological development.

But it also required, obviously, a proliferating bureaucracy, a bureaucracy that had few management and financial skills—so that enterprises owned and operated by the government soon became heavy, unprofitable financial burdens. As early as 1880, therefore, the government wisely decided to withdraw from the operation of most industrial enterprises, disposing of almost everything but railroads, arsenals, and its communications system.[7]

In this way, plants equipped with the latest machinery and staffed by the only trained employees in the whole country, passed into private hands at ridiculously low prices and under extremely favorable long-term delayed payment conditions. Many of the recipient enterprises also received long-term subsidies. To give an example or two, a copper mine whose development had cost the government ¥540,000 was sold for ¥200,000 (payable over twenty-five years, for the mine and equipment) and ¥73,000 (payable over sixteen years for the inventory); a glass factory built at a cost of ¥189,000 was "transferred" at a price of ¥80,000, payable over fifty-five years after a deferment period of five years. Properties transferred in this manner included fifty-two factories, ten mines, fifty-one merchant vessels, and three shipyards. Thanks to such governmental largesse, these enterprises became the nuclei of the huge industrial complexes controlled by the *zaibatsu*, or big financial combines.

One of the two chief *zaibatsu* is Mitsubishi, which was formed by Yataro Iwasaki. After the "restoration," he established the Tsukumo Trading Company, the name of which he changed, in 1873, to Mitsubishi Shokai. In February 1872, the central area of Tokyo, which included Marunouchi, burned down, and the whole area became a charred and useless mass of ruins. The government moved in a contingent of troops and built barracks near the Imperial Palace grounds in Marunouchi. Later these barracks were moved to Azabu and the government offered the Marunouchi area for sale.

Coincidentally, Heigoro Shoda, chief *banto* of the Iwasaki family, happened to be in London, where, walking one day through the City, he thought what a splendid thing it would be if Tokyo had a comparable financial center. Thus, when the news reached him that Marunouchi was for sale, he telegraphed back recommending that Mitsubishi buy it. His recommendation was accepted, and the Mitsubishi Estate Company bought what came to be known as Mitsubishi-ga-hara—Mitsubishi field. Later Mitsubishi erected a number of red brick, Western-style buildings, modelled after Lombard Street in London. By 1899, Mitsubishi field became the financial and economic center of the country. Mitsubishi paid ¥1,500,000 (then about US$1,300,000) for the entire property. Today it is worth several hundred million dollars, and it is still considered as an address of prestige for any financial organization.

Another Iwasaki employee was instrumental in establishing the form that Japanese corporations were to take. This was Eiichi Shibusawa, who was sent by the shogunate in 1867 as one of a delegation to attend the Paris World Exhibition. Shibusawa, then twenty-eight years old, was an Iwasaki accountant and so was especially interested in learning Western methods not only of accountancy but also of banking, the buying and selling of securities, bookkeeping, the establishment of a joint stock company, the corporate form, and the like. He also went to London, where he was permitted to study at the Bank of England and the British Mint. It was obvious to him that Japan's methods of doing business were woefully inadequate by European standards.

He returned to Japan to find the shogunate defeated, the Emperor restored to power, and the last Tokugawa Shogun, Yoshinobu, living in seclusion at Shizuoka. Shibusawa went to Shizuoka to confer with Yoshinobu and thereafter established a semi-official

35

joint-stock company. This company developed into Japan's first *kabushiki kaisha* and was engaged in banking as well as commerce and finance.

After the *kabushiki kaisha* system was introduced by Shibusawa in the second year of the new reign, a number of similar corporations were formed. In 1873, Nihon Tsuun (known as Nittsu) was established, and two years later came the formation of the Daiichi ("First") National Bank, on Shibusawa's urgent recommendation that Japan's currency needed to be put in order. Japan's paper money had been printed in Germany (¥153 million worth in the two previous years), but now a factory was built at Takinogawa, in Tokyo, so that Japan might print her own paper money and an Italian expert was invited to come to Japan to teach the new techniques. He made copper plate portraits of senior statesmen for the new money, which by 1883, had entirely replaced the old. With English help, a new mint had been established in Osaka as far back as 1871.

Shibusawa was also instrumental in the erection, in the fifth year of the reign, of an official silk factory at Tomioka, Gunma Prefecture, whose product was intended for export. French technicians came to assist in the organization of the new factory, but—so the story goes—the girls whom they were to teach refused to work with them because the French drank red wine, and to ordinary Japanese girls it looked as though they were drinking blood! Girls of the samurai class knew better, however, and as they also were in need of money and were more conscious of the national interest, they became Japan's first silk factory workers. Once again through Shibusawa's intervention, a young Japanese who was studying at London University went to Manchester in 1880 to learn British spinning methods. When he returned, he and Shibusawa established Japan's first modern spinning factory in Osaka—the present Toyo Boseki K.K. (Toyo Spinning Co.).

In the first years of the new reign, the famous old English steamship company, the P. & O., used to make frequent calls at Nagasaki and Yokohama, but according to their log-books the traffic suddenly stopped after 1876. This was due to Mitsubishi's determined efforts to operate steamships flying the Japanese flag and to take over the liner trade. P. & O. boats once again call at Japanese ports on their round-the-world voyages, but thanks to Mitsubishi's aggressive determination it took many years for them to reenter the trade.

Yataro Iwasaki, the founder of the now huge Mitsubishi enterprises, was of samurai origin, and it has been estimated that of Tokyo's leading 250 merchant houses, forty-eight were of samurai descent. But the transition from samurai to merchant was not an easy one, and often it was a painful and disastrous failure.

The period preceding the "restoration" of the Emperor was on the whole peaceful, with the class system rigidly enforced. At the top strode the two-sworded samurai, the warrior; then came the farmer; then the artisan; and way at the bottom stood the merchant, the man engaged in "the unspeakable business of buying and selling." If the Meiji government was going to build a nation that was strong both economically and militarily, the system would have, to a certain extent, to be reversed. The merchant and the banker would have to be granted the respect that they received in other countries, and the Imperial Army would have to be composed of "warriors" of all classes. The transformation, before it was complete, was to partake of some of the elements of a revolution—generally unbloody, but a revolution nonetheless, while vestiges of the old system lingered on for many years. As recently as thirty years ago, for purposes of official records, all Japanese had to be registered as either *shizoku* (samurai) or *heimin* (ordinary people). I shall not go into the question of the *eta*, the outcasts, since they did not then, and do not now, belong anywhere in the hierarchy; recent Japanese claims that they no longer exist are, however, false.

In the fairly peaceful last days of feudal Japan, the samurai had little practical employment for their sharp swords. Apart from an occasional demonstration of their arrogance and skill by cutting down *heimin* on the highways (and later by murdering a foreigner or two), they were idle and dissolute. Their moral eclipse as a caste became final with the abolition of the clans in 1871. National conscription two years later obliterated whatever *raison d'être* they may have thought themselves still to possess, for if a peasant could become a warrior, of what use was a samurai? Further indignities were imposed on them: they were forbidden to wear swords; they were ordered to cut off their top-knots; government officials among them were required, in 1876, to wear Western clothes. Stripped of rank and privilege as of sword, top-knot, and swashbuckling dress, they were left with nothing but their claim to be the best soldiers in the land. Then even that claim was proven hollow when they were defeated by an army composed of peasants in the insurrection of 1877. The daimyo, having lost their great feudal holdings, could no longer support their retainers; the samurai, therefore, had to seek employment. But what on earth were they to do? Untrained and unskilled, they were mostly unemployable—and many, unwilling to admit that their caste had ceased to exist as a social unit, refused even to try.

But not all. There were some who accepted the new world they suddenly found themselves in—and became leaders of it. A new "establishment" came into being, led in large part by former leaders of the defunct caste. Samurai who were able to fill the new national needs and who were willing to renounce the narrow objectives of caste and clan for the infinitely wider possibilities of the new national state became the leaders who, although bound in many ways by traditions of caste and clan, aspired to build a nation based on the common tradition of the Japanese people.

The founder of the Sumitomo group gave up his samurai status in order to open a shop. The Konoike exchange house, which developed into today's Sanwa Bank, the leading house in Osaka, was founded by a samurai who went into saké-brewing. Mitsui also claims to be of samurai extraction,[8] but there seems to be some doubt about the validity of the claim. Former samurai from Ōmi province came to Tokyo, where they enjoyed such great success as shopkeepers that they were called "Ōmi robbers"—presumably because other merchants of Tokyo were envious.[9] Some samurai spoke Dutch (for, during its isolationist period, the shogunate had maintained relations of a sort with Holland even after it had broken them with all other Western countries), and some were acquainted with foreign technologies and foreign methods in industry and banking. Thus, there did exist a very real cadre of potential administrators among the samurai caste.

In making the transition from warrior to merchant, the samurai were encouraged by the fact that the new enterprises had been established by the government, acting in the name of the emperor, and were considered necessary to build a militarily strong nation. That they were, therefore, "in the national interest" solved to a certain degree the awful samurai problem of "saving face." This matter of "face," and consequent identification with the national interest, is still prevalent in the private sector, as evidenced by its closeness to government and by the weight given to the bureaucracy in both decision-making and operations. On a lower level, the objection to "trade" in the old class system affected then, and continues to affect, the Japanese attitude toward selling: salesmen were at the bottom of the totem pole. And the Japanese, to this day, are rarely good salesmen. The average "salesman" in a big company is, in fact, often little more than an order-taker; no one likes to be known simply as a salesman. Euphemisms have therefore been invented, such as "sales technicians," or "technical sales representatives," or "marketing staff."

It may be noted in passing that many of the samurai who were unable to cope with the drastically changed conditions of the early Meiji period passed into oblivion. Some became farmers. Some undertook such humble employment as umbrella-making. It was samurai of this sort who give rise to the Japanese phrase, *buke no shoho*, which means literally merely "the samurai's way of doing business" but which carries the implication that whatever he may do, the samurai has no idea how to make money, so that even if he becomes a mere umbrella-maker, he will probably still fail at the task.

Yet some samurai, perhaps foreseeing that revolutionary change was inevitable, had shifted to the merchant class even before the Meiji Restoration, and it has been suggested that those who were most successful in exploiting the samurai were merchants of samurai origin.[10] They both understood the samurai mentality and enjoyed the confidence of samurai who were not merchants. Thus, during the last decades of the Tokugawa period, the merchant class had increased its wealth, if not its power, largely through acting as bankers to the daimyo (who were chronically short of money) and skillfully exploiting peasants as well as samurai. These, then, were the men who had the capital available to take advantage of the government's largesse in selling, on extremely favorable terms, the enterprises it had established. And these were the men who became the nation's great bankers, a subject I shall enlarge upon a little later in this chapter.

Meanwhile, the government continued to retain certain very definite controls on the overall direction of most enterprises, and in many cases it participated in actual management. Such devices as state protection and subsidies (as well as tariffs later on), coupled with the need for reliance for funds on state-owned or -controlled banks, provided the government with powerful weapons by means of which it could force the entrepreneur to comply with national policy. As Japanese industry prospered, the power of such banks within industry increased correspondingly, since their sole function for many years was to provide funds for industrial enterprises. The new industry, therefore, fell under government control to an unprecedented degree. Nor, as I have mentioned above, did the government turn over all enterprises to private ownership. It even took a new flier in industry, establishing the Imperial Iron Works at Yawata, the present Yawata Iron and Steel Company, which I shall discuss, along with its president, later in this book.

In pursuing its new industrial path, Japan was fortunate in the possession of large numbers of skilled artisans. These had been able to function peacefully and to perfect their skills because the topography of Japan, unlike that of China, has always tended to restrain internal military adventure. Skilfully exploiting this fact, the shogunate restricted the warlike proclivities of the clans by establishing an elaborate system of checkpoints on roads and mountain passes that permitted villages to live long years in peace and its artisans to prosper. Some clans encouraged the growth of certain skills, and small industry, as well as cottage industry so-called, tended to develop highly trained workmen.

As far back as the beginning of the eighteenth century, local artisans had learned how to cast cannon, to make fine steel, to weave cotton and wool, and to use dyes for design. The Japanese sword was unsurpassed in all the world, save perhaps by the finest Toledo blade; and hand-dyed cloth, still identifiable as to its place of origin, is greatly admired today. In addition to metal workers, there were workers in wood who found more uses for the lowly bamboo than any foreigner had ever conceived of, masons, and paper makers; there were small shipyards, saké distilleries, mines, ceramic kilns, and silk-spinning mills. The Japanese probably knew more about fish and fishing than any other people—for fish was, and is, second only to rice as a staple of Japanese life.

Tokyo, now the most populous city in the world, was a very big city even as far back as the beginning of the nineteenth century, perhaps the third largest in the world at that time. And even then it was known to be an expensive place to live, as it is now.[11] A commercial center, it became also a center of learning, leaving Kyoto to slumber in its semi-feudal past.

The unparalleled three hundred years of peace that Japan enjoyed during the Tokugawa period permitted not only the development of local skills but also brought great progress in education in general. Most communities had at least one teacher, even if only in the "shrine or temple school," and the literacy rate in Japan in the 1800's was equal to that of the most developed countries of Europe. Higher education was usually in the hands of the clan schools. By 1868, the number of private elementary schools (terakoya)* totalled twenty-eight thousand.

After Meiji, elementary education was made compulsory and

---

*Literally means "temple school," so-called because the private schools were frequently located within the shrine or temple grounds. It is now used for any grouping of students brought together for teaching. Recently, due to the disturbances in the universities, groups of students have been brought together for coaching and instruction in such unlikely places as inns, hotels, etc. This also is termed "terakoya-style."

interest in foreign studies received keen government encouragement. A large number of students were sent abroad to study, and at the same time foreign teachers were imported into Japan, enticed by the high salaries offered as well as by the obvious eagerness of their pupils to acquire whatever knowledge the teachers had to impart. In 1868, there were seven thousand foreign teachers in Japan.

Progressive samurai sent their sons to the School for Foreign Studies in Tokyo or to a school run by an English missionary. That remarkable American, Dr. Hepburn, not only taught English but also devised a system for the romanization of Japanese characters that bears his name and is currently in general use—despite pre-war jingoistic attempts to invent a "nationalistic" system, which is considered now to be much inferior to Hepburn's.

Yet despite the encouragement given to foreign studies, a traditional Japanese education was still considered to be preferable. Students who had received a traditional education and who passed the higher civil service examinations received better jobs and higher salaries than technicians who had been educated abroad. Presumably the students who fared best were those who had received, first, a traditional education in Japan itself and then a technical education abroad.

The return on an educational investment is always difficult to assess, but in Japan, ever since Meiji, it has been considered to be extremely high. There has been great eagerness to learn, not only to secure the best jobs but also to advance the national interest. Because Japanese culture is so homogeneous and because a knowledge of Japanese, however thorough it may be, offers no assistance in the learning of a Western language, the tendency has been for Japanese educated abroad to return to Japan to work. These factors, combined with the high rate of literacy and the national eagerness to learn, were of enormous importance in Japan's rapid industrial growth.

Despite Japan's isolationist policy during the Tokugawa period, the country had not been altogether without foreign trade. This, so far as the West was concerned, was restricted mainly to the Dutch, but there had long been coastal traffic as well as trade with both

Korea and China, and there had also been a considerable and lucrative amount of smuggling by the *wako*—a Chinese word which was originally applied to Japanese pirates and raiders, then later to smugglers. All these traders had acquired their experience the hard way: they knew a good deal about movement of goods, about markets, charter of vessels, conditions of carriage, and about risks and opportunities. Thus, when the new government early felt the need to develop a foreign trading arm, it found men already knowledgeable and it appointed them foreign trade agents. Mitsui, the leading exchange house, was the first; others, with similar experience, soon followed. In the bustle of its new life, Japan, in spite of its previous isolationism, found a class of entrepreneurs ready to take over its foreign trade and to develop trading facilities.

As any foreigner who was in Japan during preparations for the Olympic Games of 1964 can testify, when the Japanese decide to tackle a project, particularly one that is considered to be of national interest, they tackle it wholeheartedly. The men of Meiji were no exception. Realizing that the knowledge they required lay in the West, they were avid both in the hiring of Western talent and in sending Japanese abroad to study. The fact that the first railroad in Japan, between Tokyo and Yokohama, was largely financed by British loans and built by British engineers accounts for the British gauge and the left-hand drive; the latter was later extended to road and highway traffic.

Even the Japanese national anthem, "Kimigayo," was—at least in part—inspired by the West. According to Jean Lequiller, the composer was English and the harmonizer German.[12] According to another story, the first version of the anthem was composed as far back as 1870 by a Frenchman at the request of the Satsuma clan, which had the only Western-style band in Japan. Six years later, use of this score was discontinued, and a Japanese composer wrote a new melody, for which a German bandmaster in the Japanese Navy did the instrumentation. Whatever the true version, it is obvious that not only were popular songs imported from the West but Westerners also had a hand in the composition of the National Anthem.

Inevitably, borrowing on such a large scale—laws, systems, methods, ideas as well as technology—led occasionally to indiscriminate acquisition of useless knowledge, but on the whole this remarkable experiment was a dramatic success. Using what I have termed their "valuable inheritances," the Japanese accommodated themselves to borrowed wisdom and techniques that the West had taken hundreds of years to accumulate, and they did it so quickly that, in less than thirty-five years, Japan was sufficiently industrialized and had sufficient national cohesion to be able to fight a war with Russia—and to win it.

The Russian war is an example of the second major factor that, as I suggested at the beginning of this chapter, has made possible the "miracle" of contemporary Japan—a factor I called "fortuitous circumstances." Japan rarely seems to have made any important changes until faced by a set of seemingly calamitous conditions: then she takes action because she has to.

Other examples of this phenomenon are the dreaded arrival of Perry's "Black Ships"; Japan's involvement in China together with the Western powers; the Treaty of Portsmouth, after the war with Russia, for which some elements in Japan bitterly condemned the United States but which brought her a certain maturity and status in naval affairs as well as new territories; and the First World War, in which Japan sided with the allied powers. It was an alliance that was extremely profitable to Japan, furthering the development of her industry with virtually no risk attached. As a result of her involvement in the First World War, Japan earned money and experience as well as further territory.

Then came the period that almost brought Japan to utter destruction. Power fell into the hands of men who were determined on military adventure, no matter how high the cost, while the average Japanese was wholly unable to inform himself about conditions prevailing in the rest of the world. That the Japanese recognize this trait in themselves is indicated by their proverbs: "The frog in his well knows nothing of the ocean"; "The blind man doesn't fear the snake." There were, of course, well-informed men in the Foreign Office and the Ministry of Finance as well as in private business, but they had neither cohesion nor voice. An economist friend of mine, when chided by an American official after the war for the inadequacy of the statistics he presented to justify certain requested imports, replied: "Had we had good statistics in 1941, we would not have gone to war." Certainly, had enough senior officers of the Imperial Army realized the vast resources and the unbelievable production potential of the United States, there would have been considerably more hesitation about provoking the conflict. There would also, of course, have arisen the seemingly unsolvable problems involved in Japanese decision-making and "responsibility."

As a result of her declaration of war on the United States, Japan almost committed suicide—but once again the gods were lenient. Despite the continued opposition of large segments of the Army, the government was able finally to effect a surrender. The occupation that followed was unbelievably benevolent; hundreds of millions of dollars were given to the conquered country. The presence of the occupation forces provided the technology, the money, and the facilities necessary for the revivification of the economy.

Some unpleasantries—such as the dissolution of the *zaibatsu*—were inflicted, but the Japanese were content to wait. They knew that this typhoon, like all typhoons, must eventually end; then the bamboo could spring back. After the occupation, the *zaibatsu* groupings were reconstituted in a modern format within a few years. Japan had lost the war, but Shigeru Yoshida, her post-war prime minister, won the peace. Continuity with the past was not forgotten.

Mr. Soichiro Honda, who in less than ten years became the biggest manufacturer of motorcycles in the world, is quoted as attributing Japan's phenomenal economic recovery to the very fact that she did lose the war. "We have done well out of losing the war," Mr. Honda said. "With everything flattened, we could start from scratch, plan from the word go and think big."[13] The Korean War, which erupted at a time when Japan was undergoing a deep depression, provided the stimulus necessary for a great economic boom (1956–57). Another stimulus was provided during the recession of 1963–65 by the procurements and expenditures of the United States for the war in Vietnam. This stimulus, as of this writing, is still active—to the extent of about $500 million in 1968.

It is fascinating to observe how, over the past hundred years, Japan has profited from her own misfortunes as well as from the misfortunes of others. Perhaps she is indeed, as she claims to be, a country sacred to the gods.

A word must be said about the role played by the banks in the development of the economy since 1868. When the rulers of Meiji Japan decided to "go Western" in order to build an industrial society that could achieve economically what it could not accomplish militarily, they found it necessary to provide for the means to accumulate capital and to create organs for trade transaction and finance.

Japan at the time possessed neither banks nor a banking system, the nearest thing to a bank being the exchange houses, such as that of Konoike, or Mitsui, or Ono, although these knew nothing about modern international or domestic banking. Thus the government found itself obliged to create a banking system, which was based on a compromise between the British and the American systems.[14] "National Bank Regulations" were promulgated in 1872, and the following year the First National Bank (the Daiichi) was founded in Tokyo. Mitsui and Ono were among its chief promoters; its president, from 1875 to 1916, was Eiichi Shibusawa.

Before the Bank of Japan was created in 1882, with the Central Bank of Belgium as its model, 143 "national banks" had been chartered. And by 1893, when the "Bank Regulations" were enforced, there were in existence 545 commercial banks, although until their reorganization in that year they were not permitted to call themselves banks.

At first merchant houses were reluctant to go into banking other than as shareholders, but many of the samurai class, who had received commutation payments, had both the funds and the knowledge to become at least embryonic bankers. Face was saved by the fact that banks had to be formed in order to serve industry, which served the state and thus the emperor. It came to be considered almost a patriotic duty for educated samurai to go into banking. The Fifteenth Bank, which was also called the Peers' Bank, was founded by the nobility.

Since no one in Japan at the time knew much about banking, there were a number of bankruptcies, but with time the men who had become bankers learned more about it, and their task was made easier for them by the fact that they were expected to follow government orders, instruction, and guidance. Very likely they did not consider themselves as individual bankers, out to make a profit, but rather as semi-governmental bureaucrats. (Remnants of this feeling are still to be found in Japan today, and some Westerners believe that there are very few true bankers, in the Western sense of the word, in contemporary Japanese banks.) In 1874, the government created the Ginko-gaku Kyoku—literally, "the Bank-learning Bureau"—and imported an English banker, Alexander Allan Shand, to teach them and to act as an adviser on banking.

It expected the bankers to follow its directives; it pampered and subsidized them; it scolded them for their early follies and ineptitudes (not to mention deliberate deviations from rectitude) but it usually protected them from the consequences; it threatened them with punishment if they objected to government direction and rewarded them for conformance. Thus, they became extensions of the central bank and of the Ministry of Finance—and still are so today, though of course to a lesser degree.

Some merchant houses were persuaded to go actively into banking on their own behalf, founding the so-called ordinary, or private, banks. Mitsui Bank was established in 1876; Yasuda Bank (today's Fuji Bank), in 1880; Mitsubishi also went into banking later on. In fact, the *zaibatsu*, which had come into being with the endorsement of the government, soon began to control a great number of banks and financial institutions. Even in the Bank of Japan, for which the government provided most of the capital, sizeable blocks of shares were held by Mitsui, Yasuda, Sumitomo and other *zaibatsu* families. This state of affairs continued up to the end of the Second World War.

47

Such family enterprises as Mitsui and Mitsubishi, partnerships in which the main family kept all control, were, of course, in the feudal clan tradition. The concept of the joint-stock company (*kabushiki kaisha*), which Shibusawa introduced, was alien to this tradition, yet the concept spread, and with it came an awareness of the necessity for cooperation between banks and enterprises.

As demands for funds and banking services proliferated, the banks became entrepreneurs in their own right, thus involving themselves deeply, both through loans and through ownership, in industrial enterprises. The tendency to intercompany cooperation, undoubtedly conditioned by the traditional "community-centered" psychology of Japan, as opposed to the cult of the individual, seemed to the Japanese to be the best way for them to learn business and finance and the best way to build a tightly knit industrial structure, thus ensuring the growth of the country.

Eiichi Shibusawa, who was one of the great leaders in this era of transition, believed that this concept of cooperation among enterprises was the chief cause of Japan's economic growth, which he contrasted with the lack of growth in China. He knew, of course, that the Chinese were as profit-motivated as the Japanese (if not more so), but he claimed that where the Japanese system of inter-corporate cooperation proved successful, the Chinese system—of the individual businessman acting for himself alone—delayed the industrial development of the nation as a whole. I believe there is a great deal of truth in Shibusawa's opinion. The Chinese is (or was, before Mao) an individualist in his business undertakings. If he was successful, his profits went into his own coffers and those of his family: his interest extended no further. His obsession with return on capital invested made him more readily understandable than the Japanese to an American, whose approach to business is much the same. This may be one reason why overseas Chinese in Asia are so often successful in taking over the most lucrative businesses (except in Japan); and it may also explain why he becomes a scapegoat in any surge of nationalism, being frequently threatened with confiscation, expulsion, or worse.

Further evidence of the close intercooperation between the

Japanese banking community and the government was provided by the war. Many banks were merged and several new "banks" were created in order to finance the war effort. Some of the latter, the so-called "wartime financial institutions," were liquidated during the occupation—and their personnel went into remaining banks or other financial institutions. Having been assigned to their positions by the Ministry of Finance and the Bank of Japan, they remained government employees wherever they went.

The Yokohama Specie Bank, rather stupidly emasculated during the occupation, finally emerged as the semi-independent, official foreign-exchange bank, the Bank of Tokyo. Since the Yokohama Specie Bank was a government bank, most of its senior staff were Ministry of Finance people and considered themselves to be government officers; much the same is, in reality, true of the Bank of Tokyo today.

Japanese banks and bankers, of necessity closely allied to and controlled by the central bank and the government, in turn impose direct and indirect controls on industry, either by government *diktat* or "window guidance." The latter term needs some explanation. The Bank of Japan seems to define this extra-legal activity as a policy measure to restrict the loan limits of commercial banks in order to effect a quantitative control over the supply of commercial credit and private investment funds. Since almost all enterprises in Japan are heavily dependent on borrowings, an enterprise always finds itself at the mercy of the commercial banks, which in turn are restricted by the Bank of Japan. Thus the government exercises effective control through the typically Japanese "window guidance" system.

Of the 706 leading enterprises listed on the Tokyo Stock Exchange, Japanese banks are frequently the major individual shareholders; they therefore have an important voice in corporate decisions. (Insurance companies are now also very large shareholders of enterprises; in some instances, their holdings exceed those of banks.) Further, every corporation in Japan must borrow. The average ratio of "own capital" to total capital employed, while slowly increasing, is still very low—perhaps 20 percent. The corporation normally leans heavily upon its "main bank" but also borrows from other banks. Since the banks are, in turn, controlled by law by the Bank of Japan and the Ministry of Finance, many pressures can, and are, brought to bear upon enterprise by government. "Excessive investment" or "over-borrowing" from banks is adequately discouraged, and banks in turn are discouraged from an apparent propensity to get into an "over-loaned" position. These factors are of very grave importance to Japanese enterprises, since the flow of funds and loans is of daily importance to operation and their availability is essential to further planning and corporate growth.

Some managers are restive, of course, under such stringent control, but there is nothing much they can do about it. Mr. K. Minami, chairman of the Kokusaku Pulp Company, was quoted in a Tokyo newspaper as saying that the banks should be messengers for industry but that in Japan they appear to rule industry.[15] This attitude is widespread but usually unvoiced.

Traditional inheritances, racial and cultural homogeneity, strong relations between the bureaucracy, industry, and business, group consciousness instead of the cult of the individual: all these were strategic factors in the rapid growth of Japanese enterprises and in establishing them within the overall industrial structure, so that basically they served the state. (Until 1954, the consumer was given little or no consideration.) Thus, a typical Japanese enterprise, while its plants and its products may be quite similar to those in the Western world, is an organization ruled by an entirely different set of values and by people with different thought processes, accepting controls and reacting to pressures quite different from those of the West.

We must now examine the present-day Japanese enterprise to see if we can discover how these differences affect interchange and to see also if, hopefully, we can develop some guidelines to motivations and values, so that communication and cooperation between the Japanese businessman and his Western counterpart may be improved. Otherwise distrust and consequent antagonism will continue to impede good relations.

Business Structure 3

"Unite your total strength to be devoted to construction for the future ... and keep pace with the progress of the world."

—H. M. The Emperor

The well-ordered universe of Japan's industrial society is made up of over four million enterprises, of which more than six hundred thousand are in manufacturing, but only seven hundred or so account for the greater part of all industrial production. Of these, incidentally, the hundred largest are responsible for 39 percent of all capital and 29 percent of gross profits.

These seven hundred companies, along with the major trading companies, the banks, and the lesser companies with which they are affiliated, constitute the enterprise structure that chiefly concerns us here, since it is with them that foreign companies have most contact. Further, these elite enterprises are so important in the total economy of the country that one may say of them, "As they go, so goes Japan." The government, for example, would not permit Yamaichi Securities Company to go bankrupt, or the Stock Market to collapse in 1964, since a large number of bankruptcies would have followed. The government, accordingly, bailed them out. Nor would it allow Sanyo Special Steel to go bankrupt, since it had incurred foreign loans. I shall have more to say about these instances later.

John Donne's famous quotation—that "no man is an island, entire of itself"—may certainly be applied to a Japanese enterprise; if anything, it is an understatement. The average industrial enterprise in Japan is bound, strongly or loosely, to a great many other enterprises. It is subject to some, superior to others; it is dependent on some, others are dependent on it. It is only theoretically equal to its affiliates, or, to use George Orwell's phrase, "all animals are equal, but some are more equal than others." Therefore one must know one's place in an extremely complex hierarchical system, an example of what Ruth Benedict, discussing the Japanese character, termed the trait of "situational adaptation." Lesser members of a group are known in Japanese as the *keiretsu kaisha*; aware that they are lesser members, they must also know their place.

Seating protocol at an officers' meeting of various affiliated companies reveals this fact very clearly. Every officer knows his company's exact status in relation to all the other companies, and he knows what his own position must be vis-à-vis comparable officers of junior and senior companies that are attending the meeting. That all are equal but that some are more equal than others is, in Japan, *atarimae*, taken for granted, a plain fact that everyone knows or ought to know.

But however plain the fact may be in Japan, it is a difficult one for the foreign executive to grasp, and his lack of understanding here frequently results in *gaucheries*, and consequent embarrassment. Because of this and because many Japanese feel ill at ease with a foreigner who cannot be assigned a definite place in the economic or social hierarchy, they prefer to avoid direct negotiation with foreign businessmen. Since the Japanese cannot figure out precisely where the foreigner fits, he feels himself at a loss.

At a mixed conference of Japanese and foreigners, the Japanese invariably pay honor to the foreigner, even though his company may be a peanut compared with the Japanese giant. His Japanese hosts at the conference table will usually indicate to the foreigner where he is to sit, which will always be the place of honor, but the unknowing foreigner may find this practice presumptuous. Once he has been seated, the Japanese take their places in order of rank and importance. Juniors often sit altogether apart, frequently seeming to do nothing but take copious notes. They only speak when spoken to. They are present at the conference but take little or no part in it.

The Japanese company, then, depending, as it does, on associated or affiliated companies, adjusts its policies in accordance with conditions prevailing in the other companies, taking into account its own status in its special community of enterprises. It is also influenced of course by pressures from many other sources, including government. The key word in the quotation from the Emperor, that I have given at the head of this chapter, is "unite."

During the occupation, largely because of misguided ideological zeal, the holding companies and the great financial combines (the *zaibatsu*) were broken up. As a result, much damage was done to the Japanese economy. It was not irreparable, for the combines have since regrouped, but the former tight cohesion is unrecoverable and a certain amount of fragmentation continues. The so-called Democratization of Securities distributed shareownership into many new hands. Consequently, while inter-company shareownership continues, ownership is no longer concentrated in a comparatively few hands, as it was before. This is, perhaps, a blessing of doubtful value in Japan, where the present tendency is again to get shares into strong (and affiliated) hands.

Nevertheless, a glance at the principal owners of shares of companies listed on the Tokyo Stock Exchange reveals some interesting facts. Of the 695 companies listed by the *Oriental Economist* in its issues for August and September, 1967, it appears that 196 companies were dominated by *zaibatsu* enterprises[16] while sixty major companies had most, or a very large part, of its shareholders listed as "clans," e.g., single or multiple family owners. Others are of the clan-ownership type but are dominated by "insiders or insider organizations." Mitsukoshi Department Store is an interesting example of the latter. Mitsukoshi Clinic, the major shareholder (11 percent), Mitsukoshi Aigo-Kai (a kind of welfare association), and Mr. Kuruo Kitazawa (the auditor) hold 19.45 percent of total shares outstanding, with a "controlling rate" of 52.4 percent.

Intercorporate shareholdings in companies other than those of the clan type clearly indicate that most enterprises are (a) in one of the main former *zaibatsu* groupings; or (b) in the new power groups that have arisen since the end of the war, such as the Fuji-Yasuda monetary group; or (c) in one of the lesser industrial groups such as Furukawa, Nissan, Meiji, and Kawasaki. Many, however, have connections with more than one group, and most use not only the group bank but other banks as well. Thus, while banks (other than the Fuji-Yasuda group) may not control or have a strong voice in an enterprise through shareholding, they can and do bring powerful pressures upon management by other means. I shall revert to this very important subject later.

As I outlined in the previous chapter, certain modern Japanese enterprises developed out of clan, group, home, or family industries, while others grew out of the going concerns inherited or purchased from the Meiji government. The former retained their identification, of varying degrees of intensity, with a particular family, clan, or locality; the latter were, and are, tied to the umbilical cord of the government that gave them birth.

Of the latter, the leaders developed into the great *zaibatsu* empires which—before the Second World War—controlled almost 50 percent of all private banking and financial institutions, 35 percent of all investment, and over 32 percent of all heavy industry. Obviously, then, they wielded strong political influence; closely connected with both the government and the military establishment, they were rather like governmental appendages. On occasion, in fact, their operations were almost fully directed by the government and the military. (From 1935 to the end of the War, the Ministry of Munitions controlled and directed most plants.)

A few clan or familial industries also grew large and so became concerned with the government and its controls, but most large present-day enterprises derived mainly from government-owned industries or from entrepreneurs or groups (houses) appointed by the government as approved agents.

Mitsui and Company was the first such "house" to be appointed to negotiate foreign trade arrangements. It is, therefore, the oldest trading company in Japan, and perhaps the largest. As agent for the South Manchurian Railroad, it was a quasi-government military-directed organization, somewhat like the British East India Company, to which it has compared itself. It was the trading arm of the South Manchurian Railroad and, in the words of its managing director, "engaged in extensive activities in this field to contribute to the exploitation of Manchuria."[17] Mitsui to this day obviously identifies itself with the government—and perhaps with good reason: at the time of its dissolution, its annual income was equivalent to the whole national budget.

Mitsubishi also sees itself in much the same way. A coined name meaning "Three Diamonds," it was first used by Yataro Iwasaki in 1873 and became the name for the holding company of the Iwasaki family. Today the Iwasaki clan has lost control, and there are several hundred large shareholders, but the identification of the company with the government seems undiminished. Indeed, the president of Mitsubishi, Mr. Fujino, spoke of it recently as Japan & Co. in a Tokyo newspaper.[18] While he identifies his company with the government and seems to suggest that "Japan & Co." is motivated as much by national interest as by the profit motive, if not more so, he also admits that its shareholders feel it has the duty to make a profit. In fiscal 1967, it claimed 11.7 percent of Japan's foreign trade and 2 percent of all domestic wholesale sales.

The slogan of the Nippon Sheet Glass Company is "to render service to the country and society through the manufacture of glass"; the Matsushita Electric Company begins its working day with a hymn to country and company (see Chapter 5). Examples of this state of mind could be very nearly endless. The fact is that no company, however hard it struggles, can free itself from bureaucratic influence. Some, such as Idemitsu, have fought against government controls from time to time, but in the long run they are always brought to conform and to serve the national goal. To this end, the government makes use of a number of pressures, of which "administrative guidance" is a very powerful one. Like "window guidance" in banking, "administrative guidance" is a peculiarly Japanese invention. It has no foundation in law; it is, in fact, outside the law and so in the eyes of purists is quite illegal—but it works. It is part and parcel, of course, of Japan's long history based on the paternal or feudal concept of authority, and it is a factor that the foreign businessman had better reckon with.

Since almost no enterprise can exist alone in Japan, the dissolution of the *zaibatsu* enterprises during the occupation and the passage of the Antimonopoly Law were untenable. The result would have been to produce a system and a set of conditions not only alien to Japanese practices but inconceivable to both business and government—and incompatible as well with the actual working of Japan's economy.

Generally speaking, a Japanese enterprise is one entity in a maze of interconnected entities, all related to each other in a variety of ways and in varying degrees. In most groupings, top managers of affiliated companies have their own "club," a sort of overall board of directors which meets regularly to discuss matters affecting the whole group as well as the strategy of individual companies within the group. In the United States, such alliances might well be held to be "collusion," or "in restraint of trade," or any of the other dreadful bugbears the American antitrust people have devised for the perpetuation of the bureaucracy and the enrichment of the legal profession; but in Japan they are common practice, and by means of them the aims of each individual company are always subordinated to the aims of the group as a whole.

To name a few examples of such "clubs," the Mitsubishi Kinyo-kai is made up of the presidents of twenty-three companies and the Mitsui Getsuyo-kai, which is made up of the presidents of twenty-six companies. Mitsui recently announced a new top executive group, the Sewa-nin-kai, headed by three Mitsui presidents, with such senior advisers as the chairman of Mitsui Bank and the chairman of Toyo Rayon. (I shall discuss this new group in somewhat greater detail at the end of this chapter.) Similarly, Mitsubishi has formed a new top "panel," headed by Mr. Fujino. There are, of course, a few large companies that have developed outside any particular group or have been built up by energetic entrepreneurs, such as Matsushita, Honda, Sony, and Idemitsu, but these are relative newcomers and remain rarities in the Japanese business structure. And even they, as time passes, tend to become more and more attached to one or more groups, frequently through banking affiliations; in Japan, the maverick must, sooner or later, join the club—or fail.

Even with foreign companies, particularly joint ventures, or marketing and sales agreements, the government tries to importune the foreign partner to agree in writing to conform to existing Japanese business customs and practices.[19] "To conform" is the keynote: it is expected that the non-Japanese businessman will refrain from introducing foreign concepts that may disrupt the harmony, the *wa*, which so many Japanese businessmen, like Sazo Idemitsu, accept as their corporate philosophy.

Just as a Japanese enterprise bears a strict, almost hierarchical, relation to other enterprises, to the group, to the bureaucracy, and to the nation, so everyone who works for the enterprise knows his place within it. Its human resources—what Robert Owens called its "vital machines," as opposed to its "inanimate machines"—are required to conform, just as the enterprise itself does; individualism, in top management or in a worker, is discouraged. The changes that have occurred recently in this area will be discussed later.

The staff of a Japanese enterprise, like all enterprises everywhere, is made up of the management, the administrative functionaries, and the office white-collar workers (called "salarymen"); then there are also of course the production staff, the plant engineers, the scientists, the technicians (who are also considered to be white-collar rather than blue-collar), and the laborers, janitors, and so on (called *ko-in*). All are divided into two groups, "regular" and "non-regular" workers, and rules of employment vary somewhat between the two, but the hierarchical system prevails throughout and life employment is customary. In certain kinds of labor, such as road and construction work or stevedoring, the enterprise does not form the hierarchy but rather the "boss system," the *oyabun*, since the "boss" is himself the supplier of labor.

But the group that chiefly concerns us is the "salarymen," the white-collar workers, who are destined to become managers and perhaps eventually executives. Of course, employees from the production side frequently move into management, and some advance to top management and executive levels; as such, they would come to be included in the rather broad class of salarymen. The technical staff, although it is generally recruited and employed under the same hierarchical advancement system, usually receives somewhat different treatment, particularly in matters of retirement and pay, from the salaryman; this is particularly true of those engaged in scientific and technical research. Technicians, in any case, rarely have contact except on technical matters with the foreigner: it is almost always the salaryman with whom he has to deal. And nowhere do the differences between Japanese and Western business and administrative principles and practices reveal themselves more clearly than in this all-important personage, the key figure in the human resources that have created, that now operate, and that will develop further Japan's industrial society. I shall discuss the salaryman at length in Chapter 5.

Here I should like to look for a moment at the complexities of the industrial organization that the foreign businessman has to take into account when he attempts to deal with a single enterprise, which will generally, in his case, be a manufacturing company. Chances are it will belong to one of the major industrial groupings: Mitsui, Mitsubishi, Sumitomo, Fuji, Kawasaki, Hitachi, Furukawa, or Nissan. There are, of course, lesser industrial groupings, and there are other smaller groups—such as Tokyu, Shinko, and Toyota—that customarily concentrate on a narrower area of industry or service.

The company with which the foreigner becomes associated has a known and generally acknowledged status in the family of companies, and it has duties and obligations to many, if not all, of the other family members. Just as any human family has degrees of relationship, so are there degrees of corporate relationship and identification with the "immediate" family companies. However complex these may be, the Japanese manager, as I have indicated earlier, knows almost intuitively exactly where his company belongs, and he and his personnel are expected to act accordingly. The foreigner also needs to have some knowledge of these relationships if his own association is to be successful.

Each enterprise enjoys certain benefits as a result of membership in its group, usually in the form of financial and business protection, security, and status; each enterprise, in return, has certain obligations to the group. Before any important decision may be made, its effect upon other members of the group must be carefully considered: there must be consultation with other companies in the group, with the bankers concerned, with the government, and then with the association. The agreement or endorsement of all of these must be obtained before the decision becomes final. The analogy between the enterprise within its group and the employee in his enterprise was not an idle one: each benefits from the association and has in return certain inalienable obligations.

A very brief description of one of the tighter—i.e., less diffused—groups may give some idea of the complexities of the Japanese industrial structure. Tokyo Shibaura Electric (Toshiba), which may be thought of as the General Electric of Japan and of which, General Electric in the United States owns 10.62 percent, has about seventy subsidiaries that, in turn, own some sixty lesser companies. There are also 120 sales companies in the Toshiba family. (Incidentally, Toshiba has forty-five company baseball teams in its own league, volleyball teams for girls, soccer teams, ping-pong and even sailing teams.) The Toshiba group itself is, in turn, closely related, although not through share ownership, to the greater Mitsui family group.

In actual practice, the junior corporate member will usually leave all foreign negotiations in the hands of the senior member company. This may be due to the fact that the junior company lacks self-confidence in dealing with foreign businessmen, but it is also indicative of the reliance that the junior company places upon the senior member of the group and of the obligations that the latter has toward lesser members. Groups generally chart their organizations. Mitsubishi, for example, has its immediate family (the Mitsubishi companies), its subsidiary companies (*kogaisha*), its

59

affiliated companies (*keiretsu kaisha*), and its associated companies (*kankei kaisha*), as well as others, all sheltering under the Mitsubishi umbrella.

Ruth Benedict[20] has given a succinct account of the rights, duties, obligations, and responsibilities (the *giri* and the *on*) that Japanese have toward each other, depending on the nature of the relationship, and her explanation may be of help to the foreigner in understanding the same phenomenon as it occurs in the industrial structure, for intercorporate relationships in Japan, more perhaps than elsewhere, reflect interpersonal relationships. Although the foreigner who wants to do business in Japan must attempt to thread the maze of these intercorporate relationships, I think it is unlikely that he will be altogether successful. There are simply too many complexities. Although some groups may seem fairly self-evident, there will also be relationships outside the group with other, seemingly independent groups as well as traditional relationships that are not evident at all but that are, nonetheless, extremely powerful.

Foreigners frequently complain that after negotiating with Japanese businessmen, for however short or long a time, they had believed a final agreement was reached—only to find that the agreement was not final at all. Perhaps some last-minute change was introduced, or perhaps nothing may have happened after the "final" agreement. Only silence, dead silence! And sometimes, even after contracts have actually been signed, nothing has been done to implement them. Then the foreigner finds that no one is able, or willing, to give him an acceptable reason for the apparent dead end.

Admittedly, this is extremely annoying to the Westerner as well as wasteful of both time and money. The reasons for the dead end, which may never be truly explained, will usually be found somewhere within the Japanese group relationships or in relations with the bankers or the bureaucracy: opposition may have come from any one of them. What to a Westerner is a very simple decision, one easily made by any manager, may not be simple at all in Japan, and it may take an unconscionable length of time. An awareness on the part of the Westerner of this possibility, of the factors that enter into Japanese decision-making and of the various pressures that act on a Japanese enterprise, might bring better understanding and with it greater patience—for patience is all.

In the early 1950's, I was faced with an extremely difficult negotiation (involving several companies, a bank, and the government) which had arrived at an impasse for reasons that were mysterious to me and that could not, apparently, be explained by the Japanese. Knowing that I, as a foreigner, could neither force a solution nor precipitate a favorable decision, I called on a friend in the Foreign Office with my problem. "Give it time!" he said; and his advice turned out to be correct. In time, somewhere in the Japanese group, a decision was somehow mutually found—and the decision turned out to be an extremely favorable one.

I spoke, a few pages earlier, of the fact that before any important decision may be made, consultations must occur not only with other group members, with bankers, and with government but also with the association. To this I should add the fact that the manager of an enterprise, in attempting to find a decision, must also be careful to obtain the understanding of other companies in the same business who are therefore competitors but who are also committed to each other under a variety of cartels or cartel-like agreements. I should like to give here a brief description of the role played by associations and cartels in the Japanese industrial structure.

As I noted earlier, antimonopoly laws and laws against restraint of trade, forbidding cartels and certain types of mergers, were put in effect during the occupation, but it soon became obvious that these laws were in large part unenforceable and in need of revision, whereupon a great many exceptions were allowed. When the depression of 1953 began to take its toll, "rationalization cartels" in most industries came into being, and so also did "export associations" (*yushutsu-kumiai*), the main purpose of which was to prevent "excessive competition" by enforcing minimum prices. Thereafter, associations wielding various degrees of control proliferated through trade and industry.

No one can say how many such associations there are in Japan today, although it is known that they exist in over 120 sectors of industry. Similarly, the number of cartels or cartel-like agreement is unknown. Some estimates give a figure of 850 cartels, covering over 2500 products; others maintain that, in addition to the known cartels, there are over a thousand "hidden" cartels, covering a further 2100 products in 212 sectors of industry. Cartels extend even into the service industries, as a result of which there are, of course, geisha associations. The most prestigious in Tokyo is the Shimbashi Geisha Association.

Obviously, then an enterprise must belong to its particular association and must consent and conform to the cartel arrangements. To the Japanese, associations, cartels, affiliations, trade restrictions, monopolies, and all the other arrangements to be expected in a controlled economy are *atarimae* (natural), normal and indeed necessary. The government Monopoly Bureau is still in existence and maintains its monopolies of salt, tobacco, and camphor. Under such conditions, the industrial harmony (the *wa*) that I have spoken of earlier and that seems so desirable to the Japanese must obviously prevail. It is, in fact, to the Japanese, the only sensible basis for the conduct of economic relations.

One of the results of this remarkable intercorporate solidarity is that once an enterprise is a member of the group, it benefits by all the group's affiliations so long as it continues to cooperate and conform. The outsider is kept outside, while the member is inside and can remain inside. He may not get all the share he wants of business and profits, but he will get a share. He will not be pushed to the wall. His fellow-members will never "break his rice bowl"; rather, if he gets into trouble, they will bail him out.

At the same time, this solidarity does not mean that there is an absence of competition. For example, profit margin against sales of Japanese trading companies is said to be as low as 0.5 percent; they therefore compete energetically to increase their outlets to increase profits. There are at present some ten thousand Japanese in New York working for Japanese trading companies—figures that compare very favorably with those of European countries that have traditionally had strong ties with the United States. Further, all major Japanese exchange banks have agencies in New York, indicating how keen competition among them is. No matter how remote the place, such as in the under-developed countries of Africa, it is unlikely not to have been exploited to a certain degree by Japanese trading companies; middle-class and small businesses seek energetically to develop markets in places where large Japanese companies have not yet entered. Such keen competition may result in practices of doubtful value, such as double investment, overstaffing, and the like, but at the same time it demonstrates to what a great extent the national energy of the country is responsible for its recent economic growth within the capitalist framework.

On the other side of the ledger, there have been numerous cases of "rescue," such as that of the Yamaichi Securities Company, which I mentioned earlier and which I shall here examine in some detail. Other instances that might be cited are Sanyo Special Steel, the Kanematsu Trading Company, and Nitto Chemical. But the story of how the government, along with friendly companies, saved the Yamaichi Securities Company from the bankruptcy it faced in 1964–65 has elements of special interest.

In 1963, the Japanese stock market collapsed, and in the course of the decline most leading security companies were caught with large holdings they had acquired during the boom and could not now liquidate; faced with the disappearance of income, they were unable to meet payments or to cover the expenses of over-extended and recklessly expanded branches, along with personnel, acquired during the boom days. Yamaichi Securities Company, the second largest in Japan, with over eight thousand employees in some forty-eight branches, was the first to admit that it was on the point of bankruptcy.

In the boom years of 1960 and 1961, Yamaichi had taken over large issues, traded on the second section or over-the-counter, which, when the boom ended, were impossible to sell. Further, Yamaichi had engaged in large-scale speculative buying and selling on its own account, partly by using the shares it held for its customers under the system called *unyo-azukari*, "working investment deposit." Yamaichi, whose capital at that time was ¥8 billion had more than ¥50 billion worth of stock in "investment deposit," and the outstanding balance of its investment trusts at the end of April, 1965, amounted to about ¥250 billion. Its borrowings having exceeded ¥70 billion, yearly interest payments required some ¥8 billion. A provisional statement of account for the period between October, 1964, and March, 1965, showed a loss of about ¥2 billion, bringing accumulated losses to over ¥10 billion.

On May 21, 1965, a rehabilitation plan for Yamaichi Securities Company was announced by a group consisting of the president of Yamaichi, the president of Fuji Bank, the president of the Industrial Bank of Japan, and a vice-president of Mitsubishi Bank. The plan was also supported by both the Yasuda and the Mitsubishi Trust and Banking Companies. This rehabilitation plan provided for the closure of about twenty Yamaichi branch offices and the dismissal of some two thousand employees. Further, a syndicate of eighteen banks was to grant a moratorium on monthly interest payments of about ¥150 million.

Announcement of the plan caused considerable apprehension among investors. Cancellations of investment trusts, which had totalled ¥21.1 billion in April, rose to ¥32 billion in May. The exact amount of the cancellations of "investment deposit" contracts cannot be given, because these figures are not reported, but for Yamaichi cancellations between May and September of that year amounted to some ¥23 billion. The stock market reacted quickly with a further decline; seven days after the announcement of the plan (on May 28), the Dow-Jones average fell below the 1,100 mark.

At a press conference that evening, the Minister of Finance and the Governor of the Bank of Japan announced that Article 25 of the Bank of Japan Law (which provides for "unlimited, unsecured" emergency credits) would be invoked in order to support Yamaichi. (This was the first time since the financial panic of 1931 that this article was resorted to.) Under its provisions, the Bank of Japan was to give credit to Yamaichi through the latter's three main banks—Industrial, Fuji, and Mitsubishi—to the amount of ¥28.2 billion. (Nineteen other securities companies in the "investment deposit" business were given credits as well, and the Oi Securities Company was granted a moratorium on interest payments by the banks it dealt with.)

After protracted negotiations, another rehabilitation plan for Yamaichi was agreed upon. A new company—Yamaichi, Ltd.—was to be capitalized at ¥9 billion and was to take over the business of Yamaichi Securities Company. The capital of the new company was to be provided by the old company (¥4 billion), the three main banks (¥900 million each), and other creditor banks and related companies (¥2.3 billion).

The new company was to repay the old company its ¥4 billion in return for the good will and business of the old company, and it was, in addition, to pay a certain percentage of the commission proceeds exceeding a certain limit for a period of five years, in order to repay outstanding debts. The old company was then to repay the "special loans" granted by the Bank of Japan in monthly instalments of ¥214 million over a period of eighteen years and eight months. Actually, Yamaichi hopes to speed up the repayment and to complete it within ten years. The new company, Yamaichi, Ltd., was established on September 1, 1966; on the preceding day, Yamaichi deposited ¥750 million in repayment of its debts to the Bank of Japan.

The plan further provided that the outstanding debts of the old company to the three main banks (¥7,052 million) were to remain frozen on its books for three years. The debts to the fifteen other banks (¥14 billion) were to be taken over and repaid by the new company. The three-year moratorium was extended to interest payments (estimated at ¥2.2 billion) due to all eighteen creditor banks from June, 1965, to September, 1966, when the new company was established.

According to the plan, the repayment of the Bank of Japan's "special loans" comprises a "fixed part" (¥274 million) and a "variable part" (depending on the business of the new firm). Of the "fixed part," ¥67 million was to be applied to the amortization of the principal; ¥147 million to interest payments. The "variable part" was to be equal to one-third of the income of the company exceeding ¥16 billion a year during the first three years and ¥18 billion during the next two years. Yamaichi's income was estimated at ¥1,250 million a month (10.5 percent of the Tokyo Stock Exchange's average daily turnover of 120 million shares is handled by Yamaichi).

The Ministry of Finance wanted to reduce the interest rate on the loans of the fifteen banks to 1 *sen* per hundred yen per day (3.65 percent p. a.), but the banks objected to being held responsible for Yamaichi's bad management, and the interest rate was finally fixed at 1.7 *sen* (6.205 percent). The interest rate on the "special loans" of the Bank of Japan at that time was 1.6 *sen* (5.84 percent).

On August 31, 1968, Yamaichi Securities Company made repayment of ¥1,192 million, reducing its outstanding liabilities to the Bank of Japan to ¥21,936 million.

In the case of the Oi Securities Company, a similar arrangement was worked out by the Ministry of Finance and the Bank of Japan with the Industrial Bank and Mitsui Trust and Banking Company. Other banks—Fuji, Sumitomo, Tokai, Sanwa, Dai-Ichi, and Yasuda—were also involved.

The capital of the new firm, fixed at ¥3 billion, was made up in the following way: ¥1 billion from the old firm in the form of good will and the transfer of business, ¥600 million from the Industrial Bank and the Mitsui Trust and Banking Company, ¥200 million from the other six banks, ¥300 million from three securities companies (Nomura, Nikko, and Daiwa—all competitive companies), and ¥900 million from other financial institutions and related companies.

Oi Securities Company received "special loans" from the Bank of Japan amounting to ¥5.3 billion, for which repayment is to be made in monthly instalments of ¥40 million over a period of eighteen years. Loans of the Industrial Bank and Mitsui Trust and Banking Company amounted in all to ¥3.1 billion; interest payments on these loans are to be suspended for three years, after which the rate fixed is 1.5 *sen* (5.475 percent) to Mitsui Trust and Banking Company and 1 *sen* (3.65 percent) to the Industrial Bank. Loans from the other six banks, amounting to ¥600 million, were to be taken over by the new company, with interest payable at a rate of 1.7 *sen* (6.205 percent).

The government's direct intervention in what was supposed to be a free stock market and its deliberate bailing out of a major company that had reached the point of imminent collapse through years of over-expansion, bad judgment, and speculation, although contrary to western practice, undoubtedly achieved the results that were intended: thousands of people were saved from heavy losses and great hardship.

The case of Sanyo Special Steel Company was rather different, in that there seems to have been doubt as to the accuracy of the company's books of accounts. Sanyo is a leading producer of certain types of special steels; it belongs to the Fuji Steel group, and its main banks are the Kobe, the Mitsubishi, and the Fuji.

The chief reason for the failure of the company was excessive investment in equipment, a large part of which was imported by floating a loan shared jointly by a Belgian and an American bank. As is customary, a leading Japanese city bank, Mitsubishi, guaranteed to repay the loan plus interest should Sanyo fail to do so, and the arrangement was approved by both the Ministry of Finance and the Bank of Japan. Presumably all the parties involved in the transaction examined the company's accounts and were satisfied with its credit status and its financial stability.

Losses that began to appear in April, 1962, were not revealed for a time, but soon after the funds had been extended by the foreign banks, it came out that Sanyo had not paid its sub-dealers or contractors and that it was, in effect, bankrupt. At the trial of the former president of the firm, Hajime Ogino, the charges were falsification of accounts by fictitious entries of profits, illegal dividends, illegal remuneration of directors, and illegal acquisition of the company's own shares. The amount involved was ¥3 billion.

Nevertheless, Sanyo did not go through bankruptcy. Instead, it applied for—and obtained—permission to undergo a voluntary reorganization. At the time of its application for rehabilitation, Sanyo's total liabilities amounted to ¥50.6 billion, of which ¥2.8 billion was due to about 570 subcontractors.

While large companies are rarely allowed to go bankrupt in Japan, bankruptcy is frequent among small- and medium-sized businesses because of their weak finances and their inability to obtain adequate bank loans. The deferred payment system, whereby one company pays another for materials or products with a note of hand (*tegata*) due in ninety or 120 days, or even longer, is prevalent in almost all industry and on all levels and only serves to aggravate the condition. If a company's notes are dishonored and become uncollectable, its smaller creditors go to the wall. When, therefore, a large company gets into financial difficulties, the inevitable "domino effect" that follows knocks over a number of smaller companies down the channel of supply. In 1960, there were 1,172 bankruptcies; in 1967, the figure had risen to 8,486 (these were all bankruptcies involving liabilities of over ¥10 million).

Generally speaking, no great personal stigma appears to attach itself to a bankrupt in Japan, as it does in England or New England, but there have been cases where men who have had to go through bankruptcy in Japan have assumed full responsibility, often for the iniquities of others, and taken the full burden very much to heart.

The extent of intercorporate cooperation in Japan—a factor the foreign businessman must keep constantly in mind—is indicated by an item that appeared in a Tokyo newspaper at the end of 1967: "In a bid not to be left behind the rival Mitsubishi Group, the Mitsui Group will launch early next year an organizers' body to bolster the solidarity of its somewhat loose corporate grouping."[21]

Mitsui, which already has two regular group meetings, one of board chairmen and presidents of seventeen companies and the other of senior executives of twenty-seven companies, has thus been obliged to establish a third. The new organizers' body, according to a Mitsui spokesman, will be headed by Tatsuzo Mizukami, president of Mitsui and Company; Hideo Edo, president of Mitsui Real Estate Company; and Kyubei Tanaka, president of the Mitsui Bank. Kiichiru Sato, chairman of the Mitsui Bank, and Shigeki Tashiro, chairman of Toyo Rayon, will act as supreme advisors.

The purpose of the new body is to study, among other problems:

the promotion of a grand merger among three Mitsui chemical companies—Toyo Koatsu Industries, Mitsui Chemical Industry Company, and Mitsui Petrochemical Company, the first two of which were successfully merged around September 1968; the creation of a huge "Mitsui Heavy Industries," combining Mitsui Shipbuilding and Engineering, Mitsui Miike Machinery, Showa Aircraft Industry, and others; and unification of sugar refineries, including Shibaura and Taito, that belong to the group.

Another aspect of this same tendency in the Japanese industrial structure is the relationship between a large company and its many small sub-contractors: dependence on the one hand, obligations and duties on the other. Toyota Motor Company, for instance, uses 120 sub-contractors to provide such products as valves, piston rings, hubcaps, plastic parts, and the like. These sub-contractors rely on Toyota, for without it they would be lost, and Toyota in return must foster them, keep them alive, and help them financially when they require help. (Suppliers of important components, such as ball bearings, springs, transmissions, axles, brakes, and tires, are in a different category: these are all big businesses.)

Thus, the contemporary Japanese industrial structure, while it may be modern, is based on ancient feudal tradition that sometimes overrules logic. Everyone, from the Minister of Finance to the man who makes hub caps, has a place in the structure—a place that is his so long as he obeys and conforms to the rules. The Japanese industrial structure is Japanese, and the Westerner, if he is to find his own place in it, must attempt to understand the profound connections, the obligations and the duties, that act and interact between the great and the small.

4 Decisions and Responsibility

*"We are to consider mankind not as
we wish them but as we find them."*
—*Samuel Johnson*

I have already touched briefly on the Japanese conception of responsibility, which is so alien to our own. I should like to revert to it here, first very generally as it has affected recent history and continues to affect the daily life of the people and then, in somewhat more detail, as it has affected and still affects the national business structure and relations between Japanese and foreign businessmen. Perhaps no other single factor in Japanese government and business seems quite so incomprehensible to the Westerner, whose whole life conditions him to the making of quick and firm decisions, for which he then assumes responsibility.

Captain Ellis Zacharias, of the United States war-time Naval Intelligence, is quoted as having said: "No Japanese, regardless of rank or position, is so constituted that as an individual he is willing or able to assume responsibility for important decisions without the benefit of lengthy and repeated discussions sufficient to convince him that he does not carry the responsibility alone."[22]

Presumably the Imperial decision to surrender, after Japan's long agony of defeat in the Pacific War, is an exception to this statement of Captain Zacharias. But, as always when it comes to assessing not only the actions but also the words of a Japanese Emperor, one is hampered by the reticence that overtakes those who were most intimate with him. Marquis Kido, for example, who was the present Emperor's keeper of the Privy Seal and who was one of the first men to realize that Japan, in provoking the United States into war, was doomed to defeat, has refused to make any public utterance since that fateful mid-August day of 1945. Certainly, the Emperor did not, himself, write the Imperial Rescript that terminated the war by announcing Japan's acceptance of the Potsdam Proclamation; the Rescript was written by men appointed by the Cabinet and was worked over by the Cabinet itself. The Emperor may, indeed, alone have made the momentous decision that saved Japan from annihilation; or it may have been made, after "lengthy and repeated discussions," by the Emperor's advisers, using his "charismatic power." Perhaps, some day in the future, the historian will have at his disposal the documents necessary to sift the truth; perhaps those documents will never become available. After having lived in Japan for over twenty years, I incline toward the latter supposition.

Another example of this Japanese reluctance to come to a decision, since someone has to be responsible for it, is furnished by the fall of the Kishi Cabinet in 1960 as a result of his handling of leftist agitation against ratification by the Diet of a new Security Treaty between Japan and the United States. As a newspaper poll showed a few weeks later, only 8 percent of the Japanese people were in favor of the demonstrations against ratification of the Treaty; but Mr. Kishi had been forced to resign, nonetheless, because his attitude was thought to have been too high-handed toward the anti-Treaty minority. The Japanese are psychologically incapable of understanding why 51 percent of votes can overrule 49 percent, and they consider it improper ("un-Japanese") for the majority to ride roughshod over a minority. This factor has been most intelligently dealt with by Mr. Richard W. Rabinowitz, an American lawyer resident in Tokyo, in a lecture on "Law and the Social Process in Japan."[23]

This reluctance of the Japanese to let the majority decide and to go ahead, ignoring the minority, is prevalent not only in government but in business as well and must be taken into account by the foreigner who comes to Japan to do business. A justice of the United States Supreme Court will very often write a dissenting, or minority, opinion; but it does not obviate the fact that five votes have outweighed four—and that those five votes constitute a decision binding on the whole American people. In Japan the strictly legal aspect of majority rule does not have the same importance and is not so readily resorted to as in the West. If the majority takes what is called a "high posture," overriding dissenters, violent and widespread repercussions usually follow. The fact that consideration must be given to minority opinion creates difficulties and delays in decision making in all spheres of Japanese life—including business.

One of the chief problems in the decision to surrender was how to do it and at the same time save face. Thus, no ordinary Japanese could have made that decision and accepted the enormous responsibility that it entailed: only the "charismatic power" of the Emperor was strong enough to accomplish it—and that, considering the number of officers of the Imperial Army who felt the Emperor was being misled, was accomplished only by a hair's breadth! The same is true, though of course on a lesser scale, of day-to-day business dealings. Management's first task, in an important Japanese enterprise, is to maintain face—by which is meant its prestige, its rank, and its position within the group and the industry. All other considerations are secondary.

This fact frequently not only leads to absurdity (if Company A buys an IBM computer, Company B buys a Univac, though neither may know how to use them to complete advantage) but may also lead to disaster. This, however, is usually forgiven and the company saved by some means or other; one man, in that case, is likely to accept the onerous gift of responsibility and to retire—well taken care of.

"In Japan," writes Dr. Iwao Hoshii, "responsibility is usually only of importance as a function of success—or more often of failure. If a railroad accident took many lives, the president of the Japan National Railways assumed responsibility by tendering his resignation. The last president, Shinji Sogo, refused to submit to this tradition,which is a survival of feudal *seppuku*,"self-disembowelment.

"The resignation of the top executive of an enterprise threatened with failure is regarded as a kind of atonement for the inconvenience caused to all concerned—the personnel of the firm as well as its creditors and customers. Whether the failure was his fault or not is irrelevant. Thus it may happen that an executive who is irresponsible (at least by Western standards) squirms out of a tight spot with a slightly tarnished reputation—but a fat pocketbook, for he will receive a nice retirement allowance regardless of the financial health of the enterprise. It is his successor who will inherit the unenviable task of cleaning up the mess.

"Aside from outright and patent violations of the law, the only case in which an individual must assume responsibility for his decisions occurs when he contravenes the basic postulate, social conformity. At least in his external conduct, the individual must recognize the tenets of society, respect tradition and usage, and observe the norms sanctioned by public opinion."[24]

The concept of the *sekinin-sha* ("the responsible person") is perhaps unique in Japan in its width of application. The *sekinin-sha* is someone who is presumed to take responsibility for the actions of others, though there may be no formal commitment. He is the one who, if something goes wrong, is expected to take the necessary steps for finding a mutually acceptable solution to the problems created by or involving his charge. He is active, and indeed necessary, in many contexts, such as recommending a boy to a school, helping to find someone a position, introducing one person to another, initiating a business negotiation. A wise employer, especially in a small company, will accept a new employee only if he has a known person to accept *sekinin*, "responsibility." In such cases he is called *hosho-nin*. Then should the employee turn out, say, to be a thief and steal the company's funds, it is to the *hosho-nin* that the employer looks. Or should it become necessary to discharge the employee, the proper thing is for the employer to explain the situation first to the responsible party.

When he plays the role of "go-between," he is known as the *baishaku-nin* or, more specifically when arranging a marriage, the *nakodo*. "It is generally better," wrote Sir Francis Bacon, "to deal by speech than by letter; and by the mediation of a third [person] than by a man's self." With the latter statement, at least, the Japanese appear to have been in agreement for as long as written records exist. The go-between has played in the past, and continues to play, a vital role in the economic as well as the social life of the country.

In order to meet a person for the first time, it is not correct simply to telephone him and ask for an appointment: the "done" thing is for a first meeting to be arranged by a friend in common. (This is not true, apparently, of salesmen and reporters.) The custom is prevalent, of course, in most places in the world, but nowhere is it resorted to as constantly as in Japan. Here, where a wide acquaintanceship is so highly valued and the old school tie so important, the go-between becomes a person of tremendous influence.

The Japanese would far rather settle a problem through a go-between than by taking recourse to law; and the custom is certainly more conducive to harmony, tending to eliminate causes for internal dissension and vendetta. Indeed, in the tight, restrictive, physically crowded world in which the Japanese live, the go-between seems to be almost a necessity. The wise foreigner will make use of him to as great an extent as possible—bearing in mind always, of course, that he must be the right go-between. For years, I have had my favorite *baishaku-nin* on regular retainer. He has proven invaluable: I do not recall that he ever failed to know, and to be able to arrange a meeting with, someone of importance who could help me with the particular problem I had at the time.

During the occupation, certain less scrupulous Japanese made it their business to become acquainted with occupation officials. They then profited by *selling* introductions to these officials to other Japanese who needed help or advice but who had no idea how to approach the particular person that could give it to them. Apparently it occurred to very few simply to present themselves and ask.

In a marriage negotiation, the go-between is extremely important, since he can save face for both parties should either withdraw before the negotiations are firmly concluded. It is as if neither party existed in the marriage context until the go-between had successfully completed all the arrangements. Anyone may, of course, act as go-between, but with a marriage an effort is usually made to find someone as prestigious as possible. Many people are proud that so important a man as Mr. X was the go-between for their marriage. And many people are proud of their success in arranging marriages; a leading businessman was quoted in the press recently as boasting that he had been go-between for more than fifty!

While it is unusual for a foreigner to act as a go-between in a Japanese marriage, I found myself pressed on one occasion into such service. The marriage, I am glad to relate, is a success, and the first son is named after me. On other occasions, employees have asked me to meet the prospective partner and give my permission for the marriage to take place. A Japanese always becomes enmeshed in the personal affairs of long-time employees; it is another expression of the familial system that embraces even the foreigner who has been around long enough and has been accepted. And he soon realizes, if he is at all perceptive, how vital to the corporate as well as the social life of the country the *sekinin-sha* and the *baishaku-nin* are—if only because they contribute, when necessary, to the saving of face.

One of the prime motivations in Japanese life, face-saving is very much in the mind of Japanese management. That is why maintenance of volume of sales becomes more important to managers than profit on sales. It is the volume of sales and the "size" of the enterprise that are emphasized, for these are quantitative and may be used to make the management's "face" bigger, while profit on sales will perhaps never be mentioned by managers. "We increased sales over Company A and over our own target by x percent": such typical statements by managers omit the matter of how profitable the sales may have been and the obvious fact that the company's forward budget estimate was wrong. Japanese businessmen are addicted to the practice of setting budgets—perhaps "targets" would be a better word—and then announcing that the company has surpassed the budget so-and-so many times. This gives the managers big "face"—and incidentally supports their claims to substantial bonuses. The fact is, of course, that the way the Japanese use the word "budget"—as an estimate to be surpassed three or four times—means only that the estimate was erroneous and miscalculated in the first place. This does not, however, seem to discompose Japanese managers.

Recently, at a directors' meeting of a joint venture company, the company president proudly brought up the fact that the "budget" (in this case, production and sales targets) had been greatly exceeded. When I suggested that the targets must have been miscalculated and should in the future be continuously recalculated closer to real performance, based on known and anticipated conditions, he replied in a hurt tone that that was a harsh American way of looking at things.

Size, i.e., amount of capital is another major yardstick of prestige. "What is its capital?" is the first question asked about a company. Though it may make extremely high profits, the fact that its capital is low relegates it to a lesser echelon.

This tendency of Japanese management to consider position and status, to value quantitative sales higher than profitability, size of capital higher than return on investment, frequently leads to financial irresponsibility. Decisions are made in order to preserve the company's status in the industry rather than for corporate benefit. This irresponsibility may be of a positive nature—where management takes a financially unwise action just to keep up with the Joneses—or it may be negative, where management hides the results of its follies and ineptitudes, in a vain attempt to preserve prestige, only to the further detriment of the corporate position. It is obvious that some such positive action can, and frequently does, lead to the necessity for negative action, of the kind I have mentioned, to be taken.

The history of Japan's leading securities companies during the late 1950's and up to 1964 illustrates both positive and negative aspects that precipitated the crisis, which I discussed in an earlier chapter, when the government had to bail out Yamaichi. The others of the Big Four, as the leading securities firms are called, are Daiwa, Nikko, and Nomura, and all four, during the great boom in the "democratization" of securities and the boom of 1959, the inevitable forerunner of the depression, followed a similarly dangerous course.

They entered into an extravagant competition to get more salesmen, employing untrained people by the hundreds, to open new branches in order to sell more securities to unsophisticated and gullible customers, to buy batteries of computers and data processing equipment which they never learned to use with maximum efficiency, and to issue and sell "investment trusts"—in a word, to expand their operations (and expenses) to such a degree that when the inevitable break came in 1963, they all found themselves in grave financial straits. Yamaichi was saved by the government; others came very close to the edge.

After the bitter facts had been aired and scapegoats (not necessarily those truly responsible) found to "accept responsibility," a long-overdue retrenchment, with a tightening of regulations, was enforced by the government. The badly burned public, meanwhile, did not come back into the stock market until enticed by the 1968 boom.

I have also mentioned the case of the Sanyo Special Steel Company, which involved financial irresponsibilities approaching the criminal and which became a *cause célèbre* because it involved loans from foreign banks made to Sanyo under the guarantees of certain Japanese city banks. The fact that the company was already financially bankrupt at the time the guarantees were extended lends some credence to the claim made by many foreigners that there are few real bankers in Japanese banks; certainly, a bank credit report has very little meaning in Japan. In the investigation into the Sanyo case, the company auditor (i.e., the statutory auditor) reportedly admitted that he was aware of the financial irregularities that had occurred but felt unable to do anything that was contrary to the desires of the management. And to the manager status was—and is—more important than profitability. (Dividends paid to the shareholder frequently have little relation to profits, nor does he need to be given much serious consideration.)

Under the terms of the Japanese Commercial Code, the auditor is an officer of the company appointed by the shareholders; he is not an independent certified public accountant, nor does he actually audit the accounts, although by law he is presumed to be fully cognizant of all corporate financial matters.

In actual practice, his function is a purely nominal one. He is frequently not a working officer and may make only one or two appearances a year at the end of the accounting term, depending on whether the company closes its books once or twice each fiscal year, in order to put his seal on documents. Then, at the general meeting of shareholders, he will stand up to announce that he has received the corporate financial statements on behalf of the shareholders. This fairly meaningless ritual is usually accomplished in a few moments—unless an adverse *sokaiya* is present (about whom I shall have more to say later). For these sparse and brief appearances, the company auditor receives the full year's salary of a non-working director.

If he is a person of some age and experience, with a financial background (an ex-banker, for instance), he may be of value to the company, even though he does not run an independent audit or verify all accounts. As we saw in the case of Sanyo Special Steel, he may suspect, or even know of, irregularities, but it is most unlikely that he would ever reveal anything that was detrimental to the directors of the company.

As a result of the publicity the Sanyo case received, because foreign bankers were involved, the government took a more serious look at the role of company auditors and the reluctance on the part of companies to have independent outside audits. After a long period of study, the Ministry of Justice announced that it had completed a draft for a new Commercial Code designed to prevent the "window dressing" of corporate accounts so as to provide better protection for investors. According to a newspaper account of the announcement, "The planned revision of the auditing system for joint-stock companies has been necessitated by a series of business irregularities in recent years . . . . The inadequacy of the status and power of auditors has been believed to be making their auditing functions more or less perfunctory, and, in some cases, subject to dishonest or arbitrary decisions by the Board of Directors."[25]

The revised draft, then, not only provides for an increase in the power and independence of the company auditor but it also calls for audits of large companies by outside certified public accountants. All major firms whose securities are listed on the Tokyo Stock Exchange are to submit to the Ministry of Finance financial statements certified by auditors. At the present time, it is said that over two thousand Japanese firms make such reports, but if the new draft is approved by the Diet, more than five thousand firms will be affected. It is quite possible, however, that the final form of the new Code will be weaker than the proposed draft, since, according to the same newspaper account, "many financial companies, including banks, insurance and securities firms, have been strongly demanding exemption from the planned reform."

A company's dividends are frequently decided long before they are earned, and frequently also the dividend rate is determined by what other enterprises in the same sector are paying, for Japanese management feels it has lost face if it pays less than its competitors or fails to maintain a dividend rate. In the preparation of budgets, management often begins not with earnings per share but with dividends per share.

This practice has frequently given rise to bitter misunderstanding in joint ventures. It is not at all unusual for the Japanese partners, in explaining their financial plan at the beginning of the term, to state that they intend to pay a dividend of 12 percent at the term end. When I object to this procedure, on the grounds that it is unrealistic to decide a dividend rate so far in advance, since earnings are not predictable with such precision, and furthermore that my American principals would probably prefer to forget dividends for some years and to retain earnings, reinvesting them in the company so as to reduce its dependence on borrowings, the Japanese reaction is likely to be disbelief or distrust. The Japanese partner wants his dividends immediately, following the Japanese way, and feels the American partner must have some unexpressed motive in desiring to withhold them. Admittedly, the gap here is beginning to narrow: more and more joint ventures have come to realize that to the foreign partner dividends are less important than growth—and that there may be some merit in this approach, however disagreeable it is.

Closely allied to the deep-seated impulse to maintain face in all major decision making is the *ringisho*, an elaborate system for the vertical channeling of all proposals for corporate action and the communication of managerial decisions. By means of this process, decision making becomes a group activity—and individual responsibility is avoided. In the one direction, from the lower levels up, the decision has in essence been made before it reaches those who should be the decision-makers, thus diluting authority and consequent responsibility. In the other direction, a decision may be made at the top, for reasons known only to the top managers, or to other insiders, or to the "club," and this decision is then sent down for confirmation, once again relieving everyone of personal responsibility. It may happen that instructions or decisions sent down from above will not be acted on because of obstruction from below; in that case, nothing will happen until a group decision can be found.

These observations are, of course, only broad generalities; a thousand other considerations may be involved, at various times, in the constitution of the hierarchy and the establishment of corporate policies. A concrete illustration or two may be helpful in clarifying the problem.

An American company had licensed a Japanese company to manufacture and sell its product line. The agreement having been approved by the government, the Japanese company enlarged one of its plants, imported some machinery, and after test production finally began to produce and sell commercially. By this time, the initial license approval was about to expire, necessitating an extension or a new approval. Here government changes adverse to the foreigner were to be expected, inasmuch as that is the government's customary attitude.

Fortunately in theory—but unfortunately, as we shall see, in practice—the president of the Japanese company considered this particular project as his own pet, a fact he made no secret of. Unhappily, just at the time decisions regarding the renewal application had to be made, he fell ill. As a result, it was impossible to get any action, the reason advanced being that since this was the president's pet project, it was for him to make the decisions—and he could not be disturbed. With his death some months later, his successor took office knowing nothing about the case beyond the fact that the project was especially dear to the former president. After another delay, the foreign licensor brought pressure to bear, and the new president took over, sending sufficiently strong instructions down the line so that appropriate action was taken at last.

A second example illustrates the ingrained power of the *ringisho* system despite the desires of top management. Here, in a three-way joint venture, the advisability of transferring an existing license from one of the Japanese partners to the joint venture itself was discussed and agreed upon as beneficial to all the parties concerned. The president of the Japanese licensee company accordingly instructed his staff to do the necessary clerical work to effect the transfer.

As time went by without any action taken, questions were asked; the reply came that the company could not yet agree despite the promise of its president. When the American partner to the joint venture pressed for further explanation, there were vague references to "internal reasons" and to the fact that "it would take time." Since the other Japanese partner was equally unable to secure a clearer reply, the joint venture still awaits disposal of these "internal reasons."

It is obvious that on some echelon there are one or more officers who, for their own "reasons," are opposed to the transfer despite the benefits to the company. Since there is not unanimity, the president has retreated in the face of opposition. He cannot force the issue; only time will decide it. I had some difficulty explaining the situation to the American company and convincing the directors that it would be unwise to press the matter further. To many foreign businessmen, a situation where juniors can act in opposition to the top management and nullify their decisions will seem wholly untenable, but it happens in Japan and must be accepted without hostility.

Sometimes corporate policy in Japan will remind the bewildered foreigner of the famous words of Topsy: "I'spect I growed. Don't think nobody never made me." The fact is, however, policy *is* made—but by such a huge number of seemingly extraneous factors and influences that the foreigner (and perhaps even the Japanese himself) can hardly be expected to take all of them into account. The Japanese, however, accepts their existence: he is aware that the pressures of opinions and ideas (not necessarily correct) and of obligations constrain the operator to follow a course of action that may be unwise, or even suicidal.

One of the more "off-beat" influences that exert pressure on Japanese management is the *sokaiya* (literally, "the shareholders' general meeting man"), who is, I believe, unique to Japan and whose existence and activities are little known to foreigners. Non-Japanese are under the impression that the average individual holder of shares of a Japanese company (as distinct from institutional shareholders) is given little consideration by corporate management and has little or no interest in the company beyond the price of the shares and the dividend, since he never attends shareholders' meetings and rarely engages in proxy fights. Generally speaking, this is true: management can normally do what it wishes, after consultation with the very large institutional owners, without fear of private shareholder questioning or censorship. This would disrupt the harmony of the meeting (which is usually a brief formality for the purpose of affixing seals to documents) and would embarrass the management. It is therefore to be avoided; it isn't *junjo*, "the way things are done." Large shareholders have usually already been approached and have agreed to decisions before the meeting occurs: there is no danger from them. The general public, the individual shareholder, doesn't attend the meeting: here again there is no danger to management. But there *is* danger from the *sokaiya* ("the shareholders' general meeting

82

man"), who is also known, somewhat euphemistically, as the *tokushu kabunushi* ("the special shareholder").

The latter is, in fact, a fairly descriptive term, since he is by no means an ordinary shareholder who has invested his funds for the usual reasons—that is, to earn dividends and, hopefully, capital gains over the years. The *sokaiya* may have only one share, or at most a few shares, of stock, so his stake in dividends or capital gains is virtually nil; but the registration of his modest holding permits him not only to attend the shareholders' meeting but also to demand to see the term financial reports, which must be open to shareholders at least two weeks prior to the date of the general meeting. His only interest in these reports is the potential use he might put them to in order to make trouble. To avoid trouble, the company director in charge of General Affairs will arrange a "fee" for him (which is usually charged to some non-commital expense like research or advertising). I call him an entrepreneur, for want of a more descriptive term, since he has developed one of the oldest means of making money into a fine art—the "squeeze," the "bite" —but conducted in such a way that it is difficult for the company director who deals with him to claim any illegality or do more than protest that the "fee" demanded is excessive.

One theory of the origin of the *sokaiya* goes back to the early Meiji period, when samurai not competent enough to go into business or government had to find other means of earning a living. Some of them went into the business of providing "protection" for travelers, employing local protectors along the roads to collect money from those who wanted to be reasonably free from harassment. Some say that these "protectors" became *sokaiya* or that their better-educated descendants did; in any case, it was a field of activity that soon attracted university men who would now be outraged at being called anything more opprobrious than "businessmen"—just as a certain notorious American gangster insisted on being called a businessman in his later days.

The *sokaiya* usually operates under a "cover" organization, such as a research institute or a publishing company, though it may be composed of only one man. He never uses "enforcers"; there is no violence connected with his levy; his pressure is subtle but potent. It is said that there are only about ten really important *sokaiya* in Japan today, but each has a number of followers, called *kobun*. The prestige of some *sokaiya* is so great that they no longer bother to attend meetings (although they may send a *kobun*); their "fees" arrive punctually in any case. Others who are lower in the hierarchy will attend meetings and attempt to embarrass the management, in order to demonstrate that they are persons to be reckoned with, thus increasing both "fees" and "face." If there is a more prestigious *sokaiya* in the pay of the company, he will sit heavily on the dissenter, and if the latter is one of his own followers, he will be disciplined—for no one in Japan, even when doing wrong, must be too obviously self-ambitious. (The Mafia observes similar restrictions, though its activities are considerably more lethal.)

General meetings of shareholders in Japan have the—for the *sokaiya*—unfortunate habit of coming at the same time, in May and November, since most companies close their books twice each fiscal year, at the end of March and at the end of September. The *sokaiya* would prefer a more equitable distribution throughout the year, so that they could then "attend" to more companies. As it is, the few weeks prior to the general meeting are the time of trouble for the company director in charge of General Affairs and the time when the *sokaiya* is at his busiest. The discussion between the two will center about what I call "potentials of disputation," about whether there is to be harmony or dissidence at the meeting. For the *sokaiya* can act or he can abstain from action; he has no interest in what decisions are reached at the meeting and no stake in the future of the company. His only concern is the size of his own "fee," which is usually determined prior to the meeting. To determine just how much to pay is an exercise involving diplomacy and gamesmanship with an intuitive knowledge of the state of the market; consumer prices, employment or unemployment, costs of *geisha* parties and night club hostesses, plus a vast number of other factors. Only a company director of long experience can intelligently estimate the amount of the "fee" required by the *sokaiya*. (Such knowledge is not acquired at the Harvard School of Business.)

If he is paid enough, he becomes a company *sokaiya*, a sort of "sponsor" of the meeting on the side of management and—psychologically, at least—a threat to those stockholders or other adverse or minor *sokaiya* who might try to get out of line. The latter will then be told to be quiet or—if he is too important for such summary treatment—will be asked to discuss the matter later somewhere else. Then the company *sokaiya* shouts, "Agreed!" or "No objection!" and management breathes a sigh of relief. Where there is a potential scandal, such as in the recent case of Nippon Express (Nittsu), the *sokaiya* may anticipate substantial extra "fees" on the understanding that he will keep silent both publicly and at the shareholders' meeting.

If he is not paid enough, he may threaten to bring up unpleasant matters at the meeting, or he may decide to switch sides during the meeting and so become a bone of dreaded contention. Human nature being frail, a *sokaiya* who has been bought frequently does not stay bought. In either case, he wins—and the company, though it may sometimes find him useful, loses. The foreigner may feel that Japan's harmony is on occasion overpriced.[26]

With all these factors to be considered, it is not surprising that the foreign businessman in Japan finds it difficult to understand what a company's true corporate policy is (or even if it has one) and to discover, in any given case, what the managers really want to do or what they actually will do—since frequently what they want and what they do are two quite different things. This situation creates apparent illogicalities for the foreigner that might otherwise be explainable and so avoid common sources of misunderstanding. Foreigners also complain frequently that they are unable to find out which officer of a company can, and will, make a simple decision—for usually there is no single individual who is both able and willing to make the decision and to take the responsibility for it.

The *ringisho* system, of which I spoke earlier, is the crux of the matter: it is the basis of a set of fixed routines for all company personnel on all levels of administration. And it is coming increasingly under attack as over-rigid, ossified, and wasteful, as tending to eliminate authority and foster evasion of responsibility. Now progressive managements incline toward more horizontal inter-change, permitting more initiation and initiative at certain levels, with less adherence to rigid routine. Some companies have begun to use the *ringisho* system only as a means of communication, which would seem to be useful, rather than—as formerly—as a method of group decision-making. They are beginning to specify the authority and responsibility consistent with every level of the hierarchy. I am not sure, however, that the *ringisho* system ought to be condemned out of hand. For one thing, the system has worked. For another, if all members of a company who affix their seals to a document, in the course of its vertical journey, have really studied it, the value of the accumulated experience applied to the problem is apparent.

An editorial in *The Japan Times* (September 3, 1968) indicates the growing trend toward management reforms and the changing attitudes toward the salaryman:

"There was a time not so long ago when a salaried job was regarded as something akin to a sinecure. Once a person became a salaryman for a company, he was assured a job for life. And though we Japanese, being an industrious people, worked hard, there were more tea breaks than there should have been, and there wasn't initiative enough to find original, new solutions to problems. Come to think of it, most companies discouraged originality. They wanted their salarymen cast in the same identical mold.

"In recent years, however, there has been a definite trend away from this. The best evidence is the emphasis placed on outspoken-ness and originality by leading companies in their annual search for new employees. In a recent survey by Waseda University, 41.5 percent of the section heads polled said they looked first of all for *sekkyokusei*—positiveness—when interviewing job applicants.

"More and more companies are carrying out employee train-ing—actual work in plants, even for desk personnel—when they first enter the company and at stages in their advance with their firm. There is greater emphasis also on rating the employee in terms of his or her value to the company, rather than on age, seniority, or school ties.

"One by-product of this trend has been a boom in book sales—many of them translations of Western works—on the new economic theories, on modern management systems and practices and developments in finance, business and industry around the world. The readers are not only eager, young employees, but include department heads and high executives pushing themselves to keep abreast of developments.

"One inevitable result of this has been the de-emphasis of the so-called 'elite schools' and increasing weight on the individual worker's ability and his contribution to the company.

"One form this new emphasis on efficiency is taking is simplification of organizational structure to create more flexibility. One criticism often made of us in the past has been that we are great on organization but lack flexibility. Toyo Rayon took the initiative in 1963 by partially eliminating the *ka* (section). Hitachi, Toshiba, and Japan Development Bank are among those who have followed its example. More recently, Japan Mining and Japanese Geon have eliminated the *ka* and the *kacho* (section chief) completely.

"The *bucho* no longer has to channel his orders to subordinates through the section head. The former section head now supervises a specific project and is assigned personnel according to his needs. This flexibility makes it possible to make the best possible use of employees and their abilities. This is still a trend. But shortage of workers, rising costs and increased competition from foreign companies have compelled leading companies to overhaul their structure and modernize their business practices."

The Japan Times is, I fear, unduly optimistic in its assessment of the extent of the change. Comparatively few companies have, so far, taken up the new way of doing things; the huge majority continue stubbornly along the old path. The wind of change is blowing, to be sure, but not with the strength the editorial suggests.

Yet the fact that, as *The Japan Times* says, "this is still a trend," must not be downgraded. Other evidence of it may be found in increased recognition of the importance of training employees in new skills to improve productivity. Some companies (such as Hitachi) have long had training centers for new employees, but more and more companies now require higher officers to attend training sessions. Hitachi, Teijin, and N.E.C., among others, emphasize learning how to use computers; still others are more concerned with personnel management and modern management systems. Companies with international connections, such as joint ventures and the like, have stepped up their language training programs.

Some salarymen, however, do not agree that these trends toward pay and promotion by merit and toward changes in procedures and management rankings are all quite so desirable as they seem. For they presuppose an equivalent change in the status of the salaryman himself. He fears that his former easy life is coming to an end, and he sees his long-cherished prerogatives going with the wind of change. For the middle-aged salaryman, fearing competition from below, the new way constitutes a very real threat to the more soothing system of life tenure and promotion by seniority.

Not all proposed structural changes have been accepted without complaint. When Nippon Kokan proposed to abolish some fifty-five management positions on the *kacho* (section chief) and *bucho* (division chief) levels, the company explained that such changes were necessary in order to cope with liberalization and competition from foreign enterprises (an excuse that is almost invariably produced to justify unwelcome decisions) and that salaries and positions would not be adversely affected by the proposed changes; nevertheless, there was considerable agitation against them.

An article on the subject in the *Asahi Shimbun*[27] instances the case of Mitsumi Denki K.K., which inaugurated fairly drastic changes under the slogan: "Catch up with American companies and surpass them!" The article went on to describe the mental shock experienced by some middle-level salarymen when such changes were initiated and told how a group of wives, whose husbands had the rank of *kacho*, pleaded with a certain company that the title not be taken away even if the salary had to be reduced. The *Asahi* points out that being lowered in rank is an extremely painful experience and that title is in itself important, particularly if one lives in company housing (*danchi*). Some companies, thus, compromise by permitting rank to be ostensibly retained while reorganizing the actual work position. Tokyu Department Store is said to have changed its management structure, placing people according to ability but meanwhile continuing the old ranks for the purpose of saving face.

Japanese writers on the subject make the frequent claim that the Japanese employer takes into account the human aspect of the employee and his work while the Westerner is likely to consider only the employee's work performance.* "The American hires a hand," say the Japanese, "while we employ the whole man," and there is much truth to this claim. In most Japanese enterprises, salary and job levels have no intimate relationship with work actually performed. With the present tendency toward change, the individual may now hope to earn promotion because of demonstrated ability, or merit, while salaries and seniority will continue to be treated traditionally: the stability of the age-wage and the life-employment system will be maintained, while work-performance may be differently evaluated. The tendency, then, is to superimpose a certain degree of the Western emphasis on work on the old paternalistic system, or to attempt to integrate the two. In time it might succeed!

Meanwhile, however, there is necessarily, even in the most modern companies, a strong resistance to any change in management-employee relations, for change involves risks and creates new patterns and problems which the present managers may feel unable to cope with. (This situation does not exist to the same extent in the technical field.) Thus, no sudden drastic change is to be expected—or even desired. A whole shift to the Western system

---

*This is a Confucian concept. To quote a paraphrase from the Analects of Confucius by Dr. Cheng Tien Hsi in his book, *The Way of Confucius:* "In the employment of men, the *Jiun Tze* takes into consideration the limits of their capacity. The *Siao Yun*, in the employment of men, expects them all to be capable."

The *Jiun Tze* is frequently translated as the "superior man," but the term means rather "the man of virtue," the "man of principles." The *Siao Yun*, "the petty man," "the man of no virtue," is his counterpart.

of pay by performance and responsibility by position, with the abolition of the Japanese system of seniority and life tenure, could be such a traumatic experience that grave civil disturbance might easily result. However, there is no suggestion that the change is likely to occur quickly; it will almost certainly come about, as I have suggested, through the gradual integration of Western ideas and methods into the traditional Japanese structure; considering the make-up of Japanese management, it seems obvious that there must necessarily be reluctance to change and that it can only come slowly.

The Salaryman 5

Rui wa tomo wo yobu ("*Birds of a feather flock together*").
—*Japanese proverb*

I propose to risk a few generalizations about that peculiarly Japanese phenomenon, the salaryman, asking the reader to bear in mind that the changes I spoke of in the last chapter have rendered some of the generalizations untrue for some companies and, perhaps, if Japanese business continues to adopt Western business philosophies, it will make many of them untrue for more companies.

But meanwhile the male white-collar worker in Japan tends to pursue the path he started out on a hundred years ago when the Meiji government made its momentous decision to transform Japan from a feudal to a capitalist economy, based on the country's age-old concept of paternalism. There are now well over twenty-five million white-collar workers in Japan; called "salarymen" by the Japanese themselves, they are the present and future chief clerks, section chiefs, division chiefs, managers, directors, executives, presidents.

In most companies of any size, the salaryman is recruited on graduation from high school or college. (It is the latter that supplies the candidates for management.) Once he has been accepted and recognized as a "regular employee," the young man feels himself safe for life—so long as he conforms to the accepted code of behavior. He is on the escalator, as it is called, and he goes up automatically in status and salary as his length of service increases.

He has become part of "a large family where the membership

varies little; only that "children" are recruited from time to time."[28] He lives the rest of his working life in what sociologists call a "kinship." The rest of his group members are all pretty much like him: they have more or less the same background and went to the same kind of school. His ambitions and motivations are those of his group; he has been conditioned to think and act like the others, and as the conditioning process continues, he is confirmed in what he already believes. He knows that he is not expected to be brilliant or outstanding. Brilliance, in fact, is suspect—it is not wanted.

The company gives him a lapel badge, which he wears (like almost everyone else in Japan) at all times, to indicate where he belongs. School children, high school and college students, businessmen, lawyers, government bureaucrats, and members of the Diet all wear badges. At company receptions, the size and ornateness of the rosettas that are pinned on guests at the entrance indicate the status of the wearer, as does the value of the gifts presented on departure. At the first meeting of the Board of Directors of a newly-formed Japanese-American joint venture, one of the first items on the agenda was: "Decision as to company badge."

If our salaryman happened to work for Matsushita Electric Company, he would begin his work day every morning by singing, along with all other employees, including executives, the following song:

> For the building of a new Japan,
> Let's put our strength and mind together,
> Doing our best to promote production,
> Sending our goods to the people of the world,
> Endlessly and continuously,
> Like water gushing from a fountain.
> Grow, industry, grow, grow, grow!
> Harmony and sincerity!
> Matsushita Electric![29]

The management of this company is considered to be extremely modern, and the founder is one of Japan's great new entrepreneurs.

The suffocating closeness of the salaryman's life, in both thought and action, may help to explain his aggressiveness and recklessness when he breaks away, as at drinking parties, or on the highways, or in crowded subways. Another example of this over-reaction to over-restraint was the behavior of Japanese soldiers, before and during the War, when they were away from their own country: a trait that the Japanese have recognized in themselves for a long time. There is an old folk saying—*Tabi no haji wa kakizute*—which, freely translated, means, "The traveller, when away from home, forgets his sense of morality."

The salaryman must never do so on the job; there, conformity and harmony are essential. He must know, and abide by, his own rank in his group as precisely as his company knows, and abides by, its status within a large group of enterprises.

When he joins the company, after leaving high school or college, the salaryman is expected to have little or no useful knowledge. He is therefore given on-the-job training, and in time he is presumed to learn what he needs to know—and he usually does. At the outset of his career with the company, he will be shunted from one section to another. A generalist is considered to be preferable to a specialist, although with the advancement of technology, the demand for technicians, and the requirements of Research and Development, the necessity for specialized training has made itself felt. (Technicians, of course, are frequently required even to "over-specialize," but if they progress to management, they again must become generalists.)

After a few weeks, or a month or so, in each department, the salaryman is likely to be placed almost anywhere. This placement may have little or nothing to do with his education; graduate lawyers, for instance, may be found in most divisions, even production.

Later, if he shows some special talent, he may be kept in the appropriate department. In any event, he will never be fired—so long as he does nothing illegal. If he is habitually tardy or obviously lazy or extremely incompetent, his pay increases and bonuses may be smaller than those of others of his group after he reaches the higher clerk level, and he will soon realize that he will not reach an important position. Thus, he will in due time seek retirement receiving from the company a retirement allowance and frequently a part-time job as advisor to a smaller affiliated company.

To get his foot on the right escalator in the first place, the salaryman should be a college graduate, and his college should be as prestigious as possible. This, in turn, means graduating from a "good" high school. Competition in the field of education in Japan is fierce, for family position as an influence has been replaced to a large extent by graduation from the "right" university. But in order to get into the right university, the boy must first have attended a good high school, and here family position, or some other comparable influence, is extremely helpful, aided of course by intelligence, learning ability, and luck.

If a family, for example, is able to enter its son in Keio Kindergarten, then the boy is likely to remain at Keio throughout his entire school life, and after he graduates from Keio University, he is assured of a place in government or business or one of the professions.

It appears, in fact, that once a boy has passed his entrance examinations and been allowed to enroll in a college, any college, he need worry no longer about his future. If his college lacks prestige, then he will probably not join a very prestigious firm, but he will get his foot on some escalator going up. Apparently he need not even study very hard if he prefers not to: he will almost certainly graduate anyway. A recent book about Japan describes students who did no studying at all,[30] and I have met men who—to my amazement—were college graduates, although they appeared to have acquired no practical knowledge whatsoever.

But this appears to make little difference. The boy who graduates at the bottom of his class will probably not join so prestigious a firm as the boy who graduates at the top, but he will get his foot on an escalator all the same. If he stays on, he will eventually achieve the status he desires, and the perquisites that go with it— a large entertainment allowance, a company car, membership in a golf club, travel paid by the company, and the privilege of talking down to underlings. The man spoken down to bears the speaker no ill will, for he knows that after he moves up a notch he will speak in the same way to his inferiors. The Japanese language is full of distinctions created for this very purpose. In a society where everyone is conscious of rank and status, it is not surprising that the language too should conform. The Japanese say: "*Ue niwa ue ga aru, shita niwa shita ga aru,*" which means, "The superior has his superiors, the inferior has his inferiors."

At times the consciousness and prerogatives of rank are ludicrous. I shall give but one example—that of a friend who is chairman of a leading corporation and who, as chairman, has to use the largest car the company owns. It happens to be a Cadillac, too big to be convenient, too expensive to run, and too old to be sold for anything but scrap. My friend would much prefer a Mercedes 300—but he has to use the Cadillac. (He has tried, without success, to give it to me.)

The government bureaucracy, of which I shall speak later, is run by men who went to school together—a fact they never forget. A Westerner will be surprised at first to hear a man of sixty refer to another as a schoolmate a year or two behind or ahead of him— and he will be surprised also to discover the strategic role "the old-boy network"[31] plays in Japanese society. But we who have lived and worked here, and have needed introductions or information, are very well aware of it indeed.

In October 1967, the *Asahi Shimbun* ran an extended "profile" of a salaryman, describing his life and work. I shall tell Mr. Yano's story in the present tense, as the newspaper did, since I doubt that the situation has changed much in the past two years except for the fact that a man like Mr. Yano would now probably be somewhat more affluent.

He is not altogether typical of the salaryman, since he is a graduate of the Commercial School at Waseda University and so is one of those who, as the newspaper puts it, "run on the elite course." He decided, on graduation, to seek employment in a bank because he had taken a course on money at the University, and he chose the particular bank he did because one of his professors told him: "This bank is not yet petrified. It has a future." He was one of three applicants out of a hundred who passed the examinations given by the bank and was first assigned to a branch located in the center of the Osaka Harbor district. He soon moved from note counting to customers' man, a job at which he had to walk so much his legs became stiff. After a stint at the head office in Osaka, he worked in two Tokyo branches. He is now assistant branch manager in charge of loans.

He is thirty-six years old. His wife is thirty, the elder of his two daughters is in second grade, and the younger is only four. They live in company housing—three rooms and a kitchen on the top floor of a four-storied apartment building—for which they pay a monthly rent of ¥4,500 (US$12.50). This is no more than a token payment, since Tokyo rentals in private housing are extremely, sometimes ludicrously, high. Mr. Yano's monthly salary is ¥93,400; after taxes are deducted, he takes home ¥79,670 (approx. US$221.40). In addition to the low rent he pays, he enjoys such benefits as meal tickets, commuter tickets, and entertainment expenses. (According to the White Book on the Standard of Living, compiled by the Economic Planning Agency, for fiscal 1966, the average monthly income of an urban worker's household was ¥75,372 [approx. US$209.00].)

Some years ago, he bought a small piece of land (330 square meters) with mortgage bonds of the Housing Corporation. He plans to build a wooden house, for which the company will lend him up to ¥5 million (about US$14,000). He will have until his retirement to repay this loan.

His day begins early. He always rises at six, even if he has gone to bed as late as one or two. When he dresses, he has fifteen custom-made suits to choose from. ("Better one good suit than two cheap ones," he believes.)* At breakfast, he has eggs with bread and black tea, and looks through the morning paper—the first page, the page dealing with economics, and then local news. If a story bears on his work, such as "Increase in Discount Rate" or "Organization of a New Public Corporation," he reads it through;

---

*But custom-made suits are relatively cheap in Japan.

otherwise, he merely reads the headlines. Such items as an accident at a coal mine or a hippie demonstration do not arouse his interest: "People are not so much concerned about the hippies as the news-papers think," he says.

He leaves home at 7:15 and takes a ten-minute bus ride to the station, where he buys a business newspaper and then boards an electric train that will take him to his office in half an hour, during which time he is absorbed in his newspaper. The posters in the train advertising real estate, or the miniskirts do not distract him.

He is at his desk by 8:30, half an hour earlier than his subordi-nates. At nine he begins to interview clients—representatives of trading companies, perhaps, or firms in the amusement business, small enterprises. Mr. Yano's clients see a short man of medium weight, with his hair parted neatly at the side. He looks at them calmly, without staring, and weighs his words carefully. Both he and they are aware that where money is concerned, a wrong deci-sion may involve losses that cannot be made up by pocket money. "Banking means confidence," he says, "confidence in every single employee of the bank. If people lose confidence, banking becomes impossible."

At noon Mr. Yano lunches at the bank's canteen on the second floor,* where he talks with other employees about such sports as golf, baseball, and sumo. Health is also a frequent topic of conver-sation; many of the employees take one or another of the stomach medicines advertised on television.** Their conversation seldom

*According to a survey made by the Ministry of Agriculture, 49.7 percent of office workers brought their lunch from home, 19.1 percent lunched at the company canteen, 18.3 percent went out to lunch at some sort of restaurant or snack-bar, 7.8 percent ordered their lunch to be brought in, and 5.1 percent had lunch in some other way.

**The head of the Yawata Iron and Steel Company, in Tokyo, with fifteen hundred employees, has an average monthly attendance of twelve hundred at the company clinic. Colds are the most common complaint; digestive orders are second (over 20 percent). Says one of the doctors: "Today's patients seem to be of very delicate health. They have no well-defined symptoms, but that they cannot sleep, that they have a stiff shoulder, that their digestion is bad, that maybe it's cancer. Many seem to have some kind of mental suffering."

touches on politics. Mr. Yano himself supports the Liberal-Democratic Party. "The policies of the Socialists," he says, "are abstract, with no concrete objectives. I hate abstract theories." When asked about corruption in politics, he says, "Public opinion —the newspapers—should reprove those who are guilty." On the subject of public nuisances, he says, "I can't answer such a hypothetical question. But I don't believe that business and government overlook these problems." When asked if he thought his vote counted, his reply was: "I believe in the strength of the organized vote, which pulls the single votes together."

At three o'clock, the bank's shutters go down and the real work begins. Cash has to be counted, ledgers must balance. Mr. Yano remains until all the clerks leave. Then his eyes may meet those of his colleagues. "Have a game?" suggests one, and four of them go off to a mahjong parlor. They play until ten p.m., at which point they stop even if the game is not yet finished. Mahjong games usually occur only about once a week, and once a week also Mr. Yano goes to a beer hall with his colleagues—Dutch treat. Mr. Yano's share comes to about two thousand yen. Nothing very important is discussed; the most serious topic that arises is likely to be personnel changes; but the gatherings are regarded as conducive to making the bank run more smoothly.*

Twice a month Mr. Yano plays golf, spending each time about three thousand yen. He started playing golf seven years ago since he believes that it is now almost essential to Japanese business: the links are where a man meets customers and talks to them. "If an employee takes three customers to a Ginza bar," says Mr. Yano, "the bill is at least thirty thousand yen, but if he plays mahjong with them, he can do it for ten thousand. That's why the companies have switched from bars to golf or mahjong, and that's why the company personnel has to know how to play."

---

*A survey made by the Yasuda Trust and Banking Company gives the following figures: over 40 percent of salarymen never go to bars, cabarets, or clubs, but of employees in leading positions a large percentage go once a month or oftener. Between 60 and 70 percent of salarymen play neither golf nor mahjong.

Unless he is staying out for some reason, Mr. Yano gets home about eight o'clock. He drinks a small bottle of beer as he watches television—preferably a program concerned in some way with foreign business. He dislikes "soap operas" passionately. He reads about three books a month, books with titles like "Management Analysis of Small Enterprises," "Customer Approach," or "Personnel Management." If his wife complains about how little Yukiko (a girl child) is doing at school, his reply is: "Why worry about it? She's a child, let her play." He doesn't think mothers should be overly concerned with the education of their children (the Japanese call them *kyoiku mamas*); he believes a wife's duties are elsewhere.

On Sundays, Mr. Yano may play golf, or he may take his family on an outing. At such times he thinks a car might be handy, and if he really wants one, he'll buy it.* He may even find time to take driving lessons and get a license. Some Sundays he goes out for a walk alone. He looks at the flower gardens in front of the houses, he admires the trees and the blue sky, he relishes the mood of the season. He has no reason for dissatisfaction or worry. There hasn't even been a bad typhoon this year . . . .

In giving Mr. Yano's salary, I did not mention that he gets a substantial bonus twice a year, but that fact is extremely important to him—as it is to every regularly employed Japanese—and to the Japanese economy as well. By making do, as best he can, with the monthly salary he receives, the Japanese worker is able to put a large part of his semi-annual bonus into his savings account, or to invest it otherwise. Many companies make use of a savings system, whereby employees may deposit funds with the company itself, which then pays a high interest rate.

The ratio of savings against earnings has been extremely high ever since the Meiji industrialization and has played a vital role in the phenomenal growth of the Japanese economy. The fact that

*The Toyota Motor Company estimates that private households own 1.2 million cars. 11 percent of car owners are professional men in liberal occupations, 20.7 percent are employees in administrative jobs, 51.5 percent have clerical jobs.

Confucianism, the basis of Japanese morality, stresses the value of savings as against consumption has also contributed to this high savings ratio—although the present-day foreigner who fights his way through Japan's many crowded and expensive department stores may wonder if this particular aspect of Confucianism has not lost some of its moral force.

According to a trial calculation (made by the Fuji Bank), the total amount of the bonuses paid at the end of 1968 came to about ¥20,010 billion—an average of ¥69,000 per person. This represented an increase of over 15 percent for each person and was 20 percent higher than the total paid out at the end of the previous year. Below is a table showing the kind of bonuses given by a few representative companies to employees with ten consecutive years of service:

	YEAR-END BONUS		SUMMER BONUS	
	University graduates	High-school graduates	University graduates	High-school graduates
Fujiya Confectionery	¥262,000	¥216,000		
Toyo Rayon			¥276,000	¥130,000
Fuji Film	230,000	130,000–150,000		
Yawata Iron & Steel			250,000	100,000
Nihon Light Metal			250,000–300,000	100,000
Tokyo Shibaura Electric	215,000	113,000		
Toyota Auto Sales			200,000	150,000
Isetan Department Store			310,000–320,000(net)	265,000(net)
Asahi Glass			240,000	130,000
N.Y.K. (a leading shipping Co.)	240,000	163,000		
Japan Air Lines	250,000	180,000		
Tokyo Express	180,000–200,000	150,000		
Hypothec Bank	273,000	162,000		
Tokyo Electric Power			147,000	88,000
Kodansha (Publishers)			293,000	212,000
Nippon T.V.	243,000	207,000		

At a directors' meeting of a joint venture company, the subject of officers' bonuses was brought up as an item that ought to be decided before the imminent General Meeting of shareholders. The amounts proposed did not seem to me to be based on the usual formula of so many months' salary, so I said that, as the director for the American partner, I would like to know how the bonuses had been calculated, as I was sure my principals would want that information. I was told only that the Japanese parent company, which is extremely large and well-known, had determined the amounts according to its own formulae. That particular meeting occurred a year ago, and I have so far been unable to gain any further information. It appears that the parent company prefers not to reveal what it considers to be private aspects of a formula for evaluating the work and abilities of senior people—despite the fact that the foreign partner is obviously entitled to know how his money is spent.

An inevitable result of the Japanese system of lifelong employment is overstaffing and the carrying of a certain amount of dead weight. But the Japanese have always emphasized the overall productivity of the group rather than the productivity of each employee. A change to the "merit system," as I noted earlier, is being tried in a few companies, but even where it is being tried, it is not intended to replace the traditional system but rather it is an attempt to weld the two together. More often, no attempt is made at all. So modern a company as Idemitsu Kosan, which, under the direction of Mr. Sazo Idemitsu, has had a phenomenal growth in the past fifteen years, prides itself on its "Japan-style" management. It has no a labor union or a "time recorder to check the efficiency of its staff members, who are proud to be called Idemitsu men."[32]

The Japanese system, then, seems to require more shoulders at the wheel (and more fingers in the pie) than the Westerner would consider either necessary or desirable. The result, of course, is that a great deal of time is wasted. Many salarymen take advantage of the overstaffing to do as little work as possible, sleeping on the job, reading magazines at work, taking interminable tea-breaks. Some even indulge in *saboru*, a word coined from "sabotage," which is their own term for gross slacking on the job. Even though their immediate superiors learn about it, nothing can or will be done. These men are on the escalator as firmly as the more diligent workers, though chances are they will not rise as high.

This waste of productive time causes little comment even in the most "modern" companies. Occasional attempts to improve efficiency have few long-range results. About a year ago, a large corporation made, for Japan, the very bold attempt to measure efficiency by a sort of time and motion study conducted among the administrative and clerical staff. The study was done by a foreign company, hired for the purpose, which reportedly observed and recorded the time that employees spent gossiping, reading newspapers, drinking tea, going to the toilet, and so on. After the results were tabulated and analyzed, it appeared that if five employees worked properly they could do what was then being done by eight. Theoretically, then, three-eighths of all Japanese salarymen could be discharged and equivalent efficiency maintained by the remaining employees—provided they worked rather than wasted time. It was an interesting study that cost the company a lot of money, but I have never heard that anything was done to implement the findings.

Recently I was present at negotiations with a leading Japanese firm (which, incidentally, is active in the movement toward modern management rationalization). The Japanese firm was represented by seven men, four of whom—during the entire four hours the negotiations lasted—never opened their mouths. A couple of them seemed to be taking interminable notes, but the others just dozed. Such a waste of valuable man hours and professional time seems shocking to the Westerner—but is normal in Japan.

On another occasion I had a discussion with a Tokyo banker about the future of a very pleasant, honest, personable, and quite incompetent young man, for whom the banker had acted as *hosho-nin* (see p. 73). He decided eventually that the young man should be placed in either a government office or a large company, where there would be hundreds of others like him and where his lack of initiative, diligence, and creative ability would be scarcely noticeable, but where he would nevertheless be on a rising escalator.

One cynical observer saw a close parallel between many Japanese salarymen and many Americans in government service, where the motto "Don't do anything and you don't do anything wrong" is said to assure promotion and retirement on a pension. That this attitude is not unremarked by the Japanese themselves is illustrated by the statements attributed to "angry presidents" of companies, who say their young employees lack the "Japanese spirit" in merely seeking security and an easy time on the job for life. My own belief is that salarymen of this sort must constitute a minority, for I have known many who work unbelievably hard. Certainly the results of their efforts are obvious to the world.

A corollary to the rigidly hierarchical organization of Japanese enterprises is the deeply ingrained belief that older men of long experience merit the respectful attention that accompanies their advanced status, while younger men, no matter how clever they may be, are too inexperienced to be listened to. Many foreign companies doing business in Japan seem insufficiently aware of this attitude and unable to cope with it. Thus, they frequently send to Japan young Nisei or Sansei in the mistaken belief that these young men speak fluent Japanese (which they don't) and so will understand Japanese methods and ways of thinking. Or an American company may hire a young Japanese who has attended an American college, placing him in charge in the further mistaken belief that he will understand both East and West. If he has dealings with older members of Japanese firms, as he almost inevitably will, they may listen to him politely but they will give him neither their attention nor respect. His words, however sagacious, will go unheeded. In some twenty years perhaps . . .

The Japanese consider that not before the age of about thirty-five will a man's abilities be fully demonstrated, and it is around that age that the more obviously competent and diligent are given preference in promotion, raises, and bonuses. It is they who will be the directors of the future.

The Japanese have a proverb, *Ebi odoredomo kawa wo idezu* ("Though the shrimp may jump about, he will not leave the river."), that is particularly applicable to the salaryman. When he goes to work for a company, he expects, and his company expects, that he will be there until he retires. It is virtually a lifelong association.

Some foreign observers had predicted that mobility in the salaryman class has increased during the past five or ten years. Yet the surprising fact is that despite the adoption of some Western ways and concepts of management, despite the changes demanded by the new technology, despite the proliferation of joint ventures, mobility among the larger companies is no greater today than it was a decade ago. (It is my personal opinion that mobility is not quite so advantageous as Americans believe it to be.)

During his first two or three years in college, the prospective salaryman might—as in many other countries of the world—be a vociferous radical, he may hurl himself into violent demonstrations, he may even belong to the Zengakuren, a students' organization which is so radical it was kicked out of the Japan Communist Party. In his last year, however, he usually will tone down his activities, playing it safe so that he can get the best possible job in either government or big business. Some may take their ideals to work with them, some may even go so far as to engage in actual sabotage, but even these are usually in a short time conditioned to conform. Unions also, particularly those of white-collar workers, develop a company identification and a feeling of loyalty; on occasion they have agreed to accept lower pay rather than see some of their members dismissed. "Allegiance" is particularly strong in the old *zaibatsu* companies: strikes are shorter, disputes are more easily settled, and workers' deposits in *zaibatsu* savings plans are higher than in other companies.[33]

The most serious criticism that the Japanese make of American firms is that there is no security for the employee. He can be dismissed for reasons that are unacceptable to the Japanese: because profits are down or because he is incompetent or is growing old. In Japan, the salaryman is not an individual, he is a member of the company. His weakness, as Dr. Drucker points out, is neither looked for nor held against him.[34]

Recently, new American management, in taking over an old

and highly reputable firm, discharged the senior staff summarily in order to make room for a new youthful manager. No effort was made to place the discharged employees elsewhere or to provide for them in their old age. As a result, the reputation of the company fell so low it may never recover. The act not only flouted tradition, it was downright stupidity.

In return for the "allegiance" that the Japanese company expects from its employees, it behaves toward them as a father, or as a protector. It provides housing; lends them money at a very low rate of interest; it supplies many welfare services; it gives them free or very cheap meals; it pays for vacations and outings and a number of recreational facilities. It gives allowances for marriage; for children; for the death of near relatives. These are sometimes called "ceremonial allowances." Recently, when the father of an employee died, I sent a sizeable sum of money, as is customary in Japan, enclosed in a special "death envelope." I did not grudge it. Also it was the thing to do.

The employee, for his part, feels toward his company as he would toward a protector: he feels responsible to it and is willing to sacrifice himself on its behalf. Not only the young executive, as in America, but the ordinary worker will stay late at his job without expecting overtime pay. An obvious result of this sense of responsibility, coupled with its corollary, life-time tenure, is that a Japanese company need seldom fear that an employee which it has trained for years is likely to sell its secrets to a rival. This state of mind goes far back, of course, in Japanese history: it is well depicted in the famous story, so dear to most Japanese, *Chushingura*. It is a story of the loyalty of forty-seven samurai to their lord, and the sacrifices they bore to avenge his death.

The usual retirement age in Japan was around fifty-five, but this is now being raised in some companies. If the salaryman is destined to become a director, he will often be retained beyond the retirement age and eventually become managing or executive director, or perhaps achieve some even loftier post. If he is clearly not of managerial calibre, he will be retired at fifty-five and then either be placed with some other allied or friendly company or be rehired as a non-regular employee on a year-by-year contract, accepting a lower salary—usually about seventy per cent of his former base salary.

A man who is retired in these days at the age of fifty-five still has ten or more years of productivity ahead of him; the trend, therefore, as I suggested is toward raising the retirement age. Matsushita Electric, for example, after negotiations with its labor union, agreed to fix the retirement age at fifty-eight and to re-employ people for another two years thereafter, thus guaranteeing employment until the age of sixty. The salary for the re-employment period will be 70 percent of the salary at the time of retirement; regular increases, temporary payments, and wage base increases will be made as they are for regular employees. This is the same formula that Sanyo Electric decided on a number of years ago. Some time ago also Toyo Rayon decided to re-employ until the age of sixty, as did Toshiba and Hitachi, while Kanebo upped the age limit to sixty-five; all of them retained fifty-five as the retirement age, which meant that re-employment was on a reduced salary basis.

There is a sound economic cause for this generally early retirement-age in Japan. Employees accrue over the years a retirement lump-sum allowance, based on salary and length of service, which could become an intolerable burden on the company were there no limits to wage increases and to the accrual of retirement allowances. A ceiling must, therefore, be put on such deferred expenses.

Recently there has come into being in Japan's three largest cities, Tokyo, Osaka, and Nagoya, a new phenomenon: the so-called talent bank. The purpose of such "banks" is not to cater to the executive search—the familiar American practice of "head-hunting"—since the Japanese salaryman is notoriously reluctant to move from one company to another; it is rather to register experienced personnel from among retired people and to supply them to smaller industries, which presumably can make good use of their experience. A favorite place in which to unload such people, experienced people over fifty-five with the capacity and the desire to continue working, is in a foreign joint venture. These men are often highly competent and extremely useful, for in Japanese companies, as in the West, there is very little room at the top—and the best man does not necessarily get there. The talent banks, therefore, may fill a much-needed want in the Japanese economy, although so far as I see, they have had very little experience in fitting the right man to the right job.

One of the first questions the foreign businessman asks (for it is one of the chief causes of his incipient ulcers) is whether any immediate and drastic change can be expected in the traditional life-employment system. I am afraid the answer is a firm "No." The system is too deeply embedded in the Japanese character. Perhaps in another generation, or two . . . .

There are exceptions, of course. The Encyclopedia Britannica, for example, has rejected traditional sales channels and personnel practices; it pays by results and has been highly successful. Sony also has attempted to approximate the merit system, but it has been able to do so only because of its newness. Begun by a small group of technicians, it had no long history behind it—and no large mass of already dependent employees. It could therefore place its people more carefully as it grew and as the number of its employees increased. Chiyoda Chemical Construction Company, which is also rather new and highly specialized, uses a combined merit and life-service system—but the reaction generally has been that this is very hard on the employee.

Some American businessmen, when they first came to Japan, brashly predicted that they would soon change all that "hoo-ha," but their predictions have not borne fruit. A survey made by the Japan Federation of Employers' Associations (Nikkeiren) reveals that most foreign firms, or firms with partly foreign capital, follow the traditional pattern of seniority and life-employment.

The importance of status in Japanese life has been another chief source of frustration for the Westerner, since the graduating classes in Tokyo's three or four top schools are all "bought" annually by the largest enterprises. Smaller firms must recruit from the remainder and often have difficulty securing sufficient competent personnel.

One writer on Japanese psychology affirms that men who work for a foreign company never identify with it to the extent that they do with a Japanese company, such as, say, Mitsui, whose employees may refer to themselves as *Mitsui no mono*. Since *mono* may mean a "thing" as well as a "person," the employee is in effect saying that he is an object belonging to Mitsui. I believe, however, that if the foreign company has succeeded in integrating itself into the Japanese business society, and if those foreigners who manage it are men of experience and understanding, its employees will feel the same loyalty, pride, and identification that they do with a Japanese company.

Another aspect of Japanese business life that affects the foreigner (and the native Japanese as well) is the mistrust Japanese management traditionally feels toward any training in foreign business schools. Here again, seniority plays a strategic role. A salaryman who has left his job temporarily to study abroad will find, on his return, that he has lost his place on the escalator and that younger men have risen above him. Whatever skills he may have acquired in his study abroad may well be lost to the company, and he is equivalently frustrated.

Many companies consider foreign training, particularly of the business-school variety, to be actually detrimental. An article in *The Japan Times* for October 19, 1967, describes the plight of young men who have graduated from business schools in prestigious American universities but who cannot find a decent job on their return to Japan. In an attempt to solve this unfortunate situation, a new placement agency, designed for such men, has come into being. But company managers are generally unsympathetic. "Those young men overestimate their abilities," one objects. Or another: "Their knowledge is still very limited." "We have very little room for them," is the reply of a third. And, perhaps most telling of all: "What they have learned at a foreign university is not what our company wants."

Thus, there is serious cause for discontent among foreign-trained Japanese. If they were already on the escalator before they went away, they may, luckily, resume their place on it; and in time they swallow their frustrations and become members of the flock again. Although they could probably go to a foreign firm in Japan at a higher salary, they rarely have the courage to make the break, to withstand the pressures of obligations and duties, or to move against the strong current of Japanese nationalism.

American firms in Japan are eager to employ such men, but the image of the "dry and heartless" American enterprise, which may fire an employee or even get rid of a president at any moment, is a serious deterrent. In 1966, Pfizer is said to have spent over $45,000, plus staff time, in the United States, recruiting Japanese postgraduates of American business schools. They found four or five, and so considered the money well spent, but they could not have done the same in Japan. Recently an American firm here advertised extensively, and wrote hundreds of letters, in an attempt to recruit two or three young men of potential management calibre. So far there have been no respondents whom the company has considered worth interviewing.

Most of those who leave a Japanese firm where they may have been working for several years to join a foreign firm are the misfits, the mavericks, the men whom the Japanese firm doesn't really want. If it did, it would almost never let them leave, for great pressure can be brought to bear upon them and their families, even though they may be very young men, to keep them in the firm.

Not long ago, a young employee of a major *zaibatsu* house was introduced to me in the possibility that he might come and work for me. He himself considered that he had no obligation to the *zaibatsu* company that he had not fulfilled. He had won a one-year scholarship to a good foreign university, which the company had permitted him to accept. On his return, he was given a job doing simple routine translations, at which he had been working for two years. His talents and skills simply were not being used; in fact, the company considered them unnecessary, and the young man, as a result, saw no prospect of interesting advancement or the chance to use his brain. He had no family or other connection with the company, and no one had helped to place him there, so he bore no obligation to any "responsible person."

Taking all these things into consideration, he decided to resign from the company and to accept my offer of employment. He said he knew all the risks and was ready to run them. He had even, with great patience, been able to persuade his young wife to agree with his decision to relinquish the life-time security he enjoyed and to forget the prestige that was associated with the name of the company, going along with his desire to take the gamble on his personal abilities. Accordingly, we set a date for him to join us.

The date came and went; I heard nothing from him. Then at last he called on me, covered with shame and remorse, to announce that he could not leave his company. I told him that I could well imagine the various pressures that had been brought upon him. He described the unexpected visits to his very small house by a company director who emphasized his duties and obligations to the company and its benevolence in the role of corporate father; who emphasized also the fact that the young man was Japanese and so bore a responsibility to his country. He was grateful for my sympathy and my understanding of the many factors he had thought no foreigner could comprehend.

Shortly after, another young man in somewhat similar circumstances also decided to leave his company and join us; an almost identical course of events followed. Both men remain with their companies. One happy result of these two incidents was that because of their efforts to break away and because of this brain-drain threat by a foreign company, some realization of the abilities that these two young men possessed filtered through to their superiors—and they now have more interesting work.

On the question of a changeover to foreign ways, a recent survey, made by the Japan Institute of Labor,[35] suggests that the impact of foreign methods of pay and promotion by merit will increase as liberalization of capital develops. The Institute says further that it believes "the impact will in the long run not be a negative one for Japanese industrial relations," meaning presumably, as I suggested earlier, that the old system will be changed, but not easily or soon, and that the change will take the form of a merger of the new and the old.

It would be difficult, if not impossible, for the old ever to be altogether forgotten; nor am I sure that it would be desirable. A Japanese is not receptive to the idea of thinking of himself as an individual: he needs to belong to a group, to be dependent on it, and to have a place in it. If he does not, he feels lost. The Japanese managers of a Japanese enterprise are of course similarly affected. Perhaps nowhere in the capitalist world is there such a complex interrelational structure, requiring continual adjustment by the enterprise and its managers to the stresses and strains, the pressures and influences, the obligations and duties which are an integral part of Japanese life. The foreigner doing business in Japan who attempts to ignore this fact, or to fight it, is doomed to failure.

He will have to deal also, of course, with the government bureaucrat, and here he must deal with the same sort of man, and essentially the same sort of structure, as in the private sector of business. The close interrelationship between business and government which characterized the first days of the Meiji industrialization is still a major factor to be reckoned with.

The bureaucrat is recruited on graduation from the same universities as the salaryman in private enterprise. Although he is paid, of course, out of government funds, he is promoted and retired under the same life-tenure system. Like the salaryman, he gets his foot on the escalator and goes up automatically, largely unaffected by his talents and abilities; and like the salaryman, he is expected to conform rather than display his individuality, to show average competence rather than brilliance. He has his superiors and his inferiors, towards whom he behaves with either respect or arrogance. (The Japanese bureaucrat, like bureaucrats everywhere, can also of course be arrogant or even rude to the general public as well.) He wears his official lapel badge, which proclaims his status. As in private enterprise, the higher he goes, the more funds he has to spend for his own entertainment (although these are government funds), and the more perquisites he has at his command.

Up to the end of the Second World War, a great number of enterprises were operated by the government or were operated under government direction; therefore, regular government employees—that is to say, civil servants—were assigned to these enterprises, thus furnishing another link binding business to government. At the time of the great fragmentation, caused by the dissolution of the holding companies and deconcentration, most of such employees (if they were not purged) stayed with the final remaining enterprise.

Then, because of the purge, there developed a serious shortage of middle and, particularly top management talent to run the new splinter companies; the government, in consequence, sent in a number of surplus officials to serve as managers. Many of these, especially officials from the Foreign Office and the Ministry of Home Affairs, had little or no experience in business, but they tried to learn and—partly, because of the close cooperation between government, banking, and industry—they succeeded. It was a situation not unlike that which prevailed, as we have seen, in the early days of Meiji.

Like his counterpart in the private sector, the government bureaucrat is normally retired at fifty-five, an age when he still has many years of useful life ahead of him. Here he has a decided advantage over the salaryman, for he can almost always get a position in a semi-government organization or in a public corporation, if not in private industry. Perhaps every large enterprise has one or more retired government officials on its staff. Mr. K. Ichimura, president of Ricoh, Ltd., is quoted as saying that "ex-officials of the Ministry of International Trade and Industry and the Ministry of Finance join private business companies using influence from above."[36] The Japan Tourist Bureau is said to serve as the old men's home for superannuated bureaucrats from the Ministry of Transportation.

In view of all this, it is not surprising that the traditional dependence of enterprise on government and the traditional affinity between the bureaucrat and the salaryman are constantly being reinforced. One profound difference between the two is that the civil service has felt no breath of the wind of change that has begun to ruffle the surface of private industry. On the contrary, the bureaucrat, firmly entrenched in the life-tenure system, is clamoring for his own wages and retirement allowances to be increased, his retirement age to be extended, and guarantees of outside employment after retirement to be given.

The gap, the almost incredible gap, between the emolument of the corporate executive and that of the ordinary employee exists also in the bureaucracy. Higher officials, such as members of the Diet and of city councils, are paid many times the salary of lowly public servants, who do some kind of useful work.

This callous disregard of social justice, it must be noted, is nothing new in Japan. At the time of the Satsuma Rebellion in 1876, a policeman's salary was six yen a month. In 1881, elementary school teachers received twelve yen a month, while a university professor was paid a monthly salary of ¥125. Leading government officials did rather better. Hirobumi Ito was paid ¥500 a month for each of four posts he held: Cabinet Councillor, Minister of Industry, Director-General of the Bureau of Decorations, and Chief of the Bureau of Judicial Affairs. Aritomo Yamagata received ¥500 as Cabinet Councillor, ¥500 as Minister of the Army, ¥400 as Lieutenant General of the Army, and another ¥400 as Chief of Protocol. Kiyotaka Kuroda had two ¥500 posts in addition to his salary of ¥400 as Lieutenant General. It is always difficult, of course, to assess the value of money in the past, but the official price index for 1965 was 1,745 as compared with 1882. On this basis, Hirobumi Ito's official emoluments amounted to about ¥3.5 million a month (about $10,000), while the policeman received just over ¥10,000 (about $30).

Today's differential may be slightly less, but the cumulation of posts is far greater than in the Meiji era. Leading businessmen serve on the boards of practically all affiliated companies, and the government achieves the same result by appointing a man to several of its official committees. A former university professor who is on good terms with the (at this writing) ruling Liberal-Democratic Party may be a member of a dozen or more committees, as well as chairman of some, enjoying the corresponding accumulation of emoluments.

There are frequent articles in the Japanese press condemning government employees who are inefficient and *nonki* (lazy and irresponsible) but who nonetheless feel they deserve the "official's paradise." A story in a Tokyo English-language newspaper, for November, 1967, reported that 150 chiefs of sections and departments of the Metropolitan Government had appealed to the mayor to extend their retirement age, to increase their retirement allowance, and to assure them of jobs after retirement.

The writer of the article explains that the city government has only an internal rule about retirement (which is set at fifty-seven for section chiefs and sixty for general office workers), and that in order to induce employees to agree to retire according to the rule city management uses various devices, such as giving fifty percent more than normal retirement pay or adding fictitious years to their length of service, thus increasing normal retirement pay. The author complains that although city officials are given these great favors, they continue to clamor for even more special treatment.

He compares their lot with that of an employee of the Chiyoda Chemical Construction Company, an enterprise mentioned earlier that has largely modernized its management personnel system. At the age of forty-two, the Chiyoda employee must agree to negotiate a new employment contract, whereby he may resign or be retained under the same conditions. Two years later, depending on his work results, the company may decrease his salary, at which point he may again either resign or stay on at the lower rate. Those employees, on the other hand, who demonstrate their ability are retained and promoted. This, says the writer, is "the merit system"; he adds that it is "very hard for the salaryman." City and government officials, by contrast, he says, need not worry about their employer going bankrupt, they need make no effort to improve their efficiency against capital liberalization (Japanese industry's present bête noire), they may be as *nonki* as they please in their work, and yet when they retire, influence is exerted from above to secure jobs for them at higher salaries than they would get if they retired from private industry. No effort is being made, he concludes, to cure the evils of the "order of long service" and "nonefficiency" (by which he apparently means automatic promotion by seniority, regardless of ability).

To the Westerner, the Japanese bureaucrat does indeed appear to be less efficient than the salaryman, and even more unwilling to accept responsibility. He deteriorates far more rapidly into a sort of uniform mediocrity.

There may be several reasons for this. For one thing, a government office is not quite so closely knit a familial group as a company. Almost every large company professes to live by certain rules of conduct and to be motivated by certain, usually idealistic aims. This is not true of the bureaucracy. Thus, where the salaryman shares the ideals of his company, the bureaucrat is chiefly interested in securing the prerogatives incident to his rank—and then demanding more.

Formerly, the civil servant felt that he was a direct servant, however lowly, of the emperor, to whom he was ultimately responsible and toward whom he felt a sense of profound loyalty. The imperial presence was everywhere, and a man could take pride in serving. With the war's end, however, the status of the emperor changed. Today's civil servant, in serving the public, feels he is only serving the politicians at the top of the bureaucracy—and they are, in many eyes, rather sad substitutes for the imperial exequatur.

6 The Managers

A perceptive article in *Asia Scene*[37] makes the point that the working population of Japan today consists of three groups: those born before the close of the Meiji era (which ended in 1912); those born during the reign of his successor, Emperor Taisho (1912–1926); and those born after the present Emperor acceded to the throne, having chosen Showa as the title of his reign. (Japanese emperors, on their accession, select a name by which the reign is identified and by which they themselves will be known after their death; during their lifetime they are known as Tenno [the Emperor] or Tenno Heika [His Majesty the Emperor]. No Japanese thinks of the present Emperor, for example, as Hirohito; before the occupation, many had probably never even heard that name attached to him. Dates are customarily given as occurring in a certain year of a certain reign. The system is used by business and government offices as well as historians.)

Asia Scene points out, further, that Meiji men constitute 5 percent of the contemporary working population; Taisho men, 15 percent; and Showa men, 80 percent. However, although Meiji men are but a small minority, they wield great power and have an authority altogether out of proportion to their numbers in the Japanese economic structure. Of 1139 company presidents, 84 percent are Meiji men, 14.5 percent are Taisho men, and a mere 1.5 percent are Showa men. Thus, those approaching the age of sixty or over have the management of Japanese enterprises well under their control.

Although their actual work experience was largely post-Meiji, they were educated by pre-Meiji or Meiji men in the traditional Japanese way. They were imbued with the sense of duty and obligation and with all the biases, bigotries, and pressures inherited from the past. This fact is reflected in the way Japanese business is managed today.

Despite the radical changes that were effected in the Japanese economy during the Meiji reign, few of these men were true innovators. One exception was Yukichi Fukuzawa, who founded a private school that later developed into Keio University, the first private university in Japan. He also urged Mr. Yuteki Hayashi to establish the firm of Maruzen for the importation of foreign books. According to an editorial in the Mainichi Daily News (English edition), Maruzen, which recently celebrated its hundredth anniversary "may be termed the 'window' through which Western culture came into Japan since a century ago."[38] Fukuzawa had the courage, and the foresight, to break away from ancient feudal traditions and to stress the importance of practical learning as opposed to theoretical. Most Meiji schools, however, continued, as in Tokugawa times, to put the major emphasis on Confucian morality.

Eiichi Shibusawa (whom we encountered in Chapter 2) complained that even the newly-formed "commercial" high schools taught little that was of any practical value. Fed on a diet of lofty theorization, the student on leaving school would not have learned the bare rudiments of business life. Even Shibusawa, it must be noted, believed that along with practical training and a knowledge of the abacus, the business manager should also be well acquainted with the *Analects of Confucius* and should be able to apply both Confucian morality and traditional *bushido* ("the way of the warrior") to the conduct of business. This application of *bushido* to trade made it easier, of course, for the samurai to lower his pride sufficiently to learn to use the despised abacus.

From this initial reluctance of the schools to impart basic facts and practical information grew up the custom of on-the-job training, which is still very much in effect in Japan. When, not long ago, I interviewed a forty-five-year-old applicant for the position of manager of a company, he told me that he was an economics graduate from a well-known university, at the same time admitting that he had learned nothing that was of any practical value while he was at school. Everything he knew, he said, he had learned in his work experience. Foreign businessmen here find it difficult to believe that the possession of a degree does not also indicate possession of useful knowledge and the ability to apply it; Japanese employers, of course, do not labor under a similar misapprehension.

This lack of practical training at school may explain, to a certain extent, the fact that the average Japanese is unable to cope with even the slightest deviation from known and familiar routine. On-the-job training appeared to be the only way to teach people who had not been taught at school to think for themselves. Another factor is the Japanese tendency to learn by rote, which is partly the result of the complexities of the language. The only way to learn to read and write Japanese, lacking a photographic memory, is by continuous repetition.

Meiji men were, of course, the teachers of Taisho men, but the latter were also strongly influenced by the growing jingoism of their time that was to lead Japan to the very edge of disaster. This ever increasing militarism was not a reversion to the "ancient virtues," as symbolized by *bushido*, but was based rather on a nineteenth-century concept of the absolute state. Ultra-nationalism, which was at first taught in the schools, was later imposed on all aspects of social and business life.

A very large number of Taisho men were in the armed forces, usually as officers, or in governmental or semi-governmental wartime institutions. (One survey estimated that 62 percent of enterprise section chiefs had had military experience, and forty per cent had been officers.) This fact has had a curious and rather complex effect on Japanese life—not only before the War and during it but also after it was over.

As products of their time, these Taisho men—particularly if

they became officers of the Imperial Army—were bigoted and narrow-minded, arrogant and sycophantic; and they were also well trained. When the War ended in disaster, they found themselves dishonored and unemployed. They had to find work and to recover, if they could, some semblance of their self-respect. Being trained men, they succeeded—in at least the first of those aims. There are now about half a million Taisho men in the "middle management" group, department and section chiefs who play an important role in decision-making. These are the top executives of the future. How well they succeeded in the second aim seems to me doubtful. The disillusionment that accompanied defeat and an awareness of the sterility of their former jingoism may have resulted in a kind of cynical skepticism (which I think is not characteristic of the Japanese, who may often be skeptics but who are rarely cynical). These men, once the horrors of war had passed and they were able to set foot on the escalator, did so with the firm resolve never to step off it again—at no matter what cost, in a failure of nerve, initiative and daring.

This may account for the excessive caution that characterizes the average Japanese manager. Don't innovate, he says, don't disrupt the harmony; therefore, don't do anything in a hurry. Give it time! And since the basic time-consciousness of the Japanese is quite different from that of the Westerner, especially the American, the resultant slowness to act sometimes seems almost unbearable.

Thus, neither Meiji nor Taisho men, neither top nor middle manager, are in general entrepreneurs; upper-level salarymen, they are like upper-level bureaucrats, and they function in the same way. The *ringisho* system takes care of the paperwork, causing it to proliferate just as it does in armies or government offices; and the system permits—or rather encourages—the evasion of responsibility. If thirty or forty men have put their seals on a document, where is the Japanese company president who will not add his? The average president, in fact, is often no more than a title; most enterprises would function much the same without him. There are, of course, exceptions; there are some strong and effective executives at the top; but they are in a definite minority. The background of the Meiji industrialization is, as I have pointed out, partly to blame; and partly to blame also is the jingoism of Taisho and early Showa that resulted in the War and the consequent occupation.

I have quoted Mr. Honda as saying that the bombing of Japan's obsolete factories and the fact that she lost the war enabled her to build anew. He might also have added that the demobilization of the armed forces released a very large number of highly trained technical officers and lesser rank technicians, who then became available for the new industry that was being built. A very valuable bonus of skilled men appeared at a time when they were badly needed. Adam Smith's belief, which still seems to have general acceptance, that a military establishment is nothing but an economic waste is obviously not altogether true. I am thinking not only of the training of youth but also of the transfer of military technology to private industry for civilian purposes. For a study of the benefits that Japan's industry and economy received in the course of the American occupation, I would refer the reader to Daniel L. Spencer's "Military Transfer of Technology."[39]

Down the years, then, through both the Meiji and the Taisho periods until today, Japanese industry has been strongly influenced by traditionalism. During the Taisho period and the early years of Showa (when industry's present low-level managers were babies or were still unborn), this traditionalism was both contaminated and diluted by ultra-nationalism which reached the point of virtually complete government control of all business, regimentation of the people, and perversion of history. An incidental factor—the prohibition of the teaching and use of the English language—did grievous harm to the country by creating a serious shortage of people able to communicate with the occupying officials who were attempting to assist the country to rebuild itself.

It is the Showa men, men born after 1926, now in their early forties, who are the innovators in Japanese industry. There one hears the rumblings of reform—of attempts to inaugurate the merit system and to modernize antiques like the *ringisho*. In trying to sweep away some of the traditional cobwebs, the Showa men are taking a new look at marketing and distribution. They avidly read the spate of new magazines on modern management. Some of them have even come to the radical conclusion that if you want to sell a product, you have to get out and sell it, and that being a salesman is not necessarily dishonorable.

So far, however, the Showa men lack the power to effect their innovations. They are on the escalator, and they must stay there until they reach the top, replacing the Taisho men, who will by then have moved up to the level now occupied by the Meiji men. The escalator is not a fast one; the process will take some ten or fifteen years. Then, perhaps, profound changes in the Japanese business structure will occur but they will not all necessarily be good. Innovation for the sake of innovation is not a panacea. A great deal that people condemn as archaic or old-fashioned is, I believe, integral to the strength of Japan and so to its enterprises. Not all Western management methods are exportable to the East; but if they are adapted rather than adopted, the result will surely be increased communication between East and West that will constitute an advantage for both.

Meanwhile, the foreign businessman must deal with today's top managers, the Meiji and the Taisho men. In 1963 and 1964, a market research group conducted surveys on business executives, covering about seventy-five thousand people engaged in the management staffs of more than sixteen thousand enterprises. The findings, published in 1964, ought still to be generally valid.[40]

The survey classified managers into four groups: top management (chairmen, presidents, vice-presidents, and directors); middle management (chiefs of departments and important sections); lower management (chiefs of sections in less important departments); and branch and factory managers. As it is the top and middle managers who chiefly interest us here, I shall attempt to construct simple profiles of representatives of these two groups, using the survey as a basis.

The age of the top manager is between fifty-five and sixty-five (the majority are fifty-nine or sixty). He is married and has four children; if they are still at school, they go to public rather than to private schools. He owns his own house and dines with his family about four times a week. His house is not fully air-conditioned; he prefers Toshiba room coolers. He owns a stereophonograph, his preference there being a Victor. At the time of the survey he did not have a color television set, but he probably does by now, and probably it is a Toshiba. His fountain pen is a Parker, his watch is an Omega, his camera is a Canon.

Since he has use of company cars, he does not own his own, but if he did it would be a Toyota or a Nissan. He has made at least one trip abroad, probably to the United States by way of Japan Air Lines, where he feels more at home than on a foreign plane.

He reads at least two newspapers every day but not an English-language one (of which several are published in Tokyo). He does not subscribe to a monthly magazine; if he reads a weekly, it will be *Diamond* (a business magazine) or *Toyo Keizai* ("The Oriental Economist"). He may glance at the *London Economist*. He never reads magazines about management, presumably because he is already on top and so assumes he has nothing more to learn. He devotes an average of seventy-five minutes a day to his newspapers and eighty-two minutes to television. On holidays the time he spends looking at his television set mounts to 139 minutes. His favorite programs are the news, baseball games, and *sumo* (Japanese wrestling) matches. The latter are his preferred spectator sports.

He likes to play golf, and that is usually the way he gets his exercise. If he is among the two-thirds surveyed who smoke cigarettes, he prefers Hi-Lite. Other preferences are saké (over beer or whiskey), coffee (over black tea), and rice (over bread). He considers himself to be in good health but takes vitamins daily, and probably also geriatric medicines.

He very definitely prefers the Japanese way of living to the Western. He admires the strong men in Japanese history, like the Shoguns Ieyasu and Hideyoshi, and he particularly respects Yukichi Fukuzawa, the founder of Keio University. (He is himself, of course, a college graduate.) He does not especially admire any non-Japanese (the majority reporting listed none; among those who did, Albert Schweitzer came first; others mentioned Churchill, Napoleon, and Lincoln). His most admired book is the *Analects of Confucius*. He also enjoys reading biographies of men like Ieyasu.

He supports the Liberal-Democratic Party, prefers the democratic form of government, and likes the United States better than other foreign countries (although the American involvement in Vietnam has now somewhat cooled his admiration). He has little or no interest in religion, but he believes that youth should be taught Confucian ethics. Social studies and study of foreign languages do not impress him as being of great value. He firmly believes that it is better for a young man to remain with one company through his working life; a long list of positions held in different companies is to him no recommendation whatsoever. He gives very little time, if he gives any at all, to social welfare work. He finds his happiness, he says, in his family, his work, and his amusements, like golf.

He belongs, of course, to his company club, which is very like what we think of as a club in England or America—that is, a social organization of restricted membership, with club rooms for the members' use—save that the only people who may join the company club in Japan are managers of a certain rank. The Mitsui Club, to which sixty companies of the Mitsui group are said to belong, is one of the better known. It has club rooms and a restaurant in the center of Tokyo and a large house in the suburbs, where managers of member companies may have lunch or dinner parties, invite guests for meals, and hold meetings in one of the many conference rooms. The executive may also belong to one or more clubs, such as the Industrial Club, the Bankers' Club, the new World Trade Club, or the more exclusive and prestigious Tokyo Club or the Kojunsha.

There are, naturally, exceptions to this admittedly simplified sketch of a top manager. Many leaders of Japanese industry have become "internationalized": they are not so narrow in their point of view, so strongly opinionated, so conscious of rank, or so arrogant to their inferiors as the man I have surveyed briefly above—yet it is he who continues, as of this writing, to remain the typical representative of the top manager in the business structure.

The middle manager is younger, between forty-five and fifty. He probably lives in housing provided by the company; he spends less time with his wife and his three children than do the top men, one reason being that he is the man delegated by the company to do the entertaining of visitors and customers. He reads the same newspapers and magazines as his superiors, but he also reads sports magazines. Baseball, rather than news, is his favorite television program; on holidays he spends more time watching television than do the top men. Golf remains his favorite sport, but he is able to spend less time and money on it. He has the same preferences in saké, coffee, and of course rice; he admires the same people and has no particular respect for non-Japanese; he also believes in the Confucian morality, but as one goes lower in the management scale, there seems to be greater interest in foreign books, particularly those dealing with economics, management, and history; like his superiors, he overwhelmingly prefers the Japanese way of life, although here again percentages tend to decrease in the lower groups.

He is likelier to be a cigarette smoker than the top men, and he is not so sublimely convinced as they are that the best pen is a Parker and the best watch an Omega. He has a greater preference for Japanese products. He too owns a stereo-phonograph, and again Victor is the first choice. At the time of the survey, very few members of this group owned color television, room coolers, or cars, and very few had traveled abroad, but percentages here have almost certainly changed in the past five years.

He probably votes the Liberal-Democratic ticket (in lower management, the percentage supporting the Democratic Socialist Party increases). He is not so convinced that the United States is the ideal foreign nation; he may like Great Britain better. He believes in the life-tenure system and advises employees to stay with one company. (On lower management levels, some doubted the wisdom of such advice.)

On all levels of management, there was a feeling that more "moral education" was called for, and few were convinced that the teaching of a foreign language was necessary. On the lower level, further, there was an increase in the number of those who believed "nationalism" should be taught in the schools, as well as a suggestion that the negative attitude toward Western ideas is undergoing a change. On the whole, however, the several levels of management seem to think and act pretty much alike, and their need for conformity is so great that, as I suggested earlier, no drastic changes may be looked for until today's youth works its way up to the top and becomes the day after tomorrow's managers.

Another characteristic of present-day Japanese management is its distaste for abstraction. "The Japanese mentality," says Dr. Hideki Yukawa, Japan's foremost nuclear physicist, "is, in most cases, unfit for abstract thinking and takes interest merely in tangible things."[41] There is no need to dwell here at any length on the innumerable ways this trait is manifested, but it necessarily affects all trade and commerce. It is one reason legal niceties in contracts always seem to confuse the Japanese, to carry little weight with them, and occasionally to produce adverse reactions.

Some fifteen years ago, I negotiated a long-term crude oil sale agreement between an American producer and a Japanese refiner. The top managers of the American company had all originally been lawyers, and the final contract they sent over for signature offered abundant proof of that fact. Since it was the first such contract the American company had entered into with a Japanese enterprise, they wanted to be sure that all possible contingencies were covered.

They succeeded so well that the Japanese company was quite unable to translate the agreement. It was embarrassed by this, and perhaps also it was annoyed that the contract appeared to contain so many clauses that apparently had nothing to do with the simple act of buying and selling. Under those circumstances, the company felt it was unable to sign the contract, but the matter was urgent since the first lifting would soon be due, so I requested a meeting with the Japanese directors, at which I asked to be permitted to outline the agreement as I understood it. I explained that the American company had agreed to sell x barrels of crude oil of certain A.P.I. specifications, at so much per barrel F.O.B. Persian Gulf, with spaced liftings of approximately x tons per vessel. The loading weight as accepted by the ship's captain was to be final; payment was to be made by letter of credit so many days prior to each lifting. I then explained, as simply as I could, the meaning of Acts of God, of princes, principalities, and powers, and all the other verbiage tossed into a force-majeure clause. I said that that was all the whole lengthy contract meant. Finally the managing director replied, "Well, Adams-san, if you tell us that such is all this thing says, I will sign it," and he did.

I then set about trying to coax the American lawyers to come up with a simplified short-form contract. That took about a year, but I finally succeeded. The Japanese, of course, have now had more experience with the Americans and have become more inured to the American love of legalisms; as a result, they are less dismayed than before by the lengthy treaties American companies send over to cover a simple sales agreement. (The Japanese attitude toward law and legal procedure, in its broader implications, is dealt with by Dr. Noritake Kobayashi in Chapter 13.)

A corollary to the Japanese distrust of the business school as an institution is the firmly entrenched belief that only with age and experience can a man become an efficient manager. Executives feel that the man who can solve management problems is the man who has successfully done so over the years. This is, I find, a fairly unassailable position, though it may well tend to weaken the initiative of younger men, the ones who do study books on management and who read the magazines so avidly—if not profoundly. The fact is, systems are easier to embrace than creeds, and the new techniques of management, most of which have come from the United States, are not easy to reconcile with the old ways that, when all is said and done, have proven remarkably effective in Japan. Mr. Etsu Iwadare, who is in charge of personnel affairs at the Tokio Marine and Fire Insurance Company, is quoted in *The Japan Times* as saying: "We don't need such vague things as a master in business administration."[42] Mr. Soichiro Honda, a true modern entrepreneur, goes further. While he reportedly respects education, he has no respect for the diploma itself, which to him has less value than a ticket to the movies. "A ticket at least guarantees that you can get in," he says, "but a diploma guarantees nothing."[43]

Mr. Honda is a good example of a Japanese entrepreneur who built up a huge business in a very short time. His success came in the field of machinery, one of Japan's growth industries, which, as Dr. Hoshii has pointed out, was not founded by large concerns but developed out of small shops run by craftsmen. Later, of course, many large concerns branched out into the machinery industry.

Another self-made man who became a powerful leader of industry was the late Keita Goto, who founded the Tokyu concern, which operates a private railway as well as many other businesses, including hotels, resorts, and tour and travel services, and which has a large number of subsidiaries, such as a real estate company, a department store, and so on. Mr. Yonetaro Otani worked his way up from day laborer, *sumo* wrestler, and saké-dealer to become another of Japan's leading entrepreneurs. His main enterprise was the Otani Iron Works, but his name is more familiar to foreigners because of the New Otani Hotel, in which his family owns a major interest. Mr. Konosuke Matsushita, whom I have already mentioned, started his career as a mechanic, with very little schooling. These men all give proof of the fact that private initiative and personal ability can lead to startling success in Japan as well as in the West.

A true rags-to-riches saga is that of Mr. Yasuo Nohagi, a businessman who is not internationally famous but who is well-known in Japan and whose story illustrates some extremely laudable Japanese traits that have contributed greatly to the country's present prosperity. Mr. Nohagi was born on a farm near Tokyo in 1905. His father, a poor farm worker, died shortly after his birth; his mother, widowed at nineteen, helped on farms during the day and sewed clothes at night in order to support herself and her son. The boy himself, when he was seven or eight, began to take jobs looking after other people's children, so as to earn enough to stay on in elementary school.

After his graduation, in 1917, he worked for some wholesale distributors of dolls for a time; then in 1922, using six hundred yen of his father's life insurance money (at that time worth about three hundred dollars), he "became independent." After a few small ventures of one kind or another, none of them particularly successful, he went to Manchuria, where he became president of an outfit called the Kinshu Gunpowder Company. He returned to Japan three months before the war ended. He had no job but he did have a little money, with which he bought some land at Ikebukuro in Tokyo, where he began to deal in old clothes.

Knowing nothing about the business, he established a basic premise for its conduct. When, for example, someone brought in an article of clothing that Mr. Nohagi thought could be sold for ten yen, he would give him nine yen for it, withholding a 10 percent charge, at the same time explaining that if he should succeed in selling the article for more than ten yen, he would refund that difference. He always kept his word. Outside his shop he installed a sign that read: "Buy with Humanity." His rather unusual way of doing business soon caught the public fancy, and at times so many people came to sell and to buy that the police had to be called to keep order.

When government control of textiles was abolished, Mr. Nohagi changed the shop to a store that sold new articles of clothing, and he also opened a restaurant. Now the Kinkado Company, of which he is chairman, operates a chain of both clothing stores and restaurants. He says, "My business is for people with small incomes, who are most of the people. My aim is to please them and to make them happy. In order to do that, we sell goods of the highest quality at the cheapest possible prices. Our prices are nearly 20 percent lower than those of department stores for the very same goods." He instituted his own system of distribution and sales. His income last year was reportedly ¥72,715,000, slightly more than two hundred thousand dollars. Kinkado Company's sales have increased forty times over the past twenty years; his goal for the coming year is to sell ¥10 billion worth (about $28 million). The chairman owns more than 60 percent of the business; the president is his eldest son, and the general manager is the husband of his second daughter. The company pays a dividend of 100 percent per annum (100 percent of the par value of the shares).[44]

Compared to the giant organizations, of course, Kinkado is in the medium or small business category, but its founder is a good example of the successful, post-war, self-made entrepreneur, and as such, his philosophy of life and business may be of interest. Recently, a widely-read weekly magazine published a long article about him, called "Rich Man in Japan."[45]

The article says that because his mother was so very poor, his first thought was always of what she would have liked best—and it was with this thought in mind that he started his now highly successful business, which he regards as a legacy to poorer people. His own family precepts are his mother's: don't become a guarantor for other people and don't lend them money, don't sue them, don't cause them any trouble. These precepts he has attempted to pass on to his children. When his son entered the company, after graduating from Waseda University in 1967, he gave him the following rules of conduct:

Saké is not a requisite for doing business. No entertainment is to be done in order to buy or sell. If you feel a sense of obligation, then give a present with a sincere heart.

When you go out, always go "dutch treat." Where that is not possible, take the lead in paying.

Don't take any presents with you should you go to borrow money. If you believe it would be difficult to borrow without a present, then don't do it.

Don't drink at a teahouse by yourself, and when you go to restaurants, don't be stingy about tipping. Always give something to the people who serve you, even if it is only a small amount.

In the company cafeteria, there are notices pasted on the walls that say things like "Don't waste food" and "Don't leave any rice."

When Mr. Nohagi goes to the cafeteria, he presses his hands to-gether and gives thanks for the food that he and the others are about to eat, expressing the hope that it will enable them all to live a better life. A similar "grace" is printed on the chopstick covers at his chain restaurants, along with the statement: "No work, no food."

"All my employees," he says, "grow up in the company from youth. I like to hear them laugh together or complain about the business together. When someone tells me he is going to get married, I take pleasure in the knowledge that he has now grown up."

He believes that he, as chairman, has the obligation to say good-morning to all the employees, who, of course, bow to him. The idea that he should greet everyone first is a reflection of his conception of the proper relations between master and servant or between employer and employee, and it suggests that the old ways are by no means obsolete, even in a new and modern business. When Mr. Nohagi says good-morning to his officers and em-ployees, it means that he welcomes them, accepts them, and en-closes them in his protective aura. It is his duty, he feels, to let every employee know in such a way that he is welcome and protected.

One idea of his is that by being a patient in a hospital, a man comes to understand people. "When," he used to say to his sons, "people come to see you in the hospital, you will find that they fall into three categories—those who come to flatter, those who come on business, and those who come because they are genuinely worried about you. When you can distinguish between them, then you will be able to give them the right jobs to do. Staying in a hospital, you should heal not only the illness that brought you there but your ways of thinking as well."

One of the men he most admires is General Nogi, whose portrait, along with that of the general's wife, hangs in his bedroom. He admires him because, like Mr. Nohagi himself, the general suffered terribly from neuralgia but never allowed himself to give any outward sign of his suffering; and he admires him because the general, possessing honor, position, and wealth, committed *hara-kiri* according to the dictates of his conscience. "That," says Mr. Nohagi, "was a great thing." (It is what Rabinowitz has termed "thinking with the viscera." But Mr. Nohagi, of course, does not see it quite that way.) "Although I cannot do the same," he says, "General Nogi's firm resolve is an example to me."

The only things that interest him now are his work and his family. By 1972, he plans to have sixteen large stores and twenty-eight restaurants in Tokyo. Most interesting of all, perhaps, is the fact that he also founded the Kayaku Antibiotics Research Company, which has developed several extremely useful antibiotics and is now working on a new medicine to control cancer. The leap from ragman to manufacturer of drugs has landed him firmly in the Western world. His company has agreements, covering the antibiotics it develops, with a number of large foreign firms, which he and his assistants have visited and worked with.

Thus, despite his rather feudal attitude toward life, he is very much a hard-headed businessman, operating what would now be termed in the United States a "discount sales house" as well as a research laboratory and a manufacturing plant in a highly technological field. Far from being a run-of-the-mill bureaucrat, he is more like a local daimyo of the Tokugawa period, surrounded by his followers, while at the same time he retains many of the old-fashioned ways of thought of the former peasant class. His frugality is reminiscent of the small Japanese farmer who, under the shogunate, was never allowed to have more than just enough to feed himself and his family when crops were good and who came perilously close to starving when they were bad.

Mr. Nohagi's story of rags to riches, of course, is not unique in Japan. There are others who come to mind such as Mr. Ryohei Iketani, President of Iketani Seisakusho K.K., a maker of optical lenses; Mr. Sataro Ito, President of Tsukigase K.K., a very well-known chain of Japanese style confectionery stores; Mr. Ichitaro Okamoto, Chairman of Okamoto Glass Co., which introduced western styles of art glass into Japan.

He also has "soul," for want of a more exact term—a quality

he shares with a number of Japanese industrialists. Mr. Sazo Idemitsu, who operates some of the largest tankers in the world, is well-known for his interest in Zen Buddhism; the calendar that Mr. Idemitsu's company gives away every year is decorated with reproductions of Buddhist calligraphy. Mr. Matsushita, who built an electronic empire and has successfully invaded American and other foreign markets, is another example of the Japanese businessman who manages to combine the pragmatic with the spiritual, to hold on to the early virtues and at the same time achieve phenomenal success in a fiercely competitive world. This is not quite the same as the Western businessman who attempts to apply the precepts of his religion to his business life, for the Japanese are not a religious people as the word is conceived in the West. Their attitudes and practices are not doctrinal. *Ex oriente lux, ex occidente lex* ("Out of the East comes light; out of the West, law.") is an old saying that may contain a large element of truth.

The extra-curricular activities that many Japanese managers engage in are not, of course, of an exclusively spiritual or ethical nature. Many go to what Westerners might think of as the other extreme, spending a great deal of time at geisha parties (which the foreigner usually finds merely boring). I would say that the geisha party is probably the most expensive way in the world to buy a virtually inedible meal, with a few hours of childish and boring entertainment thrown in. Yet to many Japanese, these parties are an indispensible adjunct to their business life. A few years ago, an enterprising newspaper reporter toured the areas where the best geisha restaurants are located, listing the numbers and characters on the license plates of waiting automobiles. A very large percentage turned out to be government cars, as indicated by the identifying character on the plate. The reporter's story, after it was published, elicited considerable public clamor—and the government changed the plates.

While the stock market is supposed to be a barometer of business activity, perhaps an even more reliable index of the actual state of corporate profitability may be found at the Geisha Association. If the restaurants are busy and the geisha are in demand, business life is booming; if they are not, times are tough. Of course, the modern skin purveyors at Western-style cabarets, bars, and night-clubs, which are said to employ about a million hostesses, have taken quite a bit of custom away from the geisha—but she still reigns supreme, nevertheless, in her "flower and willow world," and many managers of business would find it difficult, if not down-right impossible, to entertain without her sugar-sweet presence.

Others spend their free time in other ways, as do their counter-parts in the rest of the capitalist world. One friend of mine, who is chairman of a very large company, devotes all the time he can to a trout farm he has built. The trouble is, it has been so successful he has been forced into the business of selling trout. Another, a collector of rocks and stones, has spent a fortune travelling the world, to some very unlikely places, in pursuit of his hobby. Others are amateur artists, many of whom belong to the Churchill Club, which was named in honor of Sir Winston. A former director of the Stock Exchange spent all his spare time singing and recording *nagauta*, an old kind of ballad which to the Westerner sounds uncomfortably like a very ill man having a spasm. One publisher I know takes no important action without first consulting his favorite soothsayer.

But these, as I have already suggested, are exceptions to the rule. The rule, in Japan as elsewhere, is that the average successful businessman leads a fairly humdrum existence, telling the same lies, worrying about his handicap at golf, going to baseball games or horse races, joining clubs like the Rotary or the Lions. And despite the seemingly large amount of time they spend away from home, most Japanese executives are good family men, although their attentions are directed more perhaps toward their children than toward their wives. Their marriages were almost certainly arranged by a go-between (the *nakodo*) on the basis of mutual family approval and the *o-miai* (the first meeting between the prospective bride and groom). Until recently, most men were reluctant to bring their wives to a party, but this attitude is under-going a gradual change as more women travel overseas with their husbands, meet foreigners, and join women's clubs in the large

133

Japanese cities, which are very useful in bringing women of different nationalities together.

One important factor for the foreigner to consider is the place of origin of the Japanese businessman he is dealing with as well as the company in which he grew up and received his experience— for chances are he has been stamped by both.

Just as people of one nationality are thought to possess a certain set of traits and characteristics—the Japanese, for instance, consider the American businessman to be very *dorai* ("dry")—so in Japan people of one region are held to be different from those of another, and the companies they form are considered to partake of those same characteristics. The Omi merchant was said to be a robber, and the Ise merchant a beggar. (Mitsui is Omi by origin but moved to Ise—so is Mitsui both a robber *and* a beggar?[46]) The Tokyo merchant was thought to be reckless and given to conspicuous display, while the merchant from Osaka was said to be the Jew of Japan and able to outsmart any Tokyo competitor. The term was Osaka *kuichi*, or "Osaka nine-and-one"; nine plus one equal ten, which is *ju* in Japanese.

Professor Kichimatsu Aonuma, of Keio University, in a study of 375 of Japan's largest corporations, reports that over six hundred of the fifteen hundred executives in his sample arrived at their positions of leadership by way of the escalator system and that about the same number were installed as senior executives of subsidiary companies after reaching high positions in the company they originally joined on graduation from college or university. Thus the conclusion seems inescapable that the great majority of Japan's industrial leaders have spent their entire working lives in one company or in one or more affiliated companies. In doing so, they have inevitably taken on the protective coloration of the company (which includes presumed regional attitudes) in ways that are both tangible and intangible. For one thing, every new employee must learn the house rules, which reflect the philosophy of the founders. For another, by merely listening to his superiors, he comes, almost without realizing it, to act and believe as they do. There are, I firmly maintain, subtle but nonetheless real differences between Mitsui people and Mitsubishi people; or between Toshiba and Hitachi; or Meidiya and Kinokuniya. The list could, of course, be prolonged almost indefinitely; it is a fact the foreign businessman ought to be aware of and a factor he ought to take into consideration in his business dealings.

Trading, particularly international trade, is still under the domination of the *zaibatsu* groups, with Mitsubishi and Mitsui leading the field. Here, as in all present *zaibatsu* groupings, the true entrepreneur is rare. One such is the eccentric Mr. Chubei Itoh, who built a powerful world-wide trading company from a small pre-war concern. His is probably the only really large firm in this field of commerce which has no *zaibatsu* connection (although it does have fairly strong ties with Sumitomo).

The *zaibatsu*, which were originally family enterprises, as I have noted, gave birth in the beginning to people who could probably be classified as entrepreneurs. That is no longer true. But there were other family enterprises, some of which have, for various reasons, disappeared; others still play an important role in the Japanese economy, and in these true entrepreneurs may still be found. Some of the most important construction firms, for example, although they are formally joint-stock companies, are family enterprises. So are Idemitsu Kosan K.K. (the great petroleum company), Hattori (the leading watch manufacturer), Bridgestone (Japan's major tire and rubber company), and Fujiya (a chief food company), among others.

A field of activity that appears to produce almost a total lack of entrepreneurs is that of the so-called "public corporations," those wholly or partially owned and operated by the government. They control a sizeable segment of the economy, employ a very large percentage of the labor force, and are managed by much the same kind of people who manage entirely private companies—save that the directors of public corporations lack the profit motivation of their counterparts in private companies and they are more opposed to any change or innovation. They can, nonetheless, as anyone who has dealt with the Japan Monopoly Corporation will testify, be very tough traders indeed. They also provide a safe and pleasant haven for a number of retired government officials.

Under the Civil Service law, a government employee cannot, for two years after his retirement, accept employment with a business enterprise that has had close relations with the government agency to which he belonged during the five years prior to his retirement. If the official held a rank above that of section chief, or if he is to become an executive in a private enterprise, approval by the Civil Service Commission is required. Should the approval be given, the two-year waiting period is waived.

This restriction, however, does not apply to public corporations or "special companies," which are considered by the ministries under whose jurisdiction they fall to be fiefs where they may send officials who cannot be promoted to higher posts within the ministry itself. In 1967, more than half of the 750 top executives in the 108 semi-governmental organizations were former civil servants; in forty of them, including the Japan Housing Corporation and the Japan Road Corporation, ex-officials held 85 percent of the executive posts. The largest number of former bureaucrats running public corporations came from the Ministry of Finance, followed by the Ministries of Agriculture, Forestry and Fisheries; International Trade and Industry; and Education. These executives of public corporations draw high salaries and on retirement receive an allowance of 65 percent of their former monthly salary multiplied by the number of months served. This system has in some cases been abused: the same individual has been known to be appointed successively to a top executive position in several public corporations and then receive retirement allowances for each of the positions he held.

I should like to close this chapter on Japanese managers with a "portrait" of one of them, based largely on material already published in Japanese.[47] He is Mr. Kota Hoketsu, president of the Polar Whaling Company (Kyokuyo Hogei K.K.), who has very kindly given me permission to tell the story that follows. I first met Mr. Hoketsu at a lunch party, during the course of which he remarked that he needed a whaling fleet. Jokingly I suggested that he buy it from Mr. Aristotle Onassis, who, I had read in the newspapers, had been having trouble with the government of Peru because of his whaling activities and so perhaps had become somewhat disillusioned with the whaling business. Not long after, Mr. Hoketsu initiated negotiations, during which I acted as a sort of advisor to him, and finally he did succeed in buying the Onassis fleet. A few years later, he said to me, "Adams-san, I want you to come with me to London and help me to buy the Hector Whaling Company fleet," which I did. Now, Polar Whaling is not a giant, like Mitsubishi or Mitsui, or General Electric or General Motors, but it operates in over a dozen areas of the world, where it is well-known and respected. Its story illustrates how its managers have made the best possible use of their abilities and their convictions to help lead Japan to the economic height it occupies today and perhaps bring it to even greater heights tomorrow.

As a background to Mr. Hoketsu's story, the reader should recall that in no field of industry was the need to rebuild from scratch after the war more urgent than in that of ships and shipping. By the end of the war, Japan's merchant fleet was smaller than it had been in 1935 and its deep-sea fishing fleets had virtually ceased to exist, a calamitous situation in a country where fish is the second staple of life. Today Japan has the fifth largest merchant fleet in the world and the world's largest tanker fleet.[48] She leads the world in ship construction, is second in fisheries, and—thanks in large part to the efforts of Mr. Hoketsu—is first in whaling.

Kota Hoketsu was born in Tokyo, in the Kanda area, in 1903 and grew up around Shiba Park—yet he calls himself a second-class Edokko (or Tokyoite), because his father came from Ehime Prefecture, in Shikoku, where one of his ancestors, it is said, was Lord Hoketsu Harima-no-kami. Young Kota studied at Waseda Middle School, then at Mito High School, and in 1924 entered the Imperial University law school. He graduated in 1927, after an idle last year, for he had completed the requisite number of courses in his first two years.

With three thousand yen given him by his father, he sailed off on a trip to Shanghai, Hong Kong, Malaya, and Indonesia, where his father had a rubber plantation. It had always been expected that he would enter the family business, but after experiencing the sultry heat of Sumatra, he decided that some other line of work was indicated.

Having spent all the money his father had given him, he worked his way back to Tokyo on a cargo ship and announced to his family that he had decided to enter the diplomatic service. He was one of six, out of three hundred, applicants to pass the entrance examinations. In this he was aided by the fact that since both his parents spoke English and since he had studied it at school, he had become fairly fluent in it. Although the six successful applicants entered the Foreign Office, they could not be given the high positions to which they were entitled because Japan had recently undergone a financial panic and a moratorium had been declared.

A little later, when things improved, Hoketsu was sent by his government to take a post-graduate course at Princeton University. After fifteen months of study, he obtained the degree of Master of Arts and was then assigned to his first post at the Japanese Embassy in Washington. He was disappointed to find that his daily task for the next two years was to be merely the deciphering and enciphering of telegrams. At the end of those two boring years, he was posted to Peking. En route there, he stopped off in Tokyo for a few days, during which time he had *o-miai* with several girls selected by his parents. (Eventually he married one of them, although not before three years had passed. After the marriage, both bride and groom confessed that each thought the other was a "matrimonial swindler": she, because the photograph he had sent from the States was too flattering—and she had been too shy to look at him during their "first meeting"; he, because he had been assured his prospective bride liked pets—and then it turned out she could not bear cats or dogs or even canaries. Despite these initial disappointments, the Hoketsus have now been married for over thirty years and have three grown children.)

The Manchurian Incident flared up just two days after the young diplomat arrived at Mukden, and the period that followed was a dangerous one but it was also exciting and—perhaps vital to Hoketsu's future career—it gave him experience in acting on his own judgment. In 1933 he returned to the Foreign Office, which posted him first to Geneva and then to Berlin. In the latter capital he was required to work on the tripartite pact that was to bind the Axis powers, but it was around that time that he heard, from the Japanese ambassador to England, Mr. Aoi Shigemitsu, words that were to affect the entire course of his life. "It is not enough," said Shigemitsu, "to do your job as well as you can, you must also evaluate what its consequences might be, and if you decide that what you are doing may have an adverse effect on the future of your country, you ought not to do it, even if the order comes from the Minister of Foreign Affairs himself."

When Hoketsu returned to Japan in April, 1941, he found that life was already on a war-time basis. He himself was seconded to the Planning Board of the Cabinet, where his job was to make an overall economic forecast, answering such questions as whether or not there would be a shortage of oil if war broke out between Japan and the United States. On the basis of his investigations, he declared that, because of a lack of necessary materials, Japan was in no position to wage war against the United States. Officers of the Imperial Army, who were also members of the Planning Board, refused to allow this statement to be included in the report; instead, it was changed to read: "If the war should start, the situation would become very serious but it would not necessarily be impossible," and in this form it was read at a council meeting in the Imperial presence. The Emperor, hopeful of avoiding war, is said to have commanded that the statement be "reconsidered," which was tantamount to an Imperial rejection. But the Japanese process of decision making combined with the very real power of the Army to negate any effective "reconsideration."

Later, Hoketsu served as counsellor to cabinets headed by Tojo, Koiso, Suzuki, and Higashikuni. On August 14, 1945, he was called to the Foreign Office to help in the preparation of the government's communication to the Allied powers, accepting the Potsdam Proclamation. Despite efforts by the Army to prevent the communication from reaching the enemy, it was at last sent; the following day, the Imperial Rescript was broadcast to the

Japanese nation and the world; and the Pacific war was ended.

Among the people the occupation authorities decided to "purge" was Hoketsu, but Shigeru Yoshida, then Prime Minister, intervened. He pointed out to the Supreme Commander's general headquarters that Hoketsu had been consistently opposed to the war and Yoshida at last succeeded in having the purge order rescinded. For a time, Hoketsu delivered biweekly lectures on diplomatic matters in the imperial presence, and then he was called to the Prime Minister's office, where Yoshida told him that the Polar Whaling Company was having difficulties with the occupation authorities and that its president had requested Hoketsu's help because of his fluency in English. On Yoshida's assurance that he would be recalled to the Foreign Office later, Hoketsu left it—temporarily, he thought—to become executive director and vice-president of Polar Whaling. He was indeed asked twice by Yoshida during the following years to return to the Foreign Office, but he was pressed to stay on with Polar Whaling by all three presidents under whom he served between 1948 and 1954. Hoketsu's twenty-three years in the diplomatic service had ended.

His new career, at the time he entered it, appeared far from glorious. By the end of the war, Polar Whaling, which had been established in 1937, had only two wooden catcher boats of about fifty or sixty tons. All its other catchers, along with its mother ship, had been commandeered by the Imperial Navy and had been sunk during the War. At the time Hoketsu entered the company, it had four catchers of less than three hundred tons and was just about breaking even. Although whales were plentiful in the south polar seas, the company was unable to go after them. It could neither recover insurance on its sunken vessels nor secure government aid. At last Hoketsu arranged to buy a vessel of five thousand tons, which he converted into a mother ship and which he dispatched, with five catchers, to the Antarctic Ocean. Unfortunately, by the time the fleet returned, with 222 heads of sperm whale, the price of oil had fallen drastically, and the company took a loss on the venture.

Hoketsu went to the then president, Sankuro Ogasawara, to say that he thought some sort of reduction was now unavoidable. Ogasawara replied that a man is bound to come up against what appears to be a blank wall at least two or three times in his life, but if he goes back and searches the wall, he may find a hole through which a rat might pass. Then, if he works at it, he can enlarge the hole to the point where a man can get through. Hoketsu did just that: he sent the fleet on a successful journey to the Northern Ocean, from which they brought back a large amount of edible whale meat (out of which the Japanese make a number of foods—including ham!).

From the three presidents under whom he served, Hoketsu learned several accomplishments. From the first, Tosataro Yamaji, a self-made man, he learned how to bargain. Neither his schooling, from Todai to Princeton, nor his training in the Foreign Office had taught him how to get prices reduced. But Yamaji did.

Yamaji's career is in itself rather fascinating. Young and penniless, he was determined to go abroad, so he got himself engaged as supervisor of emigrants on their way to Brazil. But he still needed money, and he devised two ways of getting it: one was pigs, and the other was bamboo. He arranged with the company that was overseeing the emigration to supply him with ten pigs as food for his charges. But the emigrants, as Yamaji had foreseen, got seasick and lost their appetites; the pigs grew plumper and plumper. As for bamboo sticks, they are cheap in Japan but fetch high prices in Brazil; to avoid paying customs duties, Yamaji arranged for each emigrant to carry one stick ashore. He sold both the fat pigs and the bamboo sticks at a large profit. By the the time he became president of Polar Whaling, it may be supposed there was quite a bit he could teach a career diplomat.

From Ogasawara, the second president of the company under whom he served, Hoketsu learned not only to look for rat-holes in seemingly blank walls but also—perhaps a more significant accomplishment—how to borrow money successfully from banks. Ogasawara made careful preparations before he asked for loans, he studied both his own situation and that of the bank, and when the moment came, he never cringed or bowed. Sometimes, Hoketsu noticed, he even shouted at the bankers—and he usually got his way. He ended his career as Japan's Minister of Finance.

From the third president, Shunji Minami, Hoketsu learned both thrift and generosity. When he bathed, Minami lifted only enough of the cover to get into the bath—so as not to waste hot water; and when he dined out, he had the restaurant pack whatever food was left over for him to take home. He always traveled third class on trains; after all, he said, all the carriages arrived at the same time. Yet when a directors' meeting lasted late, Minami would take everyone out to dinner and pay for it out of his own pocket, not the company's. When the company faced a serious financial crisis, Minami saved it with his personal fortune. On one occasion, learning that the portable shrine at Tsukiji had burned and that the annual festival would be ruined, Minami wrote out a check on the spot for half a million yen so that the shrine could be replaced. While he was president of Polar Whaling, he accepted neither salary nor bonus.

After the company's situation improved, he retired, recomending that Hoketsu succeed him. Later he telephoned Hoketsu and said that since he was no longer president of the company but only an ordinary director, he wondered how much the new president would be willing to pay him. "Whatever you like," Hoketsu replied; "after all, you accepted no money while you were in office." Minami said a hundred thousand yen (less than three hundred dollars) a month would be ample. "And thank you," he added, "thank you very much."

When he took office as president of Polar Whaling in 1954, Mr. Hoketsu called a meeting of all company personnel and explained various aspects of his own corporate philosophy. One of his chief points was that since the company could perform its fishing operations only with government permission, it should be more responsive to the demands of government and to the actual needs of the country. He pointed out that with a growing population and with natural limitations set to the amount of animal meat that could be processed at home or imported from meat-producing countries abroad, the Japanese people would have to continue to rely on fish as a prime source of protein. Thus, the fishing industry was, in large measure, and would continue to be, of vital importance to the well-being of the people.

He laid down several other guide lines for the better functioning of the company. For one thing, he said, since it was a *kabushiki kaisha*, the relationship between shareholders, management, and employees should be clarified, as should the relationship also between the company and the government. He prohibited the exchange of "gifts" and all unnecessary travel by company personnel at company expense. He pointed out further that since Polar Whaling was, after all, a fishing company, its employees ought not to turn up their noses at fishing boats and the smell of fish; they were not, he said, white-collar workers—although they were naturally expected to behave with propriety at all times.

Some two years after he became president of the company, there arose the question of buying the Onassis fleet. One reason why it seemed so vital to Hoketsu was that along with a fleet (composed usually of a mother ship, twelve catchers, a reefer, and perhaps an auxiliary tug and a tanker) went the right to take a certain number of whales out of the Antarctic Ocean. These rights are controlled by the International Whaling Commission in an effort to conserve the world's whale population, which might otherwise be entirely killed off. Japan is a member of this Commission, along with the United Kingdom, Norway, Holland, the Soviet Union, Germany and others.

But the price for Onassis' fleet was some $8 million—a sum well beyond the ability of the company at that time to pay. So, armed with the skills he had acquired from the three former presidents, Mr. Hoketsu began besieging the banks, pointing out persistently the benefits that the nation as a whole would enjoy if the fleet passed into Japanese hands. At last Mr. Hoketsu succeeded in obtaining the necessary funds—having in the process, he said later, learned how to *really* bow—and the purchase turned out to be a huge success. Along with the fleet itself, Polar Whaling had acquired the right to catch some eight hundred blue whale units.

As for the future, Mr. Hoketsu believes that with the inevitable decrease in the number of whales available, the Japanese fishing industry must make a gradual changeover to fish farming rather than merely catching, just as the breeding of domestic animals has replaced hunting as a source of supply for animal meat. As for himself, when he retires, he plans to spend the remainder of his life in Karuizawa, breeding trout and studying birds.

I think that the story of Mr. Hoketsu and the three presidents under whom he served furnishes a clear illustration of what happened in Japanese economic life after the end of the war. To recreate the vanished industries from scratch required the entrepreneurial type—and, almost as though by magic, it appeared. The purge had eliminated most of Japan's leading pre-war businessmen, and often men with little or no business experience (like Mr. Hoketsu) had to be put in charge of what was left of the economy. As a result of this lack of experienced leadership, the post-war readjustment process may have been slower and more painful than it need have been, but at the same time it gave many men an opportunity to prove their mettle and to develop their managerial talents. The fact that they received their entrepreneurial education in those hard post-war years is reflected in their philosophy not only of business but of life itself. They became top managers through their dogged determination in the face of an apparently hopeless situation, through caution combined with daring and shrewdness, through clever use of personal connections, and through just plain hard work. Although they could not fail to be strongly influenced by the traditions and mores of the Japanese business world, they were able at the same time to impress their own personalities on their companies. Behind the cold statistics of economic growth—the rows of storage tanks and miles of assembly lines, the congestion at the ports and the volume of traffic on the roads—lies the story of the individual entrepreneurs who, together with the unsung millions in factories and offices, created out of the ashes of war the phoenix that is now the world's third greatest industrial power.

Foreigners' Problems 7

"Understanding requires mutuality."
—Cheng Tien Hsi

The American Chamber of Commerce in Japan held, in January 1968, a seminar on the problems that confront the local representative of a foreign company (whom the seminar called the "oxy-exec," short for "occidental executive") in communicating with his home office. I had submitted a note to the seminar committee in which I misquoted a friend who had written, "Human relations are the first chapter of management." I said I thought they were the whole book, and I still believe this to be true (although an oversimplification), for in retrospect it seems that virtually every problem that was discussed at the seminar resolved itself into a question of personality: what the psychologists call "interpersonal relations."

The seminar produced no very startling results, and the problems that were aired were on the whole familiar ones, but the discussions did serve to focus a spotlight on the key problem: the fact that the foreign representative, particularly where he acts as the foreign stockholder's representative in a joint venture, frequently finds himself in the uncomfortable situation of having the devil on one side of him and the deep blue sea on the other. He must act as interpreter and go-between to both the Japanese company and his own head office, and he must often assume the role of instructor to students who are recalcitrant and reluctant to learn—or who, at least, seem to be.

Out of this emerged a further consideration: that the Japanese managers have in general very little understanding of the problems that the oxy-exec has to face in his relations with his home office, and that they rarely appreciate quite how valuable a sympathetic oxy-exec can be to them. I was also impressed, during the course of the seminar, by the evident sincerity of most foreign representatives in their attempts to be strictly fair to their Japanese associates and by their earnest desire to understand the Japanese point of view as well as to be good ambassadors of their home company— in other words, to be effective go-betweens. I believe that our Japanese friends might be well-advised to ponder this fact and to draw some conclusions from it.

Much of the material that follows has been taken, by permission of the American Chamber of Commerce in Japan, from tapes recorded during the course of the seminar. Direct statements made by the panellists are enclosed within quotation marks; other material that emerged at the seminar I have rearranged and condensed; for my own comments I assume, of course, full responsibility.

It should be pointed out, at the very beginning, that this chapter is mainly concerned with the foreign executive who represents a large or very large company, with joint ventures, licensing agreements, perhaps operation of plants, marketing, and the like. The executive who works for a pure subsidiary or branch also has problems, of course, with his head office, as does the man whose job is entirely one operation, such as a buyer or a sales representative for a single line, but the executive of a multi-phased operation in Japan finds that his problems are more than geometrically compounded.

He must, as the seminar made clear, toe the narrowest of lines between his Japanese associates and his day-to-day problems on one side and on the other his home office with its corporate policy. Trying to keep one eye on his work in Japan and the other on the demands, policy, and personnel of his home office, he is frequently called upon to make important decisions. If he makes a mistake, he is in trouble. And mistakes are easy to make. He may become so deeply involved in his daily problems in Japan that he loses perspective. He is very likely to decide that the home office is too concerned with company politics to have a proper perspective on Japan. They are demons or fools, he decides, or perhaps both (although I had always supposed demons to be highly intelligent—in their demonic way, of course). On the other side of the ledger, the home office may get the impression that "our man in Tokyo has gone nuts," "he's been out there too long," "he's gone Japanese on us!"

The seminar made the point (as I did earlier in this book) that many foreign executives here get so annoyed and frustrated they resign their jobs in anger and despair. (I might add that in many cases ceaseless complaints on the part of their wives do nothing to make their task any easier. A calm, tolerant, and long-suffering wife is essential in Japan—assuming, of course, that a wife is essential.) One panellist pointed out that the rate of failure among foreign representatives here was four out of five. The chief reason for this, suggested another, was the home office: "If the newcomer does not have a communications problem today, he will surely have one three months hence."

"I have known perhaps fifty people since 1950," said a third, "who have resigned because of a row with the head office. In most cases, the chap was doing a good job; his successor took two or three years to catch up and get to the same stage. It seems so wasteful! But I think that anyone who is sent out here and who wants to do a good job will inevitably feel this way once in a while. If he doesn't, he is probably too placid and perhaps not right for the demands of the job. It's a normal feeling to want to tell them where to get off every now and then—but it should be avoided." The panellist recommended talking the situation over with an older and more experienced friend—who will inevitably get started on his own, and to him more important, problems. A mutual session of that kind, the speaker suggested, would be helpful to both men.

Another stressed the importance for the foreigner of working out and adopting some kind of guiding philosophy to help him survive in what is, after all, an environment alien to him and far more alien to the people back home. It was suggested that he should regard himself as a professional peacemaker, attempting to reconcile the demands made upon him here in Japan with those made by the home office. "The Japanese associates say, 'Do that and do this.' 'That's all wrong—do this and do that,' says the boss at home. So frequently we are hit from both sides, and it seems much better to chuck it and pack it up. Any one of us could make at least as good a living in Miami or San Francisco, Chicago or New York, and the prospect of doing so seems very attractive from time to time. But if we do so, what happens? It will take the replacement three to four years to get to a level of reasonable efficiency and meanwhile the organization you worked hard to build may suffer or even collapse. Even so, the role of peacemaker is necessary and useful. If we keep plugging away, perhaps we can help to further understanding."

Monks, according to report, have always been more beset than other people by demons, one of the worst of them being the *demon meridionalis*, who came in the noon-day heat to bedevil his victims. But I wonder if the modern oxy-exec in Japan hasn't more demons to contend with than the medieval monk. They come both at noon and at night, and frequently in the wee small hours when the poor fellow is awakened, by the jangle of the overseas telephone, from the sleep that he had hoped would soothe his ruffled nerves to the point that he could continue the demon's work in the morning. Or he may find himself confronted by a demon who simply wanted a trip to Japan and has seized upon any convenient excuse; this demon is usually of the cloven-hoofed variety and is relatively easy to handle. Far more difficult is the self-confessed "expert" on Japan who comes out to solve problems, make surveys, and take back recommendations. He often succeeds in not only bedeviling the local man but also disrupting whatever harmony exists between him and his Japanese associates. This particular demon costs his company quite a bit in both time and productivity.

One of the problems that was brought up at the seminar is the result of conflict between the Japanese directors and the foreigner's head office. When a conflict does arise, the Japanese will often ask the foreigner to "front" for them. If he does, and if he is successful in doing so, the Japanese will continue to ask him to wangle all sorts of concessions and favors for them. The head office soon tires of all these requests, or excuses, and decides—not surprisingly —that their representative in Tokyo has become altogether too pro-Japanese. They may find any number of possible reasons for this unfortunate attitude.

Another problem considered was that of a joint venture which regards itself a separate and distinct company while the foreign head office thinks of it as merely a minor subsidiary in Japan and the Japanese partner considers it to be his own company. This is an extremely complex and difficult situation where the foreign representative needs not only to be peacemaker and teacher but also to possess himself of almost infinite patience. Often, as I noted earlier, he finds that misunderstandings with his own home office are more serious and more frustrating than the problems he has with his Japanese associates. One chief reason for this is that the Japanese, with all the good will in the world, are prone to personalize a relationship. Once they have accepted the foreign representative, they will look no further than him and will neglect to remember that he has principals at home with strong beliefs and desires—and that these must necessarily have an effect upon their new foreign friend. They will then act unilaterally, altogether ignoring the fact that the action should have been raised and cleared first with the foreign partner. In any case, they will say, off-handedly, Smith-san can explain it to his head office for them.

As representative of the American shareholder, I attended, not long ago, a directors' meeting of a joint venture company, where the Japanese president announced that he had signed a long lease for some property (owned, incidentally, by an affiliated company). Mildly I raised the point that this action would be considered an "important issue" and so would have required the advance approval of the Board of Directors (including me). The president, surprised and dismayed, carefully justified the lease and the terms of it. I explained that I was confident the terms were proper but that I would now have to explain to New York why the American company (a 50 percent partner) had been committed without their prior approval. I told the Japanese that this would be both embarrassing and difficult, since New York would conclude that the Japanese considered their own decisions to be the only ones that carried any weight. Now I would have to try to explain to the Americans that the Japanese had not intended to ride roughshod over their foreign partner and I would have to try to get the Americans to understand. The deal was done; an egg can't be unfried— and I, the Smith-san in this case, was well in the fire. To judge by the amount of time devoted to this particular problem at the seminar, it occurs very frequently and is not easily handled without disrupting harmony in Japan or incurring criticism at home.

I should like, at this point, to insert a parenthetical note about a subject that was not much touched upon at the seminar—the extent of communication, and the likelihood of sudden and sometimes inexplicable conflict, between the Japanese and the foreign representative in a joint venture. The seminar made the basic assumption that the foreigner communicates with the Japanese in one way or another. But I question whether he really knows what is going on or what is being said, and I doubt even more strongly whether the Japanese altogether understand him.

To advocate that every oxy-exec be bilingual is pointless because it is impossible: there are very few non-Japanese (of any nationality) who speak Japanese with complete fluency. There are, unfortunately, a good many who believe they do and who believe also that they understand everything that is being said; these people, in delicate negotiations, are the most dangerous of all.

Similarly there are far too many Japanese who believe they speak, read, write and understand English thoroughly. Every large company has its English expert, if only for reasons of face. He is usually a young man, a college graduate, who has a diploma and hence he, with the apparently universal arrogance of youth, is quite convinced that he is an English expert. The "Japanglish" which emerges in his writings is frequently ludicrous and even ridiculous, but always is rather sad. His lack of true ability is as dangerous in negotiations, as is that of his foreign counterpart. Even someone who has been long years in this country and who has the experience of long association with the Japanese runs the risk of making a serious boner because he is ignorant of some complex personal relationship among the Japanese themselves.

For example, some years ago I was asked to sit on the Board of Directors of a joint venture company, representing the American shareholders. The Japanese parent company was a prestigious family concern run by the elderly paterfamilias who was its president and who was also president of the joint venture company. My relations with him and the other directors were warm; the suggestions I made were carefully considered, and the questions I asked were satisfactorily answered. Then suddenly I began to feel a change: I was no longer, I found, being sent documents, I was no longer getting answers to my questions, I was no longer being telephoned by my fellow-directors. I told my principals that I was not useful to them any more and asked to be relieved, which in due course I was.

It was only later and by chance that I found out why a relationship which had begun so well had ended so badly. The turning point occurred at a dinner party, attended by both the elderly president and I, among others, when someone mentioned the name of a certain Japanese—whom I shall call Tanaka-san, the Japanese equivalent of Mr. Smith. I was asked about my own connections with Tanaka-san, and as it seemed obvious to me that he was in the bad graces of the president and his family, I told the truth: that I had known him during the occupation and that I thoroughly disliked and distrusted him because of his activities at that time. Much later, at a friend's house, I met the president's granddaughter, to whom I casually mentioned the mysterious cooling-off. She then told me that Tanaka-san was a close family connection and that her grandfather had taken my criticism as being directed at the entire family. "He's very proud and old-fashioned," she said, "and he took your remark the wrong way. The fact is, we are all highly critical of Tanaka-san, and won't even see him, but my grandfather believes that no foreigner may criticize him." *Saru mo ki kara ochiru,* the Japanese say: "Even a monkey can fall from a tree." And I, who had always taken such pride in my ability to deal with the Japanese, could with a hasty and thoughtless word put an end to what had been a happy relationship and to my own usefulness to the company I was serving. Did I learn anything from that unfortunate incident? I hope so—but I would not like to guarantee that some similarly frustrating experience will not recur in the future, as it must, I believe, to every non-Japanese who lives in Japan, no matter how well he may think he knows the country and its people.

To return to the seminar, the subject of visiting firemen was, as it turned out, a very sore one indeed. Everyone seemed agreed that the technical expert was both welcome and useful, but the self-styled "expert" who came out for a few days "to straighten things out" was not. Nobody, in fact, had a good word to say for him.

One panellist told about a case where a company's foreign representative in Tokyo had been negotiating an agreement over a considerable period of time. Suddenly a home office man, perhaps a vice-president, turned up. During the three or four days he was here, he met the Japanese with whom the local manager had been negotiating. They received him with great charm and cordiality, and when he left, he was convinced he had solved in a few days the presumably difficult problem the local man had been spending months over. The "small details" he left for the other to clear up. But the truth, as it turned out, was the opposite of what the home office man supposed. The Japanese were simply being polite to him because he was a visitor. The Tokyo manager had to begin the negotiations all over again—and to write to a skeptical home office that their vice-president had in fact got nowhere. Worse than that, he had probably made things more difficult for the local man, since a Japanese company wants to feel it is dealing with someone who is fully authorized to make decisions, not with mere "hired help."

A similar instance was brought up when mention was made of a company that had the practice of sending "experts" over for ten days or so whenever a problem arose, despite the fact that the company had extremely competent personnel in its Tokyo office. This company has had a record of very poor performance in Japan, and one of the panellists reported that he had asked the international vice-president what he thought were the reasons for this. He is said to have replied, "We went back over our files and studied the recommendations made by these two-week experts over a period of years, and in more than half the cases the expert made things worse than they were before." In my own experience, this is by no means as isolated case. The damage done by the visiting "expert" and the misinformation he sends back have caused huge losses to several companies. It is almost a general rule to say that the home company would have fared better if it had listened to its local representative—but Satan, apparently, can always find some mischief for idle "experts" to get into.

The same panellist went on: "I don't think any human being ever becomes an expert on doing business in Japan in two or three weeks, but when he goes home he may be critical of something here and as he is the "expert" and has ready access to the home office, you, the oxy-exec, are on the spot if you disagree with him." This question of "ready access" can indeed pose a nasty problem for the local representative, who may be six thousand miles away from the ear of his boss, while the "expert" is probably his drinking-companion and crony. One remedy that was suggested is for the local representative to convince the home office to employ a competent consultant who, because he is unbiased, will perhaps be listened to.[49]

"Because a man visited here," the panellist continued, "or stayed for a while in 1950 or thereabouts, or worse only during the occupation, even if he has had occasional visits since, he is, at home, generally believed to be the expert on Japan—but is, perhaps, because of a mild veneer, more dangerous than the part-time expert."

"The next problem is that our head office supervisor resided in Japan some years ago and has made intermittent trips here. He considers himself an expert on business, social customs, and American attitudes here. But he is out of date. Things change so very rapidly. I think that anyone is very misguided if he assumes that by living in New York and coming here once or twice a year he can be an expert. He cannot."

I should have added to this list the home-office person who has been concentrating his attention on problems in, say, Europe or Australia. He neither knows nor understands the Japanese, he may not even like them; thus, when he comes out here to "solve" a problem, he is generally incompetent to do so, usually uninterested in it, and perhaps even antagonistic to the people he has to work with.

Overcoming prejudice and educating head office personnel seemed a continuing theme at the seminar, and many ingenious suggestions were made as to how to accomplish these two necessary goals. But, as I suggested at the beginning of this chapter, the subject seemed to resolve itself always into one of personality and communication. Hence, the oxy-exec must learn patience; he must develop the ability to write clear and precise letters setting forth all the facts; if he can persuade his boss to come to Japan, he must be prepared to present facts and figures as lucidly as possible (and he would be well advised to take the visitor to one of the Chamber of Commerce's briefing breakfasts, where he can talk to other men with similar problems); if the local man cannot get the boss to come here, then he ought to go himself to the home office and do the best selling job he can, at the same time recommending books on Japan for the home office people to read. Ignorance, however abysmal, need not necessarily be permanent.

I recall that some years ago one of my clients, an American company, had on its Tokyo payroll a Japanese technician employed directly by the international part of the company. Toward the end of the year, I wrote the company that it was customary in Japan to give a bonus at New Year's time, and I suggested the amount I thought suitable. The vice-president of the international section wrote back approving the bonus and adding: "I presume you will pay it at Chinese New Year." Apparently he thought that Japan, since it was somewhere near China, celebrated its New Year at the same time as the Chinese. Even ignorance as profound as this can, I believe, be cured.

Often, however, even when the oxy-exec succeeds in getting his boss to Japan, he finds that the latter has allocated far too little time to his visit here—so little, in fact, that the Japanese partners find it rather insulting. The boss, or his representative from the home office, announces on his arrival that he already has his plane flight out. All appointments and conferences, therefore, must be squeezed into that brief period between arrival and departure. The visitor learns little or nothing and does little or no good. Sometimes his hurried visit is actually harmful, and he leaves the local manager to carry a badly beaten-up ball. "Couldn't he have stayed long enough for us to talk things out?" ask the Japanese.

There is a reverse to this coin. All too often the boss refuses to come to Japan when his mere presence would be extremely helpful. Some years ago I was asked to act for a rather well-known American businessman who is the president and major shareholder of a couple of rather important companies. I succeeded in working out, on his behalf, a highly profitable trade agreement with a top Japanese company that involved many millions of dollars. I then begged the American entrepreneur to come to Japan, if only to meet the Japanese with whom he would be doing business and from whom he would be earning profits for many years to come. (His passage, incidentally, would have cost him nothing, since he controlled the transportation.) He replied that he was too busy. "Let the Japanese come to see me," he said—and such, despite all my pleas, has remained his attitude through the years, although his various companies have continuing business in Japan amounting to many millions of dollars a year. He assumes, like many other successful American businessmen, that his Japanese colleagues must eventually come to him, hat in hand. He ignores the wise Chinese advice that the superior man will never make another feel inferior.

The seminar brought out the fact that joint venture companies face problems in other parts of the world, such as Latin America, which are similar to those that arise in Japan. (The Japanese themselves are experiencing some major problems in their joint ventures with Latin-Americans.) Such problems must also be met by American companies operating in Europe, although of course to a lesser degree than in Japan, since Europe is far closer to the United States, both physically and traditionally. Yet problems arise, and a failure to solve them may result in the failure of the enterprise.

"The underlying type of problems," said an American executive at the seminar, "runs the whole gamut of human and corporate emotions. Some of it is subjective, some of it empirical. You can get into questions of nationalism, of pride, of corporate superiority and corporate inferiority, complexes, government relations problems, technological problems, personality problems—in other words, a communications problem in the very broadest sense. This is the book—and probably a real test of management skills in international management.

"As to your Japanese joint ventures, it may be found that your problems with your Japanese associates may be a good deal less than your problems with the American side, because in some ways the Japanese way of life is to compromise, whereas the Americans think that the last word is written in the fine print of the contract, and that's a pretty tough attitude to deal with." The speaker, I repeat, was a leading American executive!

Other speakers raised the perennial problem of the physical aspects of communication—that is, sending a letter and receiving a reply. This is a constant impediment to efficiency. Even internally, within Japan, foreign companies have great trouble in getting replies from a division or section or in getting answers to their own letters or memos. As I mentioned earlier, the loss of face that might result from an inadequate understanding of an English-language communication sometimes seems to require that it be tossed into a wastebasket or filed unanswered.

One of the panellists gave the results of a poll he had made, among twenty American companies in Japan, on the question of how long it takes for a new man to learn his job. "There is, of course," he reported, "an awful lot of variation, depending on the nature of the job, who they have to do business with, but three years seems to be the most common period indicated. If a man comes out, say, from your Atlanta office who is already an expert in the making of widgets, if his job with the Japanese firm here is administrative, we must start him off with an efficiency rating of 35 percent in Japan whereas in Atlanta he might rate 95 percent. It's going to take him a long time to learn, because nearly everything seems to be done differently here than in Atlanta.* If your officers think they can send a man out from Atlanta and within one year he will beat a 95 percent efficiency level, they are being most unrealistic. The new man out of college with no training will take considerably longer to train here than the man who comes out with prior training in the home office. Of course, there are exceptions. Some of the boys in graduate schools at United States universities would perhaps be people one could start out here.** The factor of efficiency is an important one. The present system is very expensive and in many instances wasteful of both money and talent. Too many companies have a three-year tour of duty. That means, when a man is just becoming efficient, he is pulled out and replaced by a less efficient person."***

Many other interesting situations were posed at the seminar, many questions aired, and many solutions suggested. As the director of the seminar said, "There are so many problems that we could be here for three days just describing them." For reasons of space, I have extracted only what seemed to be the most interesting and pertinent of the questions and answers, the observations and suggestions, but if one goes over the entire record of the seminar, it all still seems to "boil down to the two most important, one at each end of the communications channel. They would be the personalities in the home office and the personality of the occidental executive. The interaction of the two allows communications to occur or causes a lack of them."

One of the most interesting conclusions to be drawn from the seminar, it seems to me, is that the foreign business representative in Japan seriously wants to learn how to improve his efficiency—

---

*It seems to be done differently because it *is* done differently.
**And some, as I know well, would soon have to be fired.
***Perhaps an argument for continuity in position, as against our much vaunted mobility.

assuming, that is, that the fifty or more who attended the seminar offer a fair sample. All on either the upper or top level of management, they are busy men who gave their time to the seminar because they sincerely want answers to the many questions that confront them. They are, I contend, the best ambassadors the United States has. But they have little voice in the making of foreign policy, and usually they are not even permitted to vote—although they *are* permitted to pay their income taxes. The League of American Residents Abroad (LARA) is now trying to secure voting rights for tax-paying citizens of the United States who are classified as "residents abroad." (The reader may recall that one of the causes of the American Revolution was the refusal of the first expatriates to accept the principle of taxation without representation. *Le plus ça change*, it seems, *le plus c'est la même chose*.)

Surprisingly, a question that was not raised at the seminar is the cost of sending a foreign executive to Tokyo and maintaining him there—for Tokyo, as his wife will repeatedly remind him, is the most expensive place in the world for a foreign businessman to live. This fact is often not appreciated at the home office, particularly if the company is new to the area. What sounds, at home, like a generous pay package frequently turns out to be inadequate, and if the company in question is a joint venture, there may be nothing that can be done about it. The Japanese side will rarely pay enough to maintain the foreigner, while the home office is likely to discredit his reasons for needing more money.

This is precisely what happened in the case of a young engineer, whom I was asked to help. Along with his wife and three children, he had been sent out as a technical adviser to a joint venture company, where he also was to act as shareholders' representative. Although the pay deal he had accepted seemed—at home—quite generous, he soon found that he and his wife could not live decently in Tokyo on what he was receiving and pay for their children's schooling. The joint venture refused him an increase, although he was working full time for the company, and the home office, apparently doubting his reports on the cost of living, was unsympathetic. As a result, the young man had fallen ill and, at the time I met him, seemed to be in a critical nervous condition. The friend who introduced us felt that if I wrote the home office, giving them the facts of life in Tokyo, they might take action. I did as I was asked, at the same time suggesting—for I know how stubborn managements can be—that if they did not believe me, they had better send someone out to stay long enough to see for himself. As it turned out, they did not believe me and they did send out a vice-president, who was here ten days or so. The company spent over five thousand dollars to verify what I had told them for free.

Another factor that contributes to the expense of maintaining foreign personnel in Tokyo is that the foreign company will often find it very difficult and expensive to get office space merely because it *is* foreign. It is the "outsider." The "insider," the Japanese company, can usually get all the space it needs. Here, in my opinion, the Japanese are making a very serious mistake. The people who are bringing skills and techniques to Japan and who are making a sincere effort to understand the Japanese way of life should be welcomed, and their paths made as smooth as possible for them.

In any case, no matter what the justification, the fact remains that it is very expensive to maintain a foreign executive staff in Tokyo—a staff, furthermore, as was brought out in the seminar, that functions at less than maximum efficiency, because of the need for extended learning time, because of rotation of personnel, and because of the sheer complexities of the Japanese business structure and its profound differences from the American.

The solution to this problem that is most frequently advocated would seem to be very simple: replace the foreigner by a Japanese. The people who favor this solution cite international companies—usually those operating in Europe—that have appointed nationals of the host country to management positions. Presumably this system is successful in Europe, but I submit that it will be a long time before it will work in Japan. Where it has been tried here, it has met with little success. Theoretically it is feasible to recruit and train Japanese nationals for lower echelon posts, and many companies are trying to do so (although the manpower-pool from which to draw, as I suggested earlier, is very shallow), but top management will still, for the foreseeable future, require the occidental executive. Anyone who has tried to recruit Japanese of management calibre, who are also fluent in English, for a foreign company knows how slim his chances are of finding a really good man. If a foreign company wants Japanese top managers, it will have to adopt the Japanese system: that is, it will have to hire young men out of college or university and train them on the job. Create an "escalator" and bring the young man up as he matures.

Foreigners, as I have written elsewhere, are often convinced that the Japanese businessman is stupid, evasive, dishonest, does everything backward etc. My friend, Handel Evans, one of the few true foreign experts on markets and distribution in Japan, in an article in *Marketing* of March 1966, the journal of the British Institute of Marketing, discusses the "evasive, insincere Japanese." Evans says that the Japanese businessman appears this way because we judge him by our code. He continues: "we must not forget that this man is responsible for what must be termed an economic miracle and he, too, has the desire to prosper. His methods are different, for they are dictated by his unique culture; but his aims are the same."

I think we can nicely wrap up this chapter by quoting Mr. Evans further. He is, of course, speaking mainly to the British executive, but the message is universal. He writes: "So it is not sufficient to cast an envious eye on the big Japanese market, to tack it on to Smith's next trip to the Far East, or to treat it as just another export market. Japan is a unique country with unique problems. Send your best and most balanced salesmen to Japan, well trained in the rigours of doing business under difficult mental conditions. He must have full authority, a big title, the constitution of a horse and the patience of a saint." These two last sentences should be heavily underlined as it is the best advice one could give to the bosses at home.

Growth and Prosperity 8

"The cautious seldom make mistakes."
—*Confucius*

"Vision" is one of a host of foreign-language words that have been matriculated into the Japanese language since the end of the war. Politicians and economists seem to have a special fondness for it, using it to mean what might more soberly be called a "forecast." It was employed in this sense by the late Prime Minister, Hayato Ikeda, in his "Plan for Doubling National Income," which was concocted largely to serve as a substitute for a national goal. Officially sanctioned by the Cabinet in December, 1960, the plan "envisioned," for the decade ahead, an average real rate of growth of 7.8 percent, which was to bring the gross national product in fiscal 1970 to ¥26 trillion (at 1958 prices). But the "Iwato boom," which had encouraged the Prime Minister to foresee "visions" that were thought at the time to be over-bold, pushed the nominal growth rate of Japan's economy in fiscal 1960 to 20.0 percent and in fiscal 1961 to 20.3 percent (the real rates were 15.5 percent and 13.9 percent), Thus, by September, 1961, the government was obliged to shift gears and to adopt a deflationary policy, which was followed by a number of other policy changes.

By 1966, the targets originally set for fiscal 1970 in the "Plan for Doubling National Income" had all been surpassed, and the plan had to be abandoned—not, as is the case with most development plans, because it could not be fulfilled, but because the actual growth of the economy had so far exceeded the target figures that they became meaningless. At fiscal 1960 prices, the gross national product by 1966 was up to ¥26,822.5 billion (¥35,091.6 billion at current prices). Exports, for which the ten-year plan had predicted a value of $9,320 million in 1970, amounted to $9,958 million in 1966; and imports, which were to reach $9,891 million in 1970, came to $10,019 million in 1966.

Despite the fact that the growth of the economy rendered the plan unrealistic, it did have two lasting effects. One was the strong inflationary trend that has reduced the buying-power of the yen by between a quarter and a third during the past nine years. The other was the expectation that Japan's fast economic growth would soon transform her into an "affluent society," with a standard of living equal to that of the most advanced countries in the world.

Year by year, as the decade of the sixties wore on, the Japanese consumer set his sights higher and higher. He took the better food and clothing that were available to him for granted, and presumably he did not object too strenuously to his unsatisfactory housing conditions. Accustomed to crowded living and working quarters from birth onwards, the Japanese apparently does not require the space and the privacy that the Westerner finds so desirable. But into his tiny house or apartment, the Japanese now began to pile gadget on gadget. When the electrical appliance industry brought prices down to levels corresponding to the average income of the salaryman, the first wave of enthusiasm created unprecedented sales for the consumer durables popularly known as the *Sanshu no Jingi* (The Three Sacred Treasures): a television set, a washing machine, and an electric refrigerator. The somewhat irreverent reference, of course, is to the Three Sacred Treasures of the Imperial House—the mirror, the sword, and the jewel—that were said to have been bestowed on the House by its divine founder, the goddess Amaterasu-o-mikami.

As the economy continued to prosper, consumers became more ambitious and turned their attention to the three C's: a car, a (room) cooler, and color-television. Although actual owners of these three fairly expensive C's are still relatively few, the average consumer does not feel that they are altogether beyond his grasp, indicating a state of affluence in Japanese society that would have been inconceivable ten years ago. More ambitious salarymen lengthened their list of C's to include central heating and a cottage in the country.

Another way for an affluent society to spend its money is on amusement and recreation. So, in Japan, along with the boom in consumer items not directly connected with food, shelter, and clothing, came the so-called "leisure boom." In the beginning, in an effort to escape the drabness of post-war reconstruction, Japanese flocked largely to movie theatres and to *pachinko* parlors, where row upon row of small upright "machines" still attract, according to one estimate, some ten million people a day. (If the *pachinko* player succeeds in getting the shiny metal balls he has bought into the nail-studded holes of the board, he is rewarded with a shower of similar little balls which he may exchange for cigarettes, canned food, and the like. A *pachinko* machine is rather a combination of a pin-ball machine and a slot-machine and exerts a fascination for the Japanese that is almost hypnotic, like the one-armed bandits of Las Vegas.)

Motion picture attendance reached its peak in 1959, when an estimated 1,127 million people crowded into the theatres; by 1967, there were many other distractions to choose from, and attendance had fallen to something over 330 million. Cities began to bolster their revenues by holding bicycle and motorboat races (which municipal authorities were empowered to operate), and horse racing was also a popular diversion—although, as is usually the case, more people bet on the horses than went to see them run.

Then, with the period of rapid economic growth, came the true "leisure boom." Millions of Japanese took to skiing and mountain-climbing, boating and motoring, hiking and golf. With their usual enthusiasm, bowling became so popular with younger people that alleys increased at a rate of over 20 percent a year.

Although the "Plan for Doubling National Income" had to be abandoned, "vision" has by no means been banished from the realm of economics. It has merely taken on a more streamlined look. Many government offices have been equipped with electronic computers, and every ministry tries to present the future development of the Japanese economy in a way that enhances the ministry's own functions. Thus, there has lately been a profusion of visionary forecasts and predictions, all of which have one thing in common: the conviction that Japan's economy and its material well-being will continue to grow. Many of these plans and projections are drawn up in connection with budgetary requests or to coincide with the proposals and policies of special interest groups. The targets and percentages merely form part of the "style"; calculations based on econometric models help to create the image of an industrial state that is up to date and at home with the latest twists in economic semantics.

So, while the United States and the Soviet Union vie with one another to reach the stars, the Japanese are quietly preoccupied with trying to lift their G.N.P. to astronomical heights. In October, 1968, the Econometric Subcommittee of the Economic Council estimated that Japan's nominal G.N.P. in fiscal 1970 would reach ¥65,352 billion, predicting an average yearly rate of increase of 15.9 percent between 1966 and 1970. (At fiscal 1960 prices, the gross national product would rise from ¥27,652 billion in fiscal 1966 to ¥41,734 billion in fiscal 1970, an average annual growth rate of 11.1 percent.)

According to a projection worked out by the Economic Planning Agency, published in August, 1968, Japan's rate of economic growth between 1965 and 1985 will average between 7.5 percent and 8.3 percent, and the gross national product will rise from the ¥30,440 billion in 1965 to between ¥130,000 billion and ¥150,000 billion in 1985. This would be equivalent to between $361 billion and $417 billion—about half of the gross national product of the United States in 1967 ($785 billion). Per capital national income during the same period, it is estimated, will increase from ¥320,000 to ¥1.2 million.

In 1968 Japan's gross national product surpassed that of West Germany (West Germany, $132.2 billion; Japan, $146.9 billion), but as far as per capita national income was concerned, the gap between Japan and other advanced countries remained a wide one

(United States, $3,266; West Germany, $1,567; Japan, $1,122). Thus, Japan would seem to be still fairly remote from the stage of a "post-industrial society," but the government believes that even that goal is well within reach. By 1985, according to the Economic Planning Agency, men will have to work 88,000 hours between the ages of 4 and 72 (the average life expectancy), while during the same span they will have 208,000 hours of free time. (For 1965, by comparison, the Agency calculated that men had to work 115,000 hours between the ages of 4 and 68, while their leisure time came to 158,000 hours.)

In 1985, people will spend a smaller percentage of their incomes on food and clothing and a larger share on housing and miscellaneous, while outlays for recreation will increase about five times over the present level.* Total private consumption expenditure will reach between ¥74 and ¥81 trillion (as compared with ¥14 trillion in 1965); investment in producers' durable equipment, ¥15-20 trillion (¥4.8 trillion in 1965); and residential construction, ¥10-20 trillion (¥1.7 trillion in 1965). Japanese exports are expected to amount to about $50 billion in 1985 ($8.45 billion in 1965) and to account for 8 percent of the world's total export trade (4.5 percent in 1965).

What Japan wants is to become as "big" as the United States. It is America she is emulating in her quest for the good life and in the ever-growing tendency of her people. Forsaking *bushido* and Confucius, the drive is to make material abundance the chief standard of value. Western Europe has not fired the Japanese imagination (at least, since the end of the war), and while Japanese business has made numerous technological agreements with European firms, Europe has exercised very little influence, generally speaking, on Japanese business thought and on the attitudes of Japan's entrepreneurial class. Similarly, although a large number

	1965	1985
*Food	39.3%	27.0%
Clothing	12.5%	9.0%
Housing	16.5%	22.7%
Miscellaneous	28.1%	38.3%

(*Figures for 1965 used as "base" figure.*)

of students are Marxists and although newspapers and other mass-communication media tend to speak of the left wing as "progressive," the Japanese have never given a moment's serious thought to emulating the Russian way of life; and Japanese businessmen, although increasingly interested in trade with the Soviet Union, do not consider it a serious competitor—*for the time being*—in world trade. Because of the built-in military and political bias of the Soviet industrial establishment, the Japanese are likely to disregard it in making international comparisons.

Thus, it is the catching up with the Americans in the sphere of economics, including technology, production, and consumption, that has become the burning ambition of the Japanese. So sweeping an assertion must obviously be hedged with many qualifications and reservations, and I am not for a moment suggesting that the Japanese have ever considered remodelling their country in the image of the United States. For one thing, they neither understand nor agree with the basic social and political premises of America's economic system: equality of opportunity and recognition of individual competence. But their guiding economic philosophy, since the end of the war, has, like that of America, been expansion. Their conduct has conformed to the principle (or to the truism) that economic expansion is the only way to increase the standard of living of a growing population and that keeping a dynamic economy moving forward by deficit financing is less dangerous than limiting growth in order to adhere to monetary orthodoxy. Numerous acts, both of omission and commission, that are incompatible with the full exploitation of possible growth opportunities have naturally occurred, but by and large expansion has been the key word in Japan's economic vocabulary.

It would have been truly miraculous had the Japanese avoided all pitfalls in their drive to become the world's second largest industrial establishment. Until the "Iwato boom," so called, there were occasional interludes when the market did not, almost automatically, absorb whatever could be produced, but these periods were only temporary. After the boom, however, over-capacity and over-production forced enterprises to discover how vital is the role played by the market itself in a productive economy.

This shift of emphasis from production to sales had a number of far-reaching effects. One was an enormous increase in advertising, based on the familiar and persuasive argument that it is better to spend money on promotion than to pay taxes, which in turn encouraged the growth of broadcasting systems and so the development of the electronics industries. A second, and more interesting, effect was the importance that came to be attributed (as I noted earlier) to one particular yardstick for bigness—the market share. The maintenance of the company's market share in an expanding economy became the focus of corporate strategy and was often the decisive consideration in investment decisions. Profitability, the most common victim of this approach to corporate growth, was not much considered so long as accounts could be juggled to show a paper profit sufficient to pay the "customary" dividend. Productive capacity frequently bore very little relation to the actual market potential, but enterprises found it less expensive to finance huge inventories of finished goods than to keep costly equipment idle—and they could always, of course, take final refuge in below-cost exports.

Of all the problems that confronted Japanese management as a result of the forced-draught expansion, three are of special interest to the foreign businessman because they are associated with the international relations of Japanese business.

The first is financing. The quantitative growth and, even more, the technological progress of Japanese enterprises required investments far beyond the financial capabilities of most firms. The average ratio of equity capital to total capital employed is still below 20 percent, and in the profit and loss statements of more than a few enterprises interest payments exceed gross profits. Thus, it is no exaggeration to say that, financially speaking, it is borrowed bigness that has made giants of many Japanese industrial and commercial enterprises. Unlike the situation in the United States, where leverage plays the major role in the formation of large corporate structures (particularly in putting together conglomerates through acquisition of existing enterprises) and where borrowed capital is quickly replaced by new stock issues, in Japan borrowed funds in the form of bank loans not only provide the working capital outside trade credits but also cover an important part of the fixed assets of most large firms. "Indirect financing," as it is called, where banks collect deposits from individual savers and lend these funds to corporate borrowers, has greatly contributed to the making of Japan's economic establishment a club of light-weights who have boosted one another into heavy-weights.

A second problem arises out of the fact that, while Japan ranks third among the nations of the world in gross national product, she is twentieth in per capita national income. Despite the steep rise in incomes, therefore, Japan's domestic market will have to continue to expand at an extremely rapid rate in order to absorb the output of an efficient industrial establishment. (The technological level of the large enterprises, in fact, far exceeds the standard of living of the population.) Thus, the basic need to export, so as to compensate for imports of raw materials and foodstuffs, is rendered more acute in Japan by the need to find foreign markets that will absorb the volume of output which exceeds domestic buying power. The difficulty of continually expanding exports of finished goods has already induced many Japanese enterprises to replace such exports by the foundation of joint ventures overseas which they then supply with materials, semi-finished products, and technology.

The need to secure sources of raw materials sufficient for the rapidly expanding capacity presents a third, and an equally thorny, problem. Japan's own scarcity of natural resources has sent her businessmen scurrying across the globe, looking for practically everything that is used in industrial production—except air and water. The threat to Japan's economic stability implied in this situation may not be disregarded.

Access to sources of raw material was an important factor in the shaping of Japan's pre-war policy, and her endeavor to gain control over North China and Manchuria was at least partially dictated by this basic need. The post-surrender policy statement of the Allied Powers mentioned, as a condition for Japan's survival, ensuring access to raw material sources, but no permanent institutional arrangements were made to solve the problem.

Japan's economic development in recent years revealed the gravity of the situation, as a result of which the government's attitude underwent a gradual but significant change. For a long time it had given priority to the country's balance-of-payments position in all transactions involving foreign investment without formulating a coherent policy for securing long-term sources of raw material. Officials in charge of approving foreign investment gave first consideration to the immediate impact of the planned transaction on the balance of payments, while tending to ignore its overall significance for the national economy.

A change in this attitude was first to be perceived in the field of oil. Large international oil companies had re-entered Japan under the protection of the occupation and had gained a dominant position in the Japanese oil market. The government was particularly irked by their unwillingness to accept the "guidance" of the Ministry of International Trade and Industry. Mr. Taro Yamashita, nick-named "*Manshu Taro*" because he had played an important role in the pre-war efforts to develop Manchuria, then proposed a plan whereby Japanese firms would obtain foreign oil concessions and import crude oil for domestic refining. In 1957, when the Arabian Oil Company was founded and began operations, the government gave its crude oil preferential treatment by designating it "quasi-domestic petroleum." Savings in foreign exchange provided a plausible pretext for forcing all refining companies to buy a certain portion of this crude oil. The status of "quasi-domestic petroleum" was also accorded somewhat later to the crude oil imported by the North Sumatra Oil Development Cooperation Company.

This policy of having Japanese companies acquire prospecting and exploitation rights so as to secure overseas sources of raw material was then extended to include non-ferrous metals (for which the Overseas Mineral Resources Development Company was founded) and uranium. The development of all kinds of minerals, as well as timber, by Japanese companies (or joint ventures) now receives official encouragement, and the life-or-death struggle to secure sources of raw material goes on. In addition to the Persian Gulf and Indonesia, oil is now being sought by Japanese interests (supported by the official Petroleum Resources Exploitation Company) in Canada, Alaska, and Australia. Investment in copper mines was concentrated originally in the Philippines and Canada but has recently been extended to Central and South America, Australia, the Pacific islands, and Africa; and Japanese participation in the development of copper deposits in the Soviet Union and Poland remains a possibility. The addition of new sources of raw materials not only increases available supplies (some part of which is, of course, needed to replace already exhausted resources) but also contributes to the factor of diversification of sources, the importance of which became apparent with the Middle East conflict.

Another important aspect of this expansion of sources is Japan's cooperation with developing countries. Like all other industrial states, Japan regards such economic cooperation as an opportunity for the export of capital goods, since the development of raw material sources usually involves a considerable investment in needed equipment, little of which is available locally. The Japanese investor, then, is free to have Japanese firms supply whatever machinery is necessary. This is one of the factors, incidentally, that makes foreign ventures for the development of raw material sources so attractive to the large Japanese trading companies: they make a profit both ways, on the export of the equipment and on the import of the raw material.

Many objections have been raised against this form of "neo-colonialism," but in most developing countries the need for quick results is overwhelming, and this kind of economic cooperation supplies it. Exploitation of mineral wealth offers developing countries an opportunity to earn much-needed foreign exchange, to provide new employment, and in many cases to improve their infrastructural facilities. Moreover, any other form of exploitation would require not only huge capital investments, which the country in question could not afford and which foreign investors would be unwilling to make, but also require such a long lead time that the resources would become a drag on the economy for a considerable period. Further, most such countries lack both the technical and the managerial personnel required for the exploitation of these resources. In some instances, such as low-grade oil, a certain degree of on-the-spot processing may be more economical, involving far less capital than the construction of an industry able to utilize the entire output of a given material.

For her supplies of industrial raw materials and fuels, Japan at present relies almost entirely on advanced and developing countries; imports from communist bloc countries play a relatively small role. There may be greater reliance in the future on developing and communist countries, but the change will not, I believe, be drastic and it will be caused by economic rather than political considerations. The chief obstacle to long-range development projects, now that Japanese companies or groups of companies are able to mobilize the requisite capital, is the political uncertainty that prevails in many developing countries and Japan's own unsettled relations with the communist states. Greater political stability may be expected to invite an all-out effort on the part of Japan to control raw material sources.

She is, however, in rather a weak bargaining position where those sources are concerned. A late comer among the advanced industrial states, she cannot take for granted that foreign countries or foreign enterprises will cooperate with her to make raw materials available, although for the moment her attempts to gain access to them encounters less opposition than her attempts to secure and expand markets for her finished products. But major obstacles remain. With certain raw materials, proven or commercially extractable supplies are growing scarcer; with others, such as oil, supplies may be ample but the entry of new producers aggravates an already difficult market situation. Further, although developing countries may lack the capital and the technology to exploit their natural resources, they are not obliged to allow foreigners to do so. If they agree to grant prospecting or exploitation rights, they can often obtain unilaterally favorable conditions, securing for themselves long-term advantages without any corresponding risk.

This logistical problem—of how the world's third largest industrial establishment is going to ensure reliable supplies of necessary raw materials, in view of the country's own wholly inadequate natural resources—takes on frightening dimensions and involves enormous potential risk. The ability of Japan's entrepreneurs to increase imports of raw materials to meet the demands of rapid economic expansion in the recent boom years and still remain competitive deserves high marks, but the situation continues to be precarious. The development of overseas raw material sources is far from being a perfect solution, since most such projects involve very high initial costs and will pay off only if exploitation may be continued for a reasonably long time. This means that in many cases only long-term arrangements to secure supplies of raw materials can contribute materially to the country's economic stability. But that, in turn, presupposes an already existing political and economic stability at home as well as abroad, and it also implies that no revolutionary technological change will make the raw material superfluous or obsolete. The risks that industry must take, however, when investing in foreign raw material sources seem small compared with the danger of having to close down plants for lack of materials.

The fact that post-war animosity against Japan has largely vanished does not mean that Japanese investment is invariably welcome. Nationalism always implies a certain amount of xenophobia, particularly in developing countries, where foreign control of raw material sources is identified with colonialism, neo-colonialism, and other real or imagined threats to national independence. Some countries have adopted an official policy of encouraging the inflow of foreign capital, but many impose severe restrictions on foreign investment and adopt a system of unfavorable tax treatment of foreign business concerns. Generally speaking, the enormous power wielded by the bureaucracy, by the army, or by some other privileged group—which often is a law unto itself—

contributes little to the improvement of the investment climate.

Projects for the development of raw material sources in many Southeast Asian countries must reckon with a lack of transportation facilities (roads, railroads, harbors), of adequate communication, of skilled labor and indigenous supervisory personnel (the result, basically, of insufficient educational facilities), of power (electricity), and of the manufacturing and service industries required for technologically advanced operations. The inaccessibility of raw material deposits will often require the creation of the entire infrastructure (which is frequently the case also in Australia, Canada, the Soviet Union, and Latin America). The project will then have to operate as a virtually self-contained unit, providing everything from spare parts for the maintenance of machinery to office equipment, food, housing, medical care, and recreational facilities. Obviously, only large-scale, long-term projects can carry so heavy an overhead; and the risk that development costs will make the project uncompetitive is ever-present. (These considerations affect some of the development programs proposed by the Soviet Union.)

Thus, Japanese industry is torn between, on the one hand, the urgent need to secure raw material sources and a strong desire to gain a controlling influence and, on the other, the fact that the risks involved are great and often incalculable. Further, as foreign projects increase in size, financing becomes a major problem. Recent government surveys show that Japanese corporations, during the last expansion, were able to finance a larger part of their equipment investment through internal cash flow than in former years, but no Japanese enterprise possesses reserves large enough to finance foreign foundations or invest substantially in overseas projects. The larger share of capital to be invested abroad must be borrowed, but Japan possesses no financial institutions for this particular purpose. Her unfavorable balance-of-payments position has often led in the past to the postponement of foreign investment decisions or to the curtailment of investment programs; it is only in recent months that balance-of-payment considerations have become less imperative.

The combination of these factors plus the scarcity of domestic capital in developing countries has encouraged the Japanese entrepreneur to share the risks with foreign partners. Moreover, in many parts of the world, such as Africa, Australia, Canada, and Latin America, international capital occupies a strong position and controls a large part of raw material sources. Despite fierce competition, therefore, the basic trend has been toward cooperation with international capital, and Japanese development efforts become increasingly integrated with the activities of international companies. Although there are no formal agreements or institutionalized arrangements, the tendency toward an integrated international supply-and-demand system for basic raw materials seems fairly pronounced—a tendency that Japanese development efforts may have accelerated.

Western partners in undertakings of this kind should bear in mind that foreign investment projects require government approval as well as the consensus of all the Japanese partners involved. Large-scale projects, especially, are often based on the cooperation of the particular branch of industry concerned, and the elaboration of a plan acceptable to all parties is a tedious and time-consuming process. In the course of it, Japanese firms often find themselves caught between their own government and their foreign partners.

Japan's economy, then, is an extremely vulnerable one, and her economic survival will depend largely on her ability to secure international cooperation and achieve an increasing degree of economic integration. Her reluctance to liberalize foreign trade and exchange and her continued opposition to direct foreign investment would seem to belie her protestations of a desire for international cooperation, but her business leaders are well aware of Japan's inescapable involvement in the world economy. While they strongly oppose American domination over the Japanese economy, they are convinced at the same time that they must avoid a confrontation with the United States. What they want is a *modus vivendi* which will not jeopardize Japan's establishment and which will permit the ruling elite to pursue its dream of catching up with the United States.

Japan stands a far better chance than Europe of meeting "the American challenge." No insurmountable difficulties arise out of national antagonisms or differences in economic structure, while the Japanese willingness to let the national interest supersede personal ambition makes it easy to rally business behind government. Businessmen accept the fact that they must rely on foreign technology (at the same time making strenuous efforts to develop domestic technology in such critical areas as computers and atomic energy), and they are less inclined than the government is to regard dependence on foreign licenses as a serious threat to economic autonomy.

Japan has never occupied a position of economic leadership, and her experience of political hegemony was very short-lived. Military successes during the Pacific War, or during the Meiji era, may thrill movie audiences in what is customarily referred to as a revival of nationalism in recent years, but dreams of imperial grandeur do not enter into Japan's vision of herself in the coming century. Obviously, politics will complicate and color whatever economic arrangement she makes with the United States—the renewal of the Japanese-American Security Treaty is a highly explosive issue—but if Japan's leadership continues along its present path, it will never be tempted to put political dreams before economic realities.

9 Business and Bureaucracy

"Established custom is not easily broken."
—Samuel Johnson

In earlier chapters I have described briefly the close connection between business and government in Japan and the close resemblance between governmental bureaucrats and industrial managers. I should like, in this chapter, to go into the subject in somewhat greater detail.

The Japanese government, like all governments, is a collection of higher and lower bureaucrats in a hierarchy that is topped by politicians; and like all others, the Japanese bureaucracy acts in the light of inherited customs, traditions, attitudes, practices, and prejudices. The top Japanese bureaucrats, like the top managers in industry, are mostly Meiji men, trained and educated by older, early Meiji men and by former Tokugawa samurai. Taisho men are perhaps slightly less tradition-bound than Meiji men, but one must bear in mind that Meiji men were the educators of the Taisho men and also that the extreme nationalism of the Taisho and early Showa periods resulted in rigid state control that has had an inevitable effect on the thought processes of Taisho and early Showa men. Thus, in government as in business, one must await the rise to power of the new youth, the later Showa men, for any final break with the feudal tradition.

The persistence of this tradition helps to explain, of course, why Japanese industry is willing to accept what in the West would be considered excessive governmental interference. In the words of

Dr. Iwao Hoshii, "A majority of business leaders seem to consider *dirigisme* as the price industry must pay for the State's protection. Relatively few openly complain of, or oppose, bureaucratic interference; government guidance is regarded as an integral part of the economic structure." This guidance has generally no foundation in law: the bureaucrat has no legal right to guide, nor is the industrialist under any legal compulsion to be guided. Yet, out of deference to tradition and habit, the guidance is usually both given and taken. The industrialist bows down, one might say, to the bureaucrat, but at the same time it is virtually impossible to determine where government's influence over industry ends and industry's influence over government begins. As a British report puts it, "The very intimate and manifold connections at all levels between government and industry are a most important factor in the attitudes and policies of both."[50] These connections have a force in Japan that is not to be found in any other industrialized capitalist state.

Contributing substantially to this phenomenon are the so-called "public corporations." Marshall E. Dimock writes: "I have seen estimates that as much as 40 percent of all the nation's economic activity is controlled by government enterprise."[51] Professor Dimock estimates that over a million people are employed by public corporations, and his study of the subject is based on 108 such corporations, but, as he points out, that figure "does not include all the corporate enterprises that might be listed in the public or semi-public sector, but only those that the government recognizes as its proper official concern."[52]

As I mentioned earlier, the Ministry of Finance makes use of what is called "window guidance" to exercise control over industry through the Bank of Japan and city banks; "administrative guidance" is usually given by the Ministry of International Trade and Industry, although other ministries also make use of it, and under its guise impose, on occasion, extremely stringent controls. The government can and has designated what company may manufacture what products, and how many of them; or what company may build a plant, and how big the plant may be; or what company must get out of a certain industry, and what company may stay in it. When industry is recalcitrant, the government brings about the end it desires through other pressures. It even extends its "administrative guidance" to marketing, allocation of markets, pricing, advertising, public relations, and sales inducements. (Not long ago the government decreed that sales promotional campaigns might give away television sets—but not color ones!)

This is the "guidance" that foreign investors must also be prepared to accept if they want to do business in Japan. A spokesman for the Foreign Investment Council is reported to have said not long ago: "We think, therefore, that we shall be justified in asking foreign investors . . . to respect our laws and customs, . . . to cooperate in the maintenance of order in their respective industries, . . . to avoid closures of plants or mass dismissals and avoid unnecessary confusion concerning employment and wages by paying due regard to our prevailing practices. . . ."[53] In other words, the foreigner, if he wants to do business here, must abide by accepted Japanese practices: he must not be too competitive, he must market through traditional channels, and he must follow the system of life-tenure in his labor relations. The fact that he is losing money is not considered a valid excuse for mass dismissals, nor are antagonistic union activities.

According to recent press reports, an American firm, the Avon Cosmetics Company, applied for permission to open a sales branch in Japan. The government could hardly refuse, since most other large foreign cosmetics companies were already well-entrenched here, but the difficulty was that Avon planned to sell its products directly to the consumer, as it does elsewhere in the world: a marketing method contrary to the government dictate that foreign companies must use existing distribution channels and may not even sell directly to retail outlets, let alone to the consumer. However, there were already in existence two Japanese cosmetic companies that were doing just that—Chanson and Pola (the latter is said to have studied and adopted Avon's system). The government could not justify a refusal of Avon's request, since other foreign companies were already operating in the industry and two Japanese companies were using the method that Avon had proposed. The bureaucracy saved its face in this instance by securing from Avon a promise to proceed slowly, to refrain from disrupting the market or engaging in excessive competition and to abide by other unwritten conditions. The company, thus, was obliged to accept restrictions that officially do not exist.

The imposition of controls is preceded by consultations between government and the industry concerned, a process that customarily involves several "councils," study groups, and the industry association, as well as the leaders of the industry. Thus the controls do not take the form of an outright government fiat—although to smaller enterprises, which may have little or no voice in the consultations, the result is the same. Yet politicians, those at the top of the bureaucracy, cannot afford to be too dictatorial, so the government must make compromises and adjustments in the process of imposing controls, just as industry must in accepting them. Above all, harmony must reign. That the system has been effective is obvious.

One of the ways in which industry collaborates with government, and the kind of dialogue that takes place between them, is exemplified in the career of Mr. Yoichiro Inayama, president of the Yawata Iron and Steel Company, the largest steel company in Japan and the fourth largest in the world. Mr. Inayama, born in the thirty-seventh year of Meiji, is now in his mid-sixties. After his graduation from Tokyo Imperial University, he was accepted by the Ministry of Commerce and Industry (today the Ministry of International Trade and Industry) and was assigned to the Yawata Iron and Steel Company, then operated by the government as part of its armaments program. Later, when Yawata was incorporated into Japan Steel, Mr. Inayama became a director of the company, which controlled all the steel mills in Japan.

With the end of the war, Japan Steel was broken up into four smaller companies, and since Mr. Inayama was not purged by the occupation authorities, the government placed him back with Yawata. But now he was no longer on the government payroll, he was a company man, a shift in status that he took in his stride.

Using his knowledge, ability, and drive (of the last some people think he possessed an over-abundance), he rose to be president of Yawata.

He now serves on a number of important committees, such as the Industrial Structure Research Council; he is spokesman for Japan's steel industry in its consultations with the government; and he has been decorated by the Emperor. Presumably, he has also done well for Yawata. To the question whether he is in reality a government man placed in industry or whether he is an entrepreneur of private industry, the answer must be, of course, that he is a government man in industry. In earlier days, he would have been a great entrepreneur; nowadays, he has done an outstanding job as president of Yawata in maintaining the delicate balance between the needs of government and the aspirations of industry. He is said to prefer *kyocho* to *kyoso*—that is, he believes that cooperation with government and other steel producers is more desirable than competition, and he believes that this system is better for his country's well-being and prosperity. Judging by Japan's formidable growth and Yawata's own preeminence, one can hardly claim that he is incorrect in these assumptions.

On June 1, 1969, Yawata was scheduled to merge with Fuji Iron and Steel Co., the second largest steel company in Japan. The resultant company, Shin Nihon Seitetsu K.K. (New Japan Iron and Steel Co.) would have then been the second largest in the world after the U.S. Steel Co. Mr. Inayama was scheduled to be President of the new company.

A comment on the planned merger may not be amiss. The Fair Trade Commission has perforce made the appropriate noises about this concentration of power, and has successfully blocked the merger, at least for some time. But it is by no means a dead issue. It is likely that the two enterprises will postpone their plan and await a more opportune time.

Another example of the relationship between government and business is furnished by the case of the Tokio Marine and Fire Insurance Company. Here, because of the government's attitude and its arbitrary disregard of the law, the company sustained enormous losses.

In 1963, building regulations were revised so as to remove the ceiling that had previously been put on the height of all buildings, replacing it with a volumetric formula that would permit high-rise buildings if a proportionate open area was preserved at the base. Tokio Marine and Fire, three years later, applied to the Tokyo Municipal Government for a permit to replace the old Kaijo Building in Marunouchi with a new thirty-story building. The application was rejected on the pretext that the planned building would spoil the "scenic beauty" of the Marunouchi district adjacent to the plaza in front of the Imperial Palace. The Metropolitan Government even drew up a Scenic Beauty Ordinance, but this failed to secure passage in the Metropolitan Assembly. When the national Ministry of Construction advised the Metropolitan Government that its invocation of "scenic beauty" was without legal foundation, the latter shifted its ground and rejected the application because the building area was composed of two different lots. This occurred in April, 1967, six months after the original application.

Tokio Marine and Fire thereupon appealed to the Metropolitan Building Council for a ruling on the interpretation of the municipal building regulations given by the Metropolitan Government. Of the seven-member Council, four were in favor of approving the application of the insurance company; the three who were opposed resigned in a last-ditch attempt to make a decision impossible. Tokyo's Governor Minobe, however, accepted the majority decision, and in October, 1967, the Metropolitan Government began processing the application, in the routine course of which the application was sent to the Ministry of Construction. Normally, approval by the Ministry takes no more than a week; but in this case, weeks and then months went by with no sign of action.

Naomi Nishimura, a former Minister of Construction, was known to be opposed to the plan on the grounds that the "scenic beauty" in front of the Palace plaza ought to be preserved. When the chairman and president of Tokio Marine and Fire visited Prime Minister Sato to "explain" their building plan, the Prime Minister showed little enthusiasm for the project and in fact advised the executives to cancel their construction plans without giving any reason for this "advice." Nearly a year later, the present Minister of Construction, Shigeru Hori, asked the Keidanren (the Federation of Economic Organizations) to decide the issue.

This final step may seem to make a mockery of legal process, but it is easily explicable within the terms of the controversy—for the real quarrel is somewhat different, it being a quarrel somewhat similar to a family dispute. Mitsubishi, as we saw earlier, had long ago bought up most of Marunouchi, and now has a huge investment in traditional ten-story buildings in that area. It wants no competition in the form of a skyscraper in the heart of the "Mitsubishi field." But Tokio Marine and Fire owns its own land and, while independent, is still very closely connected with the Mitsubishi group. Mitsubishi companies are very large shareholders and Mitsubishi Bank is its main bank. But in this instance Tokio Marine and Fire is rebelling. When, in the very beginning, Tokio Marine decided "to go high-rise," its president went to the Mitsubishi Real Estate Company, but the latter was absolutely opposed to the plan. According to "rumors" published in the daily press, the Metropolitan Government agreed to block Tokio Marine's construction plans in return for Mitsubishi's cooperation in developing the site of the former Yodobashi Reservoir in Shinjuku. The "scenic beauty" issue, thus, would seem to have been no more than a smoke-screen (which appealed to right-wing politicians) while the real issue was money. Whatever are the true reasons, as of this writing, the plan projected by the Tokio Marine and Fire Insurance Company has not yet received approval by the competent authorities.

Money is, of course, in Japan as elsewhere, one of the strongest links in the chain that binds businessmen and politicians together—although perhaps in Japan the tie is more obvious than in some other countries, where "harmony" is a less pervasive factor and where some sectors of business are regularly at odds with some sectors of government.

The ruling Liberal-Democratic Party relies on donations by business—companies, organizations, and private businessmen—

for the major part of the funds needed to finance the Party's activities, especially election campaigns. (The Socialist Party gets its chief financial support from Sohyo and its affiliated labor unions; the Democratic Socialist Party, from the General Federation of Trade Unions; and the Communist Party and Komeito, the political arm of the Soka-Gakkai, from the sale of publications). In addition to official party organizations charged with collecting contributions, many individual politicians have their own groups or associations through which they channel political funds.

Although in theory, under existing laws, these organizations must report revenues and expenditures to the Ministry of Home Affairs (Jichi-sho),* which publishes summary statistics in the Official Gazette, in fact control over such funds is virtually nonexistent, as is public knowledge of their origins. The only sources that need to be specified are those labelled "political donations"; all others may be lumped together as "others." For example, in the 1967 report, the Ikuseikai (an organization in Prime Minister Sato's group) reported revenues of ¥146 million, of which only ¥2 million were identified (as having come from the Japan Medical Federation); the remaining ¥144 million came from "others." Equally obscure are the purposes for which funds are spent, and the switching of them from one organization to another does nothing to help clarify the situation. "Research" and "Travel" are two favorite categories under which expenses are reported, while "Loans" and "Organizational Expenses" also account for large sums. According to press reports, the ruling party has made political donations to opposition parties in order to secure the "cooperation" of the latter in proceedings of the Diet! Many attempts have been made to impose stricter regulations—such as limiting contributions, providing for full disclosure of sources, and demanding stricter accounting—but so far these attempts have been aborted. The ruling Liberal-Democratic Party, it seems, has no desire to cut its own throat.

---

*"Jichi-sho" literally translates as "self-government ministry," (the Prime Minister's office says the correct name is "Ministry of Autonomy,") but its popular name in English is "Ministry of Home Affairs," which is "Naimu-sho." So beautifully clear is the Japanese language.

The funds involved in financing party activities are by no means negligible: political parties and their organizations reported, in 1967, having received ¥18.5 billion (approx. $51.4 million) and having spent ¥18.6 billion (approx. $51.7 million). But competent observers believe that the money actually spent by politicians is many times that reported to, and published by, the Home Ministry.

The list of recipient organizations of political funds is far too long to reproduce here but it makes interesting reading. Most leading politicians have their own "faction" organizations, frequently labeled as study groups, such as the Seikei Kenkyu-kai, the Political Economy Study Association, of Mr. Sato's faction. The really top men have several such groups or associations, some with rather odd names such as Mr. Sato's Ikusei-kai, which means "upbringing, nurturing, developing, society"; or Mr. Tanaka's Essan-kai which, as far as I can learn, has no meaning. Then there is the Hoan-kai (Peace Preservation Association) of Mr. Ishii's faction; the Seisaku Kondan-kai (Political Discussion Group) of Mr. Miki and so on.

An important group, the Kokumin Kyokai (People's Association) was established a few years ago as the official fund-raising organ of the Liberal-Democratic Party. Some of the party elders expressed the opinion that it should become the only dispenser of party money, but no attempt was made to prevent the factional organizations from handling political funds. The faction chiefs are well aware that their influence depends to a large extent on the financial help they can give their followers and naturally they are loath to lose their position for the sake of something so tenuous as "clean politics."

The extent to which business supports the politicians can be inferred from the "political donations" listed in the reports. Industry associations tend to direct their contributions to the official party organizations, but individual companies often prefer to support individual politicians, a process that demands a certain political acumen if the donor does not want to find that he's backed the wrong horse.

Attempts to prevent companies from using corporate funds for political contributions have been generally unsuccessful. For example, a few years ago a private stockholder of Yawata Iron and Steel Company filed suit to have the then president and vice-president repay the company ¥3.5 million donated to the Liberal-Democratic Party in 1960. The Tokyo District Court where the case was tried agreed with the plaintiff that political donations were outside the scope of normal corporate activities and that in donating the money the directors had violated the company's Articles of Incorporation. When the company appealed the verdict in 1966, however, the Tokyo Higher Court reversed the lower court's decision on the grounds that a representative democratic system involved the activities of political parties and that donations for that purpose were as lawful as contributions to charities.

The lower court had reasoned that the stockholders' consent might justifiably be assumed in the case of charitable donations but that there was no foundation for presuming that all stockholders would support the same political party. (This was the identical point that was stressed in an American court decision of 1904.) The higher court, however, ruled that making contributions to political parties "was an action which was useful to the company and within the sphere of its purposes, irrespective of the provisions of the Articles of Incorporation." (Lower courts in Japan tend to be more "democratic" than the higher courts in their interpretation of the law and the Constitution.)

Political donations are all too often found to be an integral part of the cases of official corruption that emerge from time to time on the Japanese scene. Like most other countries, Japan has a long and dishonorable history of the misappropriation of public as well as private funds. It was a major factor in the breakdown of parliamentary government before the Second World War, and it contributed to the first major post-war scandal (the Showa Denko case, in 1948) which led to the downfall of the Ashida Cabinet.

One of the more recent scandals involved the Nippon Express Company (Nittsu) and its daughter companies, which had many contracts with government organizations, including the Self Defense Agency, the Monopoly Bureau, and the Japan National

Railways. After a series of investigations, a number of executives and other officials of the companies were indicted for embezzlement and bribery, and two members of the Diet, Masanosuke Ikeda of the Liberal-Democratic Party and Seiichi Okura of the Socialist Party, for accepting bribes. Also accused of accepting bribes were officials of the National Tax Office. The prosecution charged that over ¥500 million had been misappropriated (of which ¥300 million was in secret "rebates" that did not appear on the books of the company). Nittsu's officers were accused of pocketing ¥325,940,000 (some of it in the form of gold bars and debentures) and of distributing ¥192.8 million to a total of forty-nine Dietmen between 1964 and 1967. Obviously, the sums mentioned were only those that the Tokyo District Public Prosecutor's Office was able to trace; it may be that the real extent of the misappropriations will never be known.

Among its government contracts, Nittsu had the exclusive right to transport rice for the Food Control Agency, which handles the government's purchases of rice from the farmers as well as the entire distribution of that first staple of Japanese life to consumers. The Food Control Agency belatedly conceded that it had over-paid Nittsu some ¥120 million.

Even more widespread than bribery of public officials is tax evasion, since politicians need not pay taxes on political donations they receive provided they use the money for political purposes; if they use it for personal expenditures, they are not granted this exemption. According to a statement made by the director-general of the National Tax Administration Agency, nearly ¥25 million in additional taxes were collected between March 16 and December 10, 1967, from fifty politicians who had concealed over ¥60 million of income.

An article in *Mainichi Daily News* of March 5, 1969, under the headline "Bribery Natural Result of MITI, Industry Ties" under-lines the government-business togetherness. It confirms that "most MITI men can find good employment in industries after their retirement." It condemns the entertainment of officials saying, "The ministry is also reported to be the place where the largest number of hired cars and taxis dispatched by companies can be seen around closing time every day," and, "No wonder many people call the ministry the 'Kasumigaseki branch' of certain companies."*

Almost every really large company in Japan maintains an office in Tokyo although its head office may be elsewhere. It is not only a matter of corporate "face," but it is a necessity to be near the seat of government. So deeply involved is government with business that a company, particularly if it is in any way concerned with foreign matters, must have convenient access to Kasumigaseki, since the greater majority of corporate plannings require government approval, or "understanding," involving mountains of paper work and hours of talk with bureaucrats. Almost every important international matter, whether a joint venture, a foreign licensing, the introduction of a technology or an overseas investment of any kind, is usually negotiated in Tokyo although the company's head office may be in Osaka. It is usually in Tokyo that even important domestic planning is decided, since the bureaucracy must be in the act. Thus, the thaumaturgists of Tokyo, the company men and the government men plan out and work out most foreign transactions and even most important domestic matters. They plan the future economy, plot the strategy and devise the means for implementation, then their trolls, the mass of employees, both government and business, go to work to bring the scheme to fruition.

In an earlier chapter I have shown that the fathers of Japanese industrial modernization tried to combine modern technologies with Confucian ethics.

Japan in the days before the militarists took over was said to be a very well-ordered community where honesty was the norm. It was said that if one dropped an item on the Ginza it would be there the next day to be recovered; that no one locked their house doors in Tokyo. Thievery and violence were rare and the bureauc-

---

*The ministry offices are in "Kasumigaseki," the district in Tokyo where most government ministries are located. So that, in this respect, "Kasumigaseki" means the "Government."

racy unbribable. This may be exaggerated but certainly the mass of the people were more imbued with Confucian ethics than are the post-war politicians. Buddhism and Shintoism do not deal with personal ethics—guidance came from the Imperial presence. Now both Confucian ethics and the Imperial presence, in that sense, are gone and nothing but the desire to be more affluent seems to have replaced them. Perhaps this is one reason for the decline in ethical standards among certain politicians. Although in my experience, Japan is nowhere near in the same league in bureaucratic perfidy as are certain other countries in Asia, the Middle East and yes, even in Europe.

Marketing and Distribution 10

> *"By nature men resemble one another;*
> *through habit they differ widely."*
> —Confucius

Marketing and distribution, it would seem, constitute the major sources of friction between the foreigner and his Japanese partners in a joint venture. Unlike technological problems, where modern techniques are dealt with in concrete terms, marketing and distribution obviously involve the human factor to a far greater degree and the human, trial-and-error approach to the solution of the problems. Furthermore, the Japanese distribution system (or, more accurately, systems) seems by Western standards archaic, inefficient, and wasteful. For example, in the typical Japanese distribution system as many as five (and sometimes more) middlemen stand between the maker and the consumer. In the United States, it may be noted, as in most other Western countries, there are usually only the wholesaler and the retailer, with in some instances the jobber.

Obviously, then, distribution costs must be higher in Japan than in advanced states of the West, a factor that is further compounded by Japan's use of the system of deferred payment notes (*tegata*), varying in length from sixty to 120 to 180 days. The temper of the Japanese people, as I have pointed out earlier, is to resist change (until circumstances make change inevitable), while the foreign businessman in Japan, confronted by what he considers a cumbersome and uneconomic distribution system, is eager to "streamline" it, to make it more like the system he is familiar with at home.

The result all too often is friction between the partners, and the foreigner's frustration is only intensified by the fact that the government requires him not to disrupt the market and to abide by the customs and habits of the particular business in which he is engaged. Since this is the area where many foreign businessmen have come to grief, a brief examination of Japanese distribution channels may be useful.

What Japanese commentators refer to as the "dual structure" of Japan's economy—that is, the existence of a comparatively few very large firms side by side with a vast number of very small ones—is nowhere so apparent as in the distribution of consumer goods. Although large department stores dominate retail outlets, they account for only about 10 percent of total national sales. 90 percent are family enterprises with only one or two employees. A survey conducted by the Ministry of International Trade and Industry in 1964 revealed the following figures:

Employees	Stores	Composite Percentage
1–2	917,871	70.4
3–4	251,305	19.2
5–9	97,880	7.5
10–19	26,296	2.0
20–29	6,204	0.5
30–49	3,732	0.3
50–99	1,617	0.1
100 or more	666	0.0
Total	1,305,570	100.0

A comparison of the total number of stores with the total population gives a figure of some 13.8 retail outlets per thousand people, as compared with a figure of 6.2 in the United States.

This duality of structure also applies of course to the producers themselves: the number of large-scale manufacturers is comparatively small, while that of small-scale manufacturers is extremely large. Obviously, then, the collection of a vast variety of finished goods from small producers and the distribution of the goods to a large number of very small consumer outlets (who, furthermore, tend to be weak financially) becomes a highly complicated process.

Another factor that has contributed to the profusion of middlemen in the Japanese economy is its relatively recent emergence from feudalism. Traditionally, each caste—from samurai at the top to merchant at the bottom—lived within a strict code that regulated not only behavior in the deepest sense but also so superficial a thing as costume. Every member of every caste knew precisely what kind of clothes were permissible, and even what colors. Thus, retail outlets had to stock a large assortment of goods to meet the demands (and the pocketbooks) of poor farmers as well as wealthy samurai or successful merchants. Since, obviously, a small shop was quite incapable of collecting all the various goods that were necessary and housing them in large quantities, it came to rely on the *tonya*, who might be called the chief wholesaler. He knew what goods would be required and he had the facilities to collect and store them, supplying them on demand to lesser wholesalers who would then pass them on to direct consumer outlets. Even present day mammoth department stores, some of which are said to stock nearly half a million different items, rely on the *tonya*.

A typical distribution pattern in contemporary Japan would be:

Manufacturer
↓
Major wholesaler
↓
Middle (regional) wholesaler
↓
Minor (local) wholesaler
↓
Retailer
↓
Consumer.

The pattern varies, obviously, depending on the type of merchandise and the size of the manufacturer, but remains fundamentally the same whatever the precise structure of the distribution organs may be.

It will, I think, be illuminating to examine the marketing system of one Japanese company, a cosmetics firm known to all Japan by its abbreviated name, Shiseido. Although it sells elsewhere in the world, the domestic market is its main strength. It has its own controlled system but the basic pattern remains typical.

Under the parent company, Shiseido has a chief sales company (which may be compared roughly to a national *tonya*, save that usually the *tonya* is a distinctly separate company, not owned by the maker). This sales company, called Shiseido Hambai Gaisha, has eleven branches of its own and fifteen subsidiary outlets. It has a further subsidiary, which acts as another lesser wholesaler, the Shiseido Trading Company, with a head office and eight branches. In addition, there is the Shiseido wholesale chain consisting of three hundred wholesalers who serve some fifteen thousand chain stores and about a hundred thousand smaller "member" shops. The wholesalers, the chain stores, and the "member" shops handle other goods, of course, as well as cosmetics and also other brands of cosmetics.

Exploiting the apparently ingrained desire of the Japanese to belong to a group, or a number of groups, Shiseido has with great success used a members' club (called the Hanatsubaki-kai) to sell consumer goods. Beauty shops (owned by Shiseido) and department stores that maintain a Shiseido "corner" register the names and addresses of good customers, who thus automatically become members of the Shiseido club. At this writing, it has about ten million members! From time to time, they are offered special bargains, or they may be offered "free" gifts, depending on how many Shiseido products they have bought during a given period of time (much as the "stamp" system is used to boost sales in the United States). The club also publishes a magazine which, in addition to glorifying Shiseido products, both old and new, publishes articles of general interest on such subjects as art, the theatre, the movies, travel, and so on. Small wonder, then, that Shiseido controls over half of the Japanese cosmetics market—despite fierce competition from over three hundred domestic companies (of which a dozen or so are rated large) and more than a half-dozen foreign companies.

Distribution and sales systems like Shiseido's will unquestionably continue to be general practice in Japan for some time to come, although changing conditions in the Japanese business world will tend to modify it to a greater or less degree in various industries. Yet the dual structure that characterizes both makers and retailers, the ingrained habits of the Japanese consumer, and the geography of the country itself, as well as the transportation system that has resulted, will all combine to perpetuate—for some time to come, at least—the kind of distribution system that Shiseido uses. On the question of change versus tradition, Handel Evans, in a perceptive article, says that "Japan is going through a period of cultural metamorphosis. There has been a massive infusion of Western ideas since 1945 which has left the old and the new coexisting in Japan. Yet through this cultural topsy-turvy the Japanese seem to move easily, for they have become 'cultural amphibia.' However, they find it hard to live an amphibious business life that would accommodate the Western businessman. Many of my colleagues in Tokyo say the old Japanese way of doing business is vanishing rapidly. But don't believe a word of it; tradition dies hard and it will take generations to change the basic thinking of the Japanese."[54]

True, there have been successful exceptions to the general rule of a complex distributional system, both among older Japanese companies and new foreign companies, but on the whole most companies that have tried to flout traditional and established channels and "go it alone" have either failed entirely or failed to achieve the results they anticipated. One example of Japanese groups that have successfully exploited the house-to-house system of selling is Toyama medicines a so-called monopolistic product; and it is interesting to note that two foreign companies that have successfully circumvented the traditional Japanese distributional system also handle what the Industrial Promotion Association terms "monopolistic" products. These are the Encyclopedia Britannica and Coca Cola (said to be the most profitable foreign company operating in Japan). The latter's success, it may be supposed, was achieved because of its custom of "monopolizing" the original flavoring, which it imports in bulk and then processes and bottles in Japan. That its success is no longer questionable is shown by the fact that the Japanese Soft Drink Association wants to stage a *demo* ("demonstration") against Coke. Other foreign companies have achieved success by compromising with the traditional system in one way or another: examples are Nestlé, General Foods (with Maxwell House instant coffee), Smith, Kline and French (with Contac), and Mentholatum.

An example of a joint venture company that attempted to invade the Japanese market without phenomenal success is Nichiro-Heinz K.K., in which the original ratio of ownership was 51 percent for Nichiro Fisheries Company and 49 percent for H. J. Heinz, the American company that is famous for its "57 varieties." When it became known that Heinz was to enter Japan, Japanese canned food makers, particularly of tomato juice, ketchup, and canned soups, grew extremely apprehensive—but, as it turns out, they need not have worried. Although some eight years have passed since the foundation of the joint venture, its market share in canned tomato products such as juice, soup, and ketchup is perhaps not even one percent.

There are, of course, several reasons for this remarkable lack of success. One was the apparent inability of the American partner to understand Japanese management and distribution systems; another, a rigid conviction that American sales methods must necessarily succeed in Japan; this resulted from a wholly false conception of the psychology of the Japanese consumer. It may well be that Nichiro was not the right partner for Heinz. Certainly there were grave differences in overall policy, particularly that concerning financing, between the two partners at top management level. The result was a virtual withdrawal by Nichiro from management, which was taken over by Heinz. The original 51 percent–49 percent ratio of ownership changed to 20 percent for Nichiro and 80 percent for Heinz. Heinz then dispensed with the Nichiro distribution system, largely traditional, and also with the distribution system of the Taisho Pharmaceutical Company (which had been handling the sales of baby foods, again in the traditional way). However, the more "streamlined" distributional system that Heinz then set up did not presumably yield the results that had been anticipated, and Heinz has now effected a compromise between its own way and the Japanese way, at least in the distribution and sales of canned soup, which are said to be improving. How Heinz will fare with its other products in the Japanese market remains to be seen.*

That the government seeks to preserve the dual structure is shown by the fact that there are a number of regulations in effect to protect small businesses. The "decontrol" of March 1, 1969, for example, now permits a foreign investor to own 50 percent of a retail shop but at the same time it restricts such shops to a maximum floor space of five hundred square meters (approximately 5380 square feet). Thus, small groceries in Japan are not—for the moment, in any case—seriously menaced by an imminent blanket of supermarkets. There are supermarkets in Japanese cities, to be sure, and their number is increasing noticeably, but both size and number are insignificant compared with the United States.

Here the experience of Safeway Stores, an American company, may be of interest, since it points up the many different factors a would-be investor in this field must take into account in Japan: size, inventory, methods of purchasing, consumer buying habits, costs, and so on. The "Safeway story" that follows is taken from an account published by the Japan Industrial Promotion Association in *A Key to the Japanese Market:* Tokyo, 1968, in English.

Safeway entered Japan under a company called the Keihin Shokai, a wholly-owned subsidiary of Sumitomo Trading Company (the original partner-to-be of Safeway), which opened a supermarket named the Nozawa Building Store, and Safeway itself sent over a representative to supervise the management. "The American way of operating a supermarket was thus inaugurated in Japan," wrote the Industrial Promotion Association, "but it turned out to be a complete failure." The Association noted that there were three profound differences between the United States and Japan—scale of operation, amount of space allocated, and manner of shopping—"but," it said, "such differences were ignored, and the American way was introduced just as it is, in spite

---

*This account of the Nichiro-Heinz company is based on a report by the Japan Industrial Promotion Association.

of everything. It is believed that this very fact was the primary cause of the failure."

Going into more detail, the article points out that American supermarkets work on the assumption that they will attract customers from within a radius of fifteen miles—while the usual distance between customer and shop in Japan is a five minutes' walk. The average Japanese housewife does not have a car at her disposal, nor is she likely to make use of public transportation to leave her immediate neighborhood in order to shop. Her habit is to buy the food she requires each day, and she prefers fresh foods (perishables) to frozen foods. This tendency of hers, as the article points out, naturally has an effect on the small, neighborhood shops that she patronizes. Since she makes a large number of very small, daily purchases, shops must stock a wide assortment of goods, but since the shops are small, they cannot afford to keep large quantities of individual items. Thus, they are required to buy through an established *tonya*.

Keihin Shokai, however, according to the Association's report, "ignored the local tradition of peculiar relationship between the wholesalers and retailers" and proceeded to do business in the American way. The *tonya*, as a result, were offended. It is also said that Safeway adopted a *dorai* ("dry" or inflexible) attitude. Further, Safeway was apparently uninformed, or misinformed, on the subject of the availability and price of land. "The business of the Safeway-Sumitomo joint store was far from satisfactory," the report concludes. "They could not have their way about the name of the store to begin with; the American consultant left for home exasperated; and the Safeway Store Japan Company was dissolved in January, 1965. The store, however, continues to be operated by the Japanese alone, and it seems they are doing better since the Americans withdrew. Judging from the result, it may be said that Safeway Stores' attempt to launch a business in Japan was a failure, and the biggest reason was the incorrect appraisal of the Japanese market."

It must be noted, however, in defense of Safeway that they may merely have been somewhat ahead of the times, for since their

196

departure, a large number of supermarkets (admittedly, on a much smaller scale than their Western counterparts) have opened in Japan and are gradually bringing about what has been called a "distribution revolution." In the beginning, the supermarkets concentrated on foodstuffs, an area where they were forced to rely on the *tonya*, but later, when they began to deal also in textiles, they discovered that the *tonya* were inadequate for their purposes. As a result, supermarkets are now tying up with large trading companies, such as Mitsui, Mitsubishi, Sumitomo, and Kanematsu, which have begun to replace the *tonya*. They supply cheap imports from Hong Kong, Korea, and Taiwan; some (notably Mitsui) lease necessary equipment to the supermarket; and even in the so-called cold chain system for cold storage perishables there is a move to dispense with the middlemen. Thus, the various elaborate systems that the Japanese have evolved for getting goods from maker to consumer are beginning to be subject to change.

But, as I pointed out earlier, it is unlikely that the change will be either drastic or sudden. The government prefers to maintain the dual structure, and in order to do so must protect the million small outlets that are comparatively weak financially. The latter, further, are required by the Japanese consumer to carry a wide variety of goods in small quantities. The small shops, therefore, must depend on the *tonya*, most particularly when it comes to perishables. Changes are naturally to be expected, but to speak of a "distribution revolution" may perhaps be premature.

Thus, the foreign company that wants to market a product in Japan must make a thorough study of the distribution system that already exists in its particular product line and then try to find a way to use the existing system to the best advantage of the company. Different channels of distribution for other types of merchandise must also be considered. The only way to find the right method to market a foreign product is by making a case to case study, and while a thorough investigation of available marketing methods is essential, so is flexibility. Stubbornness may end in disaster. The system that works in Peoria need not necessarily be a success in Nagoya or Tokyo—and a wrong decision, based on inadequate information or incompetent advice, may well be fatal.

At the same time, it is pointless to concentrate exclusively on methods: the company that comes to Japan to sell can only sell its products to people. It must, therefore, make a sincere effort to understand the Japanese as people as well as potential buyers; if it succeeds, it may also succeed in selling them its goods. Who, then, *is* the Japanese consumer? What is he like? How does he buy? What motivates his choice? Perhaps the best way to begin to answer these questions is to take a brief glance at his history.

It is only recently that manufacturers, Japanese as well as foreign, have begun to consider the consumer's needs and desires. In the past he took, uncomplainingly, what he could get—and that was precious little in the long years that elapsed while Japan was preparing for war, waging war, and recovering from defeat. A stoical and frugal people, the Japanese were willing to make do; further, their living habits, food, and clothing were rather narrowly circumscribed, so that there was little real demand for variety and even less for luxury, except among the few very rich. *Daitai*— "almost right"—was good enough for the average consumer. If an object broke down after brief use, he would not return it to the shop; such a thing was simply not done; besides, the shopkeeper would lose face. Manufacturers took advantage of this permissiveness to produce and sell the shoddiest kind of merchandise; "MADE IN JAPAN," before the war, was a term of opprobrium.

Then, with defeat and occupation, came exposure to Western ways, transfer of American technology, education of Japanese personnel in everything from the repairing of airplanes and tanks to cooking, training in quality control, insistence on inspection of materials, imposition of specifications and standards for all products that were to be supplied to the United States forces in Japan. *Daitai* was just not good enough for the hundreds of thousands of alien consumers quartered in the country, and with the passing of the years it began, at least in some areas, to be not good enough for the Japanese either. In 1952, with the beginning of the so-called Jimmu boom, native consumers went on a buying spree to compensate for the long years of austerity, and they found that manufacturers had improved the quality of their goods almost beyond measure. In world markets, "MADE IN JAPAN" became a highly desirable identifying label.

Despite this overall improvement in quality, however, the average Japanese consumer is still reluctant to complain if the goods he buys are unsatisfactory or if the services and facilities he is given are inadequate. Japanese inns are notorious for serving food cold that should be hot, at which the foreign guest would probably complain while the Japanese would not. My office in Marunouchi is in one of the newest buildings put up by the Mitsubishi Estate Company—yet the washrooms have no hot water and no towels. Mitsubishi may be one of the greatest industrial and commercial empires in the world, but its directors chose to deprive its tenants of such "unnecessary" creature comforts as hot water and towels.

Here, however, as in most other areas of Japanese life, the situation is changing, and it is changing gradually. While there is no "disruption of harmony," the Japanese consumer is slowly coming into his own. He has an increasingly wide choice among a great variety of consumer products, some of which have even been designed by well-known foreign designers. Japanese taste is often not very good when it leaves familiar and traditional paths, and Japanese manufacturers, fearful of foreign competition and of the influx of foreign capital into industry and at the same time stimulated by the success of certain foreign companies, from Coca Cola to International Business Machines, began to import foreign designers and designs. Some Japanese cars are based on Italian designs, while an American firm (Walter Landor and Associates, of San Francisco) was called in to design the Sapporo beer can, the packaging for Meidi-ya fruit juices, and the Morinaga caramel package (which had been unchanged for half a century).

The presence in Japan of Western advertising firms, including J. Walter Thompson, has also tended to make the Japanese manufacturer more conscious of the consumer, and a great number of market research companies have recently leapt into existence and seem to be prospering. However inept some of their research may be, the general trend is certainly in the consumer's favor. A. C. Nielsen, the famous television and radio rating firm, has an active branch in Tokyo; its customers are largely leading Japanese companies who want the impact of their television advertising measured.

Further evidence of this changing attitude, from neglect to protection of the consumer, is provided by the government's efforts to exercise greater control over quality, especially in foods and drugs, and also to tighten rules concerning claims made in advertisements and on labels. Although the Japanese housewife can never be fooled about the quality of kimono or obi material or of tea or bean-paste, she can be—and is—taken in by claims made for unfamiliar, Western-type goods, including foodstuffs. The Fair Trade Commission, therefore, is performing an extremely valuable function. The newly awakened Japanese consumer feels—and with reason—that the Commission is not doing enough for him. But then the question must be asked: is there any country in the world at the moment where the consumer receives total protection? The answer, of course, is "No!" In Japan at least he is now beginning to receive an increasing amount of it.

A survey conducted recently by the Statistics Bureau of the Prime Minister's Office yields some interesting information about the Japanese consumer.[55] A normal household of four people——two adults and two children—averages ¥87,400 (about $243) a month in earnings. (To this figure must of course be added the semi-annual bonus.) The household spends its money roughly as follows:

food	25.1 percent
housing	9.4 percent
light and fuel	3.1 percent
clothes	8.2 percent
miscellaneous	29.0 percent
non-consumption	8.2 percent

Of the surplus remaining (17 percent), some 12 percent goes into savings. Expenditures for liquor in 1968 increased over those in

1967, as did also expenditures for electric home appliances, television sets, automobiles, and (interestingly) Japanese-style clothes —most probably kimonos (which can be quite costly) for the female members of the household. Peak periods for the sales of more expensive consumer items are around the times of the biannual bonuses.

The average age of salarymen is 40.8 years, and the average family has 3.96 members. They are slightly more affluent in the seven large cities (presumably Tokyo, Osaka, Kobe, Yokohama, Nagoya, Kyoto, and Kita-Kyushu) than in smaller cities and towns, although the report indicates that the gap is lessening. Another prediction is that the salaryman will spend more in the future on leisure goods, household appliances, cars, and non-essentials.

Until fairly recently, the Japanese had no true consumer credit system, of the kind familiar to all Americans, but with the demand for the new, and expensive, C's mentioned earlier (central heating, air conditioning, and a cottage in the country) some form of consumer credit had to be inaugurated. It began in 1960 with department store credit and a limited form of automobile credit. Actually, banks were less interested in extending credit than in devising new gimmicks for increasing deposits. Department store credit, for example, was predicated on the customer opening a special account with a bank that cooperated with the store.

In 1961, loans for housing and education as well as savings for overseas travel were added to the consumer credit system. (On instructions from the government, savings for overseas travel were soon "de-emphasized.") Terms of automobile credit became more liberal in 1963, and banks, cooperating with manufacturers, began to give loans for the purchase of pianos and electrical home appliances. A new feature was added in 1964, when banks formed "savings clubs" for various purposes, particularly in fields connected with social, educational, or recreational activities.

Four large banks—Fuji, Sumitomo, Sanwa, and Mitsubishi— have introduced a kind of credit card system. Fuji cooperated, in 1960, in the establishment of the Nippon Diners Club and concluded a franchise agreement with the Diners Club of the United States; its cards are now honored by some six thousand hotels and stores. Mitsubishi cooperates with the American Interbank Card Association; the Japan Credit Bureau, established by Sanwa and four other Japanese banks, works with the American Express; and Sumitomo with its affiliates set up the Sumitomo Credit Service Company, Ltd., which entered into a cooperative agreement with the Bank of America, Barclays Bank, and the Royal Bank of Canada.

One of the results, evidently, of these extensive contacts with Western banks has been a general easing of rigid bureaucratic restrictions that Japanese banks formerly imposed on depositors. All commercial banks in Japan, for instance, now handle personal checks, and most now permit their depositors to use merely a personal signature rather than, as before, the elaborate *han* (or seal) that had to be specially made and registered. Most banks now also have a system of demand deposits which permits the customer to withdraw money from his account at any branch office. Dai-Ichi's bank card enables the bearer to pay by check up to ¥50,000.

By now, the Japanese consumer can buy almost anything he wants on time payment. The Economic Planning Agency, as the result of a survey made in the summer of 1968, estimated that 37.2 percent of all households made use of installment plan purchases; most of them were families with yearly incomes ranging from ¥0.9 million to ¥1.2 million. According to the Ministry of International Trade and Industry, installment sales total just over ¥2 trillion a year; other estimates, however, made in 1967, put the annual figure at ¥3 trillion. Using statistics compiled in 1965, the Ministry reported that installment sales accounted for 75 percent of all passenger car sales, 84 percent of sewing machines, 53 percent of television and stereo sets, 52 percent of refrigerators, and 59 percent of pianos. Conditions established by the Ministry for the sales of three items were: for automobiles, a down payment of 25 percent and a payment period of twenty months; for color television sets and air conditioners, a down payment of 15 percent and a payment period of twenty months. With the latter, however, the Ministry permits a 20 percent deviation, which means that the down payment may be as little as 12 percent and the payment period as long as twenty-four months.

By the end of September, 1968, outstanding consumer credit given by banks directly to clients amounted to approximately ¥294,261 million in the form of 870,000 loans. At the same period, oustanding loans by banks to companies for installment purchasing yielded the following figures:

Unit: ¥1 million

Installment sales companies	828,813
Retailers selling on installment plan (total*)	756,449
Automobile sales companies	665,807
Installment department stores	24,287
Others	66,353
Organizations issuing coupons (total)	33,091
Credit sales companies	13,335
Associations of specialty stores	19,756
Construction companies	39,272

*Figures are rounded out to the million and hence do not add up.
(Loans for automobile purchases secured by installment payment promissory notes...520,970)

Although there is no central credit information agency in Japan, various attempts are being made to integrate existing systems. Nippon Shimpan (which originated as a financing agency for installment sales by retail stores) now serves also as a credit information and guarantee agency and cooperates with other credit institutions. Similar services are provided by the Japan Installment Association and the Million Card Service (the latter being particularly active in the Nagoya area). Banks have cooperated with manufacturers of electric home appliances and musical instruments to set up a joint credit information service that was scheduled to begin operating in June of this year.

But names and numbers, figures and dates tell a dry story, and I shall return now to the promise—or, if you prefer, the threat—that I made earlier and attempt to give a brief, composite portrait of the Japanese consumer, trying to make it as comprehensive as space permits. It is only, after all, by understanding him—or, her—that the seller can hope to compete successfully on the Japanese market.

Like everywhere else in the world, the Japanese housewife is the principal buyer of most items for the home—save perhaps the more permanent and costly products, such as radio, television, or stereo sets, where the father of the family may make the decision or it may be the result of a consensus among the entire household. Thus, the buying habits of the Japanese housewife are of crucial importance to the seller, and those habits are not at all of the kind that the Westerner is familiar with.

The usual Japanese wife is rather a lonely person. Her husband is at the office, her children are at school, and she has little or no human contact until she sallies forth, around three in the afternoon, to do her shopping for the day. To be sure, she has been glancing at the family television set as she did her household chores, but it is human contact that she has been lacking, it is human contact that she needs, and it is human contact that she will get as she buys the things she requires for the evening and the following morning. Although she likes bargains, she is not going miles away, to some distant supermarket, to get them; she will patronize her neighborhood shops, and as she does, she will meet other wives of the neighborhood and exchange tidbits of gossip with them. Looking for the freshest fish and the freshest vegetables, she will also get the latest news about that notorious Suzuki-san who lives across the street. She buys only what she needs to satisfy the daily requirements of her family, and if she cannot actually see the particular food, the meat or fish or vegetable, because it is wrapped in something, she is reluctant to buy it. With families that are affluent enough to have a maid, it is often she who does the daily shopping —and the daily dose of gossip is just as necessary to her as it is to the housewife. This being true in the comparatively sophisticated and cosmopolitan environment of Tokyo, the reader may easily imagine how much truer it is in small towns and villages up and down Japan—and it takes no learned social scientist to figure out the losses that a foreign company is liable to sustain if it fails to take adequately into account the factors that motivate the housewife's choice, the quantities she is likely to buy, and the fact that she will almost certainly buy them in her own neighborhood shops. And if she happens to live in a neighborhood that has no shopping area nearby, the shops may come to her. As the fishmonger and the vegetable man make their presence known, she comes out to see what they have and there, around the carts, she finds the other housewives of the neighborhood, ready for a good gossip.

It is not enough, obviously, to think of the Japanese merely as consumers; one must be more specific: consumers of what? There is a vast market for drugs and cosmetics in Japan, for instance, but no market for shot guns. Among women, there is a growing market for brassieres and foundation garments but none for hats. Until quite recently there was no market for proprietary sunburn remedies, much less "sunburn enhancers," since proper people stayed out of the sun, but now, along with miniskirts and bikinis, teenagers have taken to suntans; and as a result, Coppertone and Sea and Ski are doing very well in an expanding market. A generation ago, it was unthinkable for the housewife to prepare the daily rice in any but the traditional way; now she uses an electric rice cooker. She also buys the so-called "instant" products—rice, noodles, and soup as well as tea and coffee, all of which poured onto the market as a result of the popularity of instant coffee. An outstanding success story, incidentally, is that of Nestlé whose Nescafé initially captured—and still enjoys—the greater market share for instant coffee, a good example of the tendency toward "brand-loyalty" of the Japanese buyer. Other similar examples are Coke, Chanel perfumes, and Parker pens.

I have suggested a few of the changes in living and buying habits among post-war Japanese, but the list might have been almost endless, for while they are a traditional people in many ways, the Japanese are also eager for novelty and they are impressed by almost anything Western so long as they find the product to be of high quality. This statement is true of everything—from machine tools to cosmetics—and it is one that I have tried repeatedly to impress on British and American companies. The fact that many packaged items in Japan are given foreign language names would indicate that there is wide acceptance of Western-style goods.

(Some of these names, such as that of an instant cream powder called Creap, are not altogether inspired.) At the same time, however, that the Japanese are now beginning to sleep in beds rather than on *futon*, to use canned baby foods, or to prepare rice in electric cookers, many of their basic habits remain unchanged. A girl may wear a miniskirt to work, but for any really important occasion she will want a kimono and an obi. She may marry in a Western-style wedding gown, but for the reception afterwards she will change to traditional dress. The contemporary Japanese is a fascinating blend of the old and the new: in certain areas the seller may not, under penalty of failure, transgress fixed rules and ingrained habits, while in others he may be as imaginative as he chooses in an effort to capture the buying public.

He must consider also, of course, the fact that this vast consumer market of a hundred million is not one market only but many. Tastes, loyalities, and buying habits vary from place to place and from one social level to another to such an extent that it is a fascinating, frustrating, and extraordinarily complex market to analyze—or indeed even to discuss. Demographically, on the other hand, it is delightfully simple, a true paradise for the advertising executive. Where else in the world will you find such concentrations of consumer purchasing power so readily accessible to all advertising media? Almost every household in the prime marketing areas possess both television and radio sets. The diffusion of television sets in the Tokyo area, the major market, has been estimated—conservatively—at 96 percent of all households, while throughout Japan itself 93 percent of households take at least one daily newspaper, and many (perhaps most) take two as well as magazines of all kinds.

Outdoor advertising in Japan is also highly developed. Some people, indeed, think it is too highly developed, but in any case it is equal to that of any other country of the world in both ingenuity and customer impact. The visitor to Tokyo or Osaka who stares amazed at the forest of neon signs towering above him in the night sky may hanker wistfully for the lanterns of Edo, but he will have to admit that the Japanese here yield pride of place to no other.

The following table gives some indication of the high rate of literacy of the Japanese:[56]

Number and Circulation of Daily Newspapers in 7 Selected Countries

Country	Year	Number	Circulation	
			Total (1,000)	Per 1,000 (population)
Japan	1967	121	47,555	474
U.K.	1965	110	26,100	479
W. Germany	1965	411	19,264	326
U.S.A.	1965	1,751	60,358	310
U.S.S.R.	1965	639	60,948	264
France	1964	128	11,872	245
India	1964	514	5,693	12

As might be expected, traditional advertising methods are also still in use, notably the colorful *chindon-ya*, a small group composed of a one-man band with two or more companions dressed in bizarre costumes. They are employed to tour—and entertain—a neighborhood, at the same time announcing the opening of a new shop or a special sale at an old shop. The Japanese equivalent of the sandwich man is also very much in evidence.

Another proof of the persistence of the traditional in Japanese buying is the fact that it is highly seasonal. The old calendar continues to affect buying habits and also, necessarily, store inventory. After May 15, for example, it is almost impossible to buy any kind of heavy clothing or underclothing, while after September 15 light-weight *yukatas* disappear from the market. Japanese poetry and painting are extremely sensitive to the changing seasons and so is the Japanese consumer: he is content to wait for the right season to return again.

One of the oldest sales methods in Japan is still prevalent today, most particularly in the field of pharmaceuticals. It began when the shogunate gave the daimyo of what is now Toyama Prefecture the right to send his salesmen of herbs and medicines throughout the country. These salesmen carried special documents that permitted them to travel freely at a time when the country was riddled with check-points, as in Eastern Europe today. The "pitch" was for the salesman to leave a year's supply of medicines at each household he visited without asking for any money. When he returned a year later, the household paid him for what it had actually used. He then replenished the stock and continued on to the next house. The "Toyama" system might well prove effective today in certain areas of the United States, as it continues to do in Japan. The emergency medicine kit in my office is a variation of this system. It cost me nothing to start with, but monthly a representative of the supplier drops by to see if anything has been used. It is then replaced, and I pay for it. Fair enough, it seems to me, and a good sales pitch to boot.

Another traditional hangover, incidentally, is "gift-giving," and it can prove a special headache for the unwary foreigner, who may unconsciously go wrong by being either too lavish or too cheap or by giving something unsuitable. Perhaps nowhere else in the world has the art of giving a present been so refined and so hedged in by protocol, and perhaps only a native-born Japanese is capable of evaluating all the considerations that enter into the choosing of a suitable gift. The foreigner is best advised to leave this thorny problem to his Japanese associates.

"Gift-giving" is at its headiest twice a year, at the two bonus times: *o-chugen* at mid-year and *o-seibo* at the end of the year. It is then that virtually every company in Japan sends out vast numbers of gifts, ranging from very cheap to very expensive depending on the relationship of the recipient to the company. Many foreign companies follow this custom (and more might be well-advised to do so), leaving the writing of the list to the Japanese themselves. All department stores and all large food, fruit, and confectionery shops make up special gift packages for these two bonus times, some so elaborate that one is reluctant to destroy the package in order to get at its contents.

Japan's department stores always astonish the first-time visitor and ought, perhaps, to be the subject of a book in themselves. Probably nowhere else in the world do department stores offer such multifaceted entertainment. The top floor is usually given over to cultural exhibits, which are often expensive for the store to assemble, troublesome for the staff, and non-productive in the sense that valuable space yields no return. But the exhibits are thought to be helpful in attracting shoppers, both paying and window, and whole families often go to a department store (usually on Sunday) spending hours there as though it were a picnic grounds. There are restaurants, snack bars, and special shops as well as other exhibits scattered through the eight, nine, or ten floors of the store; in addition, there are usually also two or three basements, devoted to food, household goods, bargain counters, and the like. The specialty shops often feature foreign goods. Matsuzakaya, for instance, has an area housing Henry Poole of Saville Row, London, which is very successful. So also is Dior's section at Isetan. Virtually every famous designer of women's clothes has found Japan to be a profitable market and the department store, presumably, to be the most suitable outlet. A prestigious department store is also, it must be noted, a status symbol. All stores have a variety of identifying shopping bags and wrapping papers, and a gift from Mitsukoshi or Takashimaya carries a cachet that a gift from the shop around the corner lacks.

It is obvious, then from this brief survey, that the already existing market for consumer goods in Japan can only increase as the years pass. Japan's standard of living is still very low, difficult though that fact may be to believe when the visitor looks at the vast quantities of expensive goods, both domestic and foreign, to be found in the department stores and the specialty shops. In 1968, Japan ranked only twentieth among the countries of the world in per capita national income. Thus, it seems clear that as her economy prospers and her gross national product rises, so must her per capita income.* The hundred million will have increasingly large sums of money to spend on consumer products, and they will be searching, as their counterparts do in other areas of the world, for new products to buy. Presumably, manufacturers will not want to disappoint them.

*Messrs. Kahn and Wiener in their book, *The Year 2000*, *op. cit.*, predict that by the year 2020 Japan will have the highest per capita income in the world. (See Table 5, in Appendix.) The Japanese Ministry of Finance is more optimistic and gives 1984 as the date (*Oriental Economist*, April 1969).

11 | The Future

"All great things have been done
by little nations."
> —Disraeli

I have pointed out some of the weaknesses, as I see them, in the present-day Japanese economic structure: the lack of almost all basic raw materials and the difficulties and dangers of ensuring their supply, an inadequate system for industrial financing, and the vestiges of feudalism in the management class that often result in overcaution where daring is needed. How then do I justify the prediction I made, in the Foreword to this book, that Japan will quite probably within the next couple of decades become the world's second post-industrial state? I shall attempt, in this chapter, to reconcile those two statements.

Admittedly, I have no crystal ball; and if I had one, I should probably use it as a paperweight. I have no great faith in any system, either occidental or oriental, for foretelling the future by means of the stars—or, indeed, by any other kind of divination. Nor do I believe that "history repeats itself" in any but the broadest terms, although I think that a study of the past can be useful in anticipating the possible future. I know that most "financial analysts," as they are called in the United States, consider certain industries to be "cyclical." In that case, perhaps the *I Ching* ("The Book of Changes"), which has been used in the East for a couple of millennia to determine cyclical changes, may be worthy of consultation.[57] The predictions that follow, I hasten to add, were not made by throwing straws or coins and then consulting the appropriate entry in the *I Ching:* they are made out of nearly thirty years of intimate day-by-day experience with the people who have accomplished the "miracle" of Japan's post-war industrial resurgence, and also by studying their past—for they are in essence the same people, despite occidental intrusions on Japanese traditionalism. Japan, as I have tried to point out, remains a tightly-knit group made up of numerous other groups that are less tightly knit. This constitutes one of her great, intangible advantages over the other industrialized nations of the world.

It seems to me there is little doubt that within the next fifteen years or so, Japan will be in control of most of the markets for manufactured goods in all of the Far East and Southeast Asia, probably including Oceania and Eastern Siberia. She will be competitive also in Central Asia (India, Pakistan, Afghanistan, Nepal, Kashmir, and Ceylon), in Arabia and the Middle East, in the Balkans and Eastern Europe. Her business relations with the United States and Canada will inevitably continue to grow. Japan has beaten her swords into electronic computers, and what she failed to accomplish with the former she will succeed in doing with the latter. (My predictions presuppose, of course, that within the next fifteen years or so, there will still be a planet called Earth.)

I presuppose also that protectionism, with its attendant animosities and countermeasures, can be eliminated on both sides of the Pacific, rather than augmented. Japanese businessmen agree with American businessmen that Benjamin Franklin's dictum, "No nation was ever ruined by trade," is a sound one. But there is always the danger that government, ever more timorous than business, will succeed in spoiling what has begun as a healthy relationship. Quite obviously, Japan needs American investments and technology, as well as her goodwill; but America must keep in mind that the reverse is also true and will continue to be true in the future, to an ever-increasing degree.

Foreign businessmen might well ask themselves what it is these Japanese do so wrong that frequently turns out so right. If they could emulate these Japanese "mistakes," the result might well be a more virile economy in Europe and a higher rate of growth of the gross national product in the United States. All too often the foreign businessman who comes to Japan suffers from the dangerous disease of complacency, although it is highly unlikely that his own company has done as well in growth, productivity, and profits as a similar Japanese company (which, according to him, does everything wrong!). *The Economist*, in the book that I have quoted from earlier,[58] has pointed out this strange anomaly, to the embarrassment of a number of British industrialists. The latter have, at long last, begun to welcome American expertise and investment, but they might, I believe, look longer and more deeply, to their own advantage, at Japanese technology and inventiveness.

The disease of complacency, however, as I have indicated, is at its most virulent (and dangerous) among government bureaucrats, including the Japanese. Although the Ministry of International Trade and Industry considers the advance of foreign enterprises into the Japanese market a stimulant to domestic industries and certainly preferable to imports, it at the same time fears that foreign enterprises may lessen the independence of Japanese industry, and so it discourages such interchange in certain important areas. Its own survey of companies in which foreign investment accounts for more than 15 percent of capital showed that sales of these enterprises constituted only 1.65 percent of total sales made by all enterprises in Japan. Thus in reality there is no such threat.

Wholly-owned foreign subsidiaries in Japan, however, according to the same survey, showed net profits that were five times higher than those of other enterprises. These are active in fields where technical improvement can be achieved quickly, where differences between Japanese and foreign technical abilities are considerable (such as chemicals, machinery, and the like), and where dependence on foreign sources of raw materials is high (petroleum and aluminum, for example). The profit ratio of these wholly owned foreign enterprises, against total used capital employed, was 13.5 percent in 1966—somewhat higher than the 3.1 percent average among Japan's main manufacturers. The lessons to be drawn from these figures are obvious: the induction of foreign technology and the melding of foreign techniques with Japanese skills can contribute greatly to the Japanese economy in the future.

Tomorrow's world—certainly the Far East, at least—will be short of food, and in helping to alleviate this shortage Japan can, and will, play a strategic role. Her food exports are already sizeable, and they are bound to increase. She knows more about rice culture and intensive farming than probably any other country in the world. (Incidentally, her poultry breeders are acknowledged as the world's experts on the sexing of chickens.) Further, as populations increase, more people will probably come to depend on fish and pelagic products for their sources of protein, and here again Japan is in a highly strategic position. The only other nation that really competes with her in whaling is the Soviet Union, but Japan not only catches more whales but also makes more profit per blue whale unit. The Japanese produce edible foods for themselves out of whale meat and also export it to England and America, most of whose dogs and cats—and that is a lot of dogs and cats—eat pet food containing whale meat caught by Japanese fleets. Operating wherever fish can be caught, other Japanese fishing fleets provide fresh or frozen fish directly to a great many world ports; in addition, canned salmon and tuna and frozen fish are exported from Japan proper to most parts of the world. Of other pelagic products, Japan has at least as much knowledge as any other nation in the world, and perhaps more: she has grown edible seaweed for thousands of years, she cultivates numerous varieties of shellfish (many of which she exports frozen), she invented the process of using the small oyster as a "mother" for cultivated pearls.

But what, the reader may ask, has all this to do with Japan's future conquest of world industrial markets? Quite a lot, I think— for in the list of the world's three basic needs, it is always food that is placed first. The rice bowls of the hundreds of millions of people who inhabit the Orient must be kept filled; while the second staple the world over is fish, and as fish-suppliers shift their emphasis from hunting to breeding, fish products may be expected to play an even more important role in supplying the population of the world with needed protein. Further, the only truly unexplored area of the earth's crust is its great bodies of water, and here Japan is far advanced. Her knowledge of the oceans and the seas as potential suppliers not only of food but also of minerals and products of medicinal virtue is famous.

One of the major factors that may inhibit, or delay, Japan's efforts to become the world's second post-industrial state is the relative poverty of her overseas monetary investments, caused in large part by the excessive caution and xenophobia of the bureaucracy. Japanese companies and private individuals must, if Japan is to continue her growth, be permitted to invest and own properties overseas. If the bureaucracy persists in its stringent controls trade will be hampered, and so in consequence will business expansion.

Further, such holdings become valuable assets in times of crisis. When the Second World War broke out, private British ownership of shares of companies and of real estate materially helped to finance British purchases of steel, food, ammunition, ships, and planes from the United States. True, according to Japan's present Constitution, she will never declare war on another state—but no one can guarantee the reverse. World peace is, obviously, the ideal condition, but until it is achieved, pacificism is tenable only so long as the pacifist country has nothing that another power does not covet. Japan's huge industrial complex would be a splendid prize for some ruthless predator. A British officer, asked recently what would be needed to take over Hong Kong, replied, "One telephone call from Mao Tse-tung. " Japan is in almost as parlous a situation: were it not for the Security Treaty with the United States, she could be taken over within a week by a foreign nuclear power.

Thus, it is in her own interests to have large investments overseas, just as it is in her own interests to permit foreign capital to enter the country more freely. The bureaucracy's fear of foreign investment may be irrational, but it is nonetheless real, and it is the chief factor that presently restrains Japan from pursuing her goal with greater speed and effectiveness. What is needed is true "liberalization" on the part of government, not mere lip service. Japan must encourage foreign investment. Furthermore, she can never become a first-class nation until the yen is as freely convertible as the United States' dollar.

Japan's future, then, it would seem, depends more on the wisdom of her legislators than on the skill of her industrialists. The latter know what they want, and they apparently know how to get it. Japanese trading firms are already established almost everywhere on the globe; Mitsubishi has about eighty overseas branches, Mitsui about a hundred; there are companies especially designed to trade with the Soviet Union and the "iron curtain" countries; and more introduction into foreign markets is planned; but ultimately, for purposes of stability, this will require ownership of foreign properties. The government, then, must pursue a path of true liberalization, and there are hopeful signs that it will. The yen is becoming a hard currency, and foreign investors look increasingly to Japan as both a safe haven and one of opportunity.

Furthermore, Japan is going forward with decontrol of direct foreign investments. The second round of capital decontrol, as it is termed, took effect on March 1, 1969, when restrictions were lifted on 155 industries. Admittedly those industries most attractive to foreigners, such as automobiles, cosmetics, certain chemical lines, electronic computers, department stores and chain stores, air conditioning, nuclear equipment, etc., are not on the list, and a report in the Japan Times, March 1, 1969, admits that this second round of decontrol is "lukewarm" but, "nonetheless [it] marks a step forward for assimilating the Japanese economy with the international economy." Japan is moving in the right direction and with "the lapse of time," to quote Mr. Ihara, President of the Bank of Yokohama, true liberalization will become a reality, although most foreign businessmen are disappointed and condemn the snails' pace at which the Japanese authorities seem to approach true liberalization, now planned for late 1971. Even then there will be some restrictions on such areas as the computer, atomic energy, munitions industries and banking.

I do not wish to appear an apologist for the Japanese. Certainly the inflow of foreign capital must be eased, but I do feel that the foreigner perhaps has lost sight of certain factors and sees only Japan's spectacular growth. They see only the 10 percent or more per year growth in GNP; the expansion of Japan's exports; the improvement in her balance of payments, but they forget other facts which, I maintain, justify a certain amount of protectionism and the go-slow approach to full liberalization.

It must not be forgotten that in 1945, at the war's end, Japan was devastated. Its economy, total capital assets, GNP, had been set back over ten years. Japan's losses put her back financially, in plant and equipment, in goods and services, to about the equivalent of 1933–35. She had lost land area, but gained only people. So, in 1946, Japan, except for the remnants of a few war industries, was in reality an underdeveloped country and in some sectors it remains so today, particularly in housing. Nor had Japan ever been a leading industrial state as had the U.K., Germany, Sweden, France— all with long years of necessary internal adjustments behind them. Japan's phenomenal growth thus served only to compound the imbalances (what some scholars refer to as the "dual structure") within the economy. Had it taken her thirty years with an annual growth in GNP of 3 percent per year, instead of ten years at 10 percent per year, such imbalances might have been automatically adjusted. There are still a vast number of medium and small enterprises which have vociferous spokesmen and they cannot be disregarded. Admittedly, in time the very small will largely disappear, but it is not yet the time, and there has not yet been enough time for adjustments and realignments. Therefore it is not to the point to consider Japan as one would consider the U.S. or West Germany and one must "give it time" to mature. There is also innate custom to be overcome. I believe that, despite the several businessmen, scholars and government officials, particularly in the Foreign Office and the Ministry of Finance, who advocate true liberalization, the great majority of businessmen and higher officials are so accustomed to the government control of business and the government's paternal protection, that they find it difficult to conceive of existence without it. Add the xenophobia which is rather strong in Japan and perhaps one can more readily understand how hard it is for the officials to designate industries to be "liberalized." Then add the very definitely precarious nature of Japan's basic economy, the very definite imbalances in many undeveloped industries, and the very definite problems of adjustment; plus the problems of protecting weak industries and weak enterprises (which is an admitted policy of the government) for at least some time until they either grow or disappear. Then, when all are taken into consideration, the prudent man would, I believe, act pretty much as the Japanese government does.

The government policy is, I am completely convinced, to achieve as full a liberalization as is possible without creating further imbalances or hardships on weak enterprises and hence confusion both economically and socially. Efforts to put pressure on the government by impatient foreigners are to be deplored since they will serve only to support the many opponents of liberalization and thus make it more difficult for the government to act positively. Within the government itself are those opposed, in MITI and particularly in the Ministry of Agriculture, which has sufficient problems of its own to solve. There are then the ever present facts of political expediency. Small businessmen comprise a very sizeable group of voters and government action towards greater liberalization may adversely affect them. This factor, to quote an official of the Ministry of Finance "increases the political strains associated with liberalization." I would hate to see the issue of "liberalization" whooped up into an inflated, or more delicate political issue than it already is by foreign pressures. I am sure the foreigner would prefer the continuation of a "liberal" Japanese government at the expense of some "liberalization."

Should a socialist government ever gain control in Japan, it would be most likely that there would be no "liberalization" whatever. One should therefore be very judicious in making demands. A friendly government in Japan is more to be desired than trade concessions.

One of the most encouraging signs for the future growth of the country is the respect paid to education and the eagerness of youth to get as much of it as they can. Japan's literacy rate is one of the highest in the world, greatly surpassing that of any European country. An illustration of this eagerness to learn is the phenomenal success that the Encyclopedia Britannica has enjoyed here. With thirty-two offices throughout the country, employing some thousand salesmen (both full- and part-time), it sells a "package" consisting of the twenty-four volumes of the Encyclopedia itself, the twelve-volume "Perspective" series, a dictionary, a Bible, and a series of "great books"—all in English—for ¥230,000 ($639). In 1967, its sales totalled $9 million; its profits were $800,000.

Quite recently Japan's government and industry, working, as always, closely together, have created a new school for international trade. The building is already under construction in a comparatively isolated area near Mount Fuji. It is expected that between three and four hundred students will pass through the school yearly, taking a high intensity course in the intricacies of international trade and finance, under specialists for each area of the world, studying techniques and systems that have proven useful or successful in other countries—and, of course, foreign languages.* A number of companies also give foreign language courses to their employees as well as courses of study directed mainly at domestic corporate affairs.

Japan has no need to be worried about the "brain drain" that troubles some other countries. On the contrary, she now exports "brains"—and she can afford to. Not long ago, the World Bank and the International Monetary Fund requested the Japanese Ministry of Finance to find suitably qualified personnel to act as technicians, scientists, and teachers in under-developed areas, where the need for such people is acute. After screening several hundred applicants, the Ministry selected seventy whom it considered to be especially well qualified. I was given the rare opportunity of interviewing over sixty of them—all of them from the private sector, of course, since the government, properly enough, is hanging on to its own cadre of "brains." Every person whom I saw would have been extremely valuable to any company in the United States or Europe; the range of talents and experience, even among the younger people, was remarkable. In discussing this with a Ministry official, I mentioned the European "brain drain" and the

*Dr. Kobayashi, co-author of this book, is on the faculty of the new school.

interesting fact that Japan was in a position to export "brains." "Ah, but we're not," the official replied, "we're only lending them. It's a kind of lend-lease of brains. When these people come back to us after a few years, they'll be far more experienced and valuable than when they went away." The United Nations, I understand, is also trying to persuade the government to lend an increasing number of Japanese "brains" for UN-sponsored or related projects in underdeveloped areas. When these young technicians of varied skills come home, after having spent several years, at little or no expense to Japan, in countries where great consumer markets are developing, their places will be taken by representatives of the trading companies.

It has been pointed out that Japan spends considerably less than the United States on research and development, slightly less than the United Kingdom and France and slightly more than West Germany and Italy. Although research and development are, as economists well know, intimately related to the rate of growth of the gross national product, Japan has been able to compensate for her relatively small expenditures (as compared with the rate of growth) by borrowing technologies from other countries—and then in many cases improving on what she has borrowed. She has bought the results of foreign research and development after they have been tested and proven, at a relatively small cost, without herself engaging in a long and costly period of trial and error. Her returns, thus, have been higher than in most other nations in respect to time and money spent, and her technological skill has enabled her to effect improvements. A typical example is the transfer of Ultra High Frequency communications technology to the Nippon Electric Company. Japan acquired the technology from the United States very reasonably, mastered it, and improved on it, and now Nippon Electric, together with Hughes Aircraft have created the Nihon Satellite Communications Co.

But for good measure, Mitsubishi Electric has recently tied up with T.R.W. Corp. of the United States also to go into the cosmic telecommunications business by satellite. How avid for knowledge, are the Japanese, and how skillful they are in adapting such knowledge is further shown by the fact that Japan will soon have its second atomic power plant, providing electricity to industry. Tokai Power Station at the "nuclear city," Tokaimura, is already in operation and a second atomic power station, the Tsuruga Power Station, is under construction. In the use of atomic energy as a fuel it utilizes the technology of the General Electric Co.

Further, in every case involving transfer of technology to Japan that I am familiar with, part of the agreement has stipulated the training of Japanese technicians. Thus, a large educational gap which might otherwise exist is at least partially bridged. The chief weakness of Japan's own research and development is a lack, not so much of expenditure, but of coordination and of cooperation between industry and the universities, which latter——stupidly, it seems to me—do not favor that kind of cooperation. To offset this, one of Japan's strengths is the innate curiosity, even inquisitiveness, of her people. I would hazard a guess, for example, that Japanese technicians receive and study more printed material from the Soviet Union than their American counterparts. Japan, certainly, is extremely well-informed on industrial developments throughout the world: she keeps abreast of new inventions, processes, and products. In this she is aided by what Westerners would call over-employment in both government and industry. Large numbers of employees can be assigned to "research" departments to do nothing but study the thousands of trade papers, magazines, reports, and the like that pour into Japan from all corners of the globe. America's far higher standard of living would not permit this apparently extravagant use of manpower. The full extent of Japanese industry's knowledge of what is going on in the rest of the world is seldom appreciated by Westerners who do business with Japan.

That the Japanese economy is on the move and is gaining momentum year by year is swiftly apparent to anyone who studies official figures or who reads Japanese trade journals. In fiscal 1967 (which ended in March, 1968), Japan's exports increased 12 percent and her gross national product was up 13.3 percent, and in fiscal 1968 exports increased a further 25.3 percent and GNP, real rate,

14.4 percent. Now let us glance for a moment at the headlines in the *Nihon Keizai Shimbun* (*The Japan Economic Journal*); they tell the story:

CHRYSLER BUYS ENGINES FROM NISSAN

ELECTRIC POWER SURVEY FOR INDONESIA

JAPAN-FRANCE RADIATION CHEMICAL INDUSTRY

CAPITAL OF U.S. SUBSIDIARIES TO BE INCREASED

JAPAN BUYING EDIBLE OIL FROM POLAND

KANSAI ELECTRIC AND KYOTO MUNICIPALITY TO FLOAT DEUTSCH
    MARK BONDS

KOREAN PROJECT BY DAINICHI LIGHT METAL

POLAND TO BUY BUS AND TRUCK FACILITIES

DAIWA, TOYOTA AND SOVIET TECHNOLOGICAL TIE-UP

BURMA SEEKS JAPANESE HELP ON OIL PROSPECTING

PETRO-CHEMICAL FIRM TO SELL BUTADIENE TO U.S.

JAPAN TO IMPORT ALASKAN AMMONIA FROM JOINT PLANT WITH
    COLLIER CARBON

AIWA STARTING GLOBAL SALES

CABLE FOR JAPAN SEA TO SIBERIA

TWO FISH MEAL COMPANIES IN PERU TO BE BOUGHT

FISHERY COMPANIES TO ENGAGE IN PRAWN FISHING IN CARIBBEAN

JAPAN TOP FREE WORLD TRADER WITH U.S.S.R.

JAPANESE INVESTMENTS IN CANADIAN RESOURCES

TRADE MISSION TO GO TO POLAND

JAPANESE CARS HUGE SUCCESS IN BRUSSELS

MULTIMILLION DOLLAR DEAL WITH AUSTRALIA. . . .

It will be noted that many of the headlines concern trade with East Europe and the Soviet Union, and a word might be said here about Japan-Soviet cooperation for the rapid development of Siberia. Under the terms of a contract recently signed for the exploitation of forests in the Maritime and Khabarovsk areas, Japan will supply machinery valued at about $163 million over the next three years and in return will take eight million cubic meters of timber over the next five years. Other cooperative ventures under consideration are the development of the Udokan copper mine, the improvement of port facilities at Nahodka, an oil pipeline in Western Siberia, a North Pole navigable route, and technology and machinery for plants (including those for the manufacture of paper and pulp). Incidentally, the exporting country that will suffer most from the Japan-Soviet lumber deal is the United States; Pacific Northwest lumber interests have recently been highly vociferous in their complaints that Japan's purchases of timber have unreasonably pushed up prices in the area. Since Japan is usually denounced by American interests for "dumping," it seems rather odd that she should now be accused of *buying* at good prices.

While the future of Japanese industry would appear to be highly favorable, its close connection with government renders it particularly susceptible to the vagaries and inadequacies of the politicians. In that respect, the year 1970 is a crucial one, for it is the year the Security Treaty with the United States comes up for renewal. There is no question that the left is making an all-out effort to use the Treaty as a means to overthrow the government. Armed struggles on the university campuses are not only propaganda campaigns against the "establishment," they are also practice runs for a revolutionary uprising. Although only a very tiny minority of the student population, militant agitators are permitted to take over campuses for weeks and months, to disrupt the entire functioning of the university, and to commit incredible acts of vandalism, often destroying equipment that is either irreplaceable or extremely expensive and difficult to replace.

The situation is a highly complex one, partly, as I pointed out earlier, because of the innate Japanese dislike for making quick decisions, for taking immediate action, and for overriding a minority even when it appears to threaten the security of the country; and partly also because of the fact that under feudalism, which is still almost within living memory, the universities were actually self-governing bodies. In combatting these claims of the militant students to be an elite above and beyond the law, the university authorities have shown themselves to be weak and irresolute as well as reluctant to abandon their "autonomy," while the government, deferring to the puerile academic conceit of the university administrators, have been equally hesitant to act firmly.

On both these issues—the renewal of the Treaty and the chaos on the campuses—the government has procrastinated, failing to make a definite statement of policy but rather confining itself to vague and often meaningless generalizations. Perhaps even more dangerous, from the long-range point of view, is its reluctance to face and attempt to solve Japan's social problems. While Japan is little troubled by such outright squalid poverty as is so evident in many advanced Western countries, part of the population is discontented—and has legitimate cause for discontent. Because of the government's topsy-turvy agricultural policies, rice-growers enjoy an unprecedented opulence while farmers who do not grow rice are far from prosperous. Big business flourishes, but many small businessmen must struggle to keep their heads above water—and often are submerged. Wages admittedly are high, but so is the cost of living, and the share of the wage earner in the national product remains far below what it should be. Working conditions are incomparably better than before the war, but housing remains highly unsatisfactory.

The salaryman is burdened with an unfairly heavy share of taxation (his income tax being deducted at the source), while professional men, traders, farmers, and certain other groups (notably politicians) pay much less than they ought to. (Doctors, for instance, may deduct 80 percent of their income as "expenses.") The inequities of the taxation system form an important factor in the general feeling of discontent with the "establishment" among middle-rank salarymen, and although they would never join the militant students |on the barricades, they would probably watch the downfall of the present government without regret—and perhaps with hope.

Generally speaking (although there are of course exceptions), Japanese businessmen are as lacking in social consciousness as Japanese politicians. Their talk of social responsiblity is seldom more than an abstract declaration of good intentions; it is rarely translated into action. If it is, it will very likely be no more than a combination of the nineteenth-century Western concept of "charity" with traditional Japanese paternalism. The fact that large enterprises and many smaller companies have truly excellent welfare facilities for their own employees does not mean that Japan's business leaders either understand or desire to understand the basic social problems of the country at large.

The corollary to this, of course, is that they are equally apathetic in the face of the vast problems that confront the earth if it is ever to become a true world community. Nonetheless, the Japanese economy is being drawn more and more into the mainstream of international business, and there is a budding awareness among the Japanese that their traditional unilateral activities in the realm of international trade are becoming less and less acceptable abroad, and that, if they are not to experience a repetition of the débacle which pre-war political and military adventurism brought upon them, they must now avoid similar adventurism in the field of economics.

Suggestive of a welcome change in attitude are the tendency to establish joint ventures with foreign firms, in order to secure foreign know-how and markets; the readiness to work out agreements acceptable to foreign business partners; and the increasing willingness to forego immediate advantages in order to achieve a lasting accommodation. The foreign executive in Japan should be sensitive to this gradually changing attitude on the part of the Japanese businessman, even though the latter may still be wholly insensitive to the various pressures that combine to form the attitude of the foreigner. The government has attempted to remedy this situation, but so far the attempts have borne little fruit. At government expense, the Japan Productivity Center has organized hundreds of missions of businessmen for travel abroad (mainly to the United States), but so far the only results have been the publication of voluminous reports, which are out of date by the time they are in print, and the making of a few superficial acquaintances. The Japanese businessman is still unready to attempt to understand the foreign point of view, and generally he makes little or no effort to do so.

The foreigner, nonetheless, must try to let the Japanese know that their efforts to achieve a cooperative solution to the problems created by their need for foreign markets is appreciated abroad. It is important also that the Japanese be made to realize that the growing internationalization of business will be of benefit to Japan as well as to the rest of the world that takes part in it. Japan will probably even be willing, in time, to participate in the development and elaboration of a world-wide supply-and-demand system. This would ensure a fair allocation of business and would eliminate most of the causes of present-day friction and tension—but it would also require whole-hearted international cooperation, so for the moment, in a strife-torn world, it must remain no more than a dream of the future. Yet when the time comes, if it ever does, I believe that Japan will be ready to carry her share of the burden, for there is a resilient spirit in the Japanese people that can, and will, prevail over minority attempts to isolate the country or turn her backward instead of forward. The Japanese say that, although crickets chirp all day in the trees and bullfrogs croak all night in the marshes, no one pays them any attention—yet when the cock crows at dawn, everyone listens. In Japanese astrology, 1969 is the Year of the Cock, and I hope the world has heard the sounds of awakening and will ponder well what they might augur for the future.

THROUGH

JAPANESE

EYES

ACKNOWLEDGEMENTS:
I should like to acknowledge the kindness of the Japanese Committee for Economic Development in permitting me to use several reports prepared under the auspices of the Committee, and of Toyo Keizai, Yamatake-Honeywell, Keio University Business School and Father Robert J. Ballon for assistance in the preparation of the various case studies used in my text. (N. K.)

Capital Liberalization 12

Japan's five-year Capital Liberalization Program, inaugurated in July, 1967, has at this writing more or less reached its half-way mark and has entered upon the second stage of its implementation. The foreign, as well as the Japanese, businessman may now therefore gauge its progress so far and may even venture to prognosticate what its future is likely to be. According to the aim of the Program itself, the close of 1971 should see practically all fields of Japanese industry open to foreign investors on at least a fifty-fifty joint venture basis, save for certain reservations that may be made by the government in isolated sectors of what are called "strategic industries," such as automobiles, petrochemicals, and electronics.

But will the five-year Program actually effect the kind of liberalization that foreign investors desire? I think most of them are doubtful that it will. So far neither the speed nor the scope of Japanese efforts toward liberalization have satisfied the expectations of foreign investors, and probably they see no reason to believe that the second half of the Program will be markedly more effective than the first. Most foreign businessmen who are interested in investing in Japan claim that the chief cause for this disappointment is the close relation—or, perhaps more accurately, collaboration—between Japanese government and business. They say it works against their being able to do business effectively in Japan, and they wonder why Japanese business should be thus helping the Japanese government to impede the progress of liberalization when only liberalization can put Japanese business into a world-wide perspective. At the same time, of course, that it can increase profitable relations between Japanese businessmen and businessmen abroad, it can also open a relatively new and certainly profitable market for foreign money. Swift and easy capital liberalization ought, therefore, to be the aim of Japanese business and government as well as of foreign investors.

What, then, is the reason for the apparent unwillingness of Japan to liberalize as speedily and broadly as foreigners had hoped? What role does government play here and what is the exact nature of the relation between government and business? Does the collaboration really work against foreign interests? If so, how may foreign investors best deal with this apparent "conspiracy"? And how much true liberalization may they expect by the end of the five-year Program? These are some of the questions that I shall attempt to answer here.

Let us begin with an imaginary situation—but one that is by no means unfamiliar. Let us suppose that an American wishes to invest both money and technology in Japan. He consults his lawyer, who almost certainly advises him that because of Japanese law, the establishment of a wholly-owned foreign company is virtually impossible, and that the only practicable way to operate a business in Japan is by means of a joint venture with a Japanese partner. Our American investor, therefore, goes to Japan, finds a reliable partner, and begins negotiations toward the establishment of a joint venture and the granting of technological licenses.

During the course of the negotiations, the representative of the American investing company is perplexed by the fact that his Japanese partner makes regular "informal inquiries" of government officials in an effort to determine whether or not he should agree with the American partner on such important issues as equity division, royalty rate, and sales territory division. These are all matters that the American partner feels should be kept secret, at least until the signing of the agreement.

Once the agreement has been signed, the contracts have to be sent to the government for official validation (required by existing foreign exchange and investment control laws) before the American partner has the right to bring his technology and money into Japan, with the right of remittance. Usually, because of language difficulties, it is only the representative of the Japanese partner who goes to the indicated government office to apply for the necessary validation. The American partner, at this point, is further perplexed by the fact that, in spite of all the "informal inquiries" the Japanese partner had made during the "private" negotiations prior to the signing of the contract, the government now makes the validating process still more difficult by offering a great deal more "informal guidance."

The American partner now discovers that government officials never turn down an application with an explicit "no." Rather, they make suggestions for amendments to the agreement. The implication is that unless the suggestions are complied with, the government will withhold its validation. In attempting to grapple with this problem, the American will now ask to see the "suggestions" and have them translated; whereupon, he will be told that they have all been made orally from government official to Japanese partner. Nothing has been written down.

The American's perplexity increases when he attempts to discuss with his Japanese partner ways of making the "suggested" amendments more favorable. The latter, reluctant to argue with the government official, merely asks his American partner to agree to the government's "suggestions." Unless he acquiesces, the American learns, the necessary validation will rarely, if ever, be granted. At this stage (unless he just gets mad and goes home), he will probably throw up his hands and agree to all the government's "suggestions," however unsatisfactory he may consider them. He realizes that this is his only hope of extracting any profit from the joint venture.

Confronted by an experience of this nature, the American may decide that Japanese business and government are in collusion against him. Or he may decide that Japanese capitalism partakes of none of the elements of laissez-faire that are so familiar to him;

rather, that it is government-sponsored capitalism. Or he may agree with Mr. Norman Macrea, of the *London Economist*, who argued that "[One of the seven keys] to the risen sun lies in the [economic] planning itself" which is made and administered by "the most intelligent bureaucracy." "Some of the most intelligent young men in Japan" attend the formulation of plans and collaborate closely with business, aiming for internal growth while protecting it from outside threat.[59]

That there is a basis for the belief that both Japanese government and business share both the "foreign-capital phobia" and a kind of "enterprise nationalism" cannot be questioned. Japanese history would make such concepts almost inevitable: the long isolationism of the island race has imbued in its people a pride in both their racial purity and their independence as well as a deep respect for group loyalty within the confines of their island society. That same isolationism has resulted in a state of profound ignorance among most Japanese about conditions prevailing in the rest of the world. It was that ignorance which permitted the imperial Army to embark on its nearly fatal course of conquest in the earlier part of the century, and it is that same ignorance which now, as the century approaches its three-quarter mark, tends to promote fear of the foreigners who come to do business in Japan and suspicion as to their motives.

"Just look at the challenge America poses in Europe!" is how the fear and suspicion may express themselves. "If capital liberalization is allowed to expand as freely as the foreigners desire, Japan may be subjected to a similar threat. We must, therefore, at any cost defend our poor islands from foreign exploitation." Whether or not there is any objective justification for these fears, they do exist, and business and government do join hands in attempting to ward off possible threats. The two tend to act together when they fear that the national interest may be threatened.

At the same time, mere recognition that this type of sentimental communion exists does not satisfactorily explain either the actual mechanism of the government-business relationship in Japan or its impact on the foreign investor. The latter has sometimes reacted to

232

this relationship with distaste and sometimes with an outright refusal to have anything more to do with it, but such reactions do little to clarify the complicated nature of the relationship. The foreigner who refuses to make any attempt to understand it is hardly likely to succeed in doing so. However desirable it may be to find the simplest answer to a complicated question, the fact remains that complex problems usually require complex solutions— and the nature and effect of the relationship between business and government in Japan is probably the most complex problem that the foreigner who comes to do business here will ever be called upon to solve.

Its roots, as I have indicated, lie far back in Japanese history and its results, as we approach the eighth decade of the twentieth century no longer lie open to question. The hand of government on industry is far heavier in Japan than in America, heavier probably than in any Western capitalist state. The interested foreigner who reads Mr. Norman Macrea's account in *The Economist* might well be tempted to conclude that all business activity in Japan is subjected to rigid government control and is regulated by predetermined governmental programs. There is, indeed, good evidence for this belief. When, for instance, the government advocated a "doubling of income" program, income was doubled; and when the government issued a warning against the over-heating of the economy, business was quick to respond with a remarkable slowdown in its pace of expansion. The Economic White Papers published annually by the government have consistently pointed out the success of its programs in regulating private industry.

To read the series of White Papers, however, and to conclude from them that business is wholly under government's thumb is a little like putting the cart before the horse, since it tends to make final evaluations only from results. I believe that Japanese business is far more independent of government control than is apparent to the Western observer, and if I were asked whether credit ought to be given to government for creating favorable conditions for business operations or to businessmen for voluntarily fulfilling government's expectations, I would surely vote for the latter.

If the White Papers give a different impression, I would suggest that one very good reason might be the vast amounts of the taxpayers' money the government is in a position to spend gathering information and then hiring economists to put that information into the most favorable light—most favorable, that is, to the government itself. It is not surprising, therefore, that the White Papers often give a highly ingenious, pro-government explanation of results that have in fact been achieved by businessmen. As for predictions about the future of the economy, certainly the government—with the abundant data it has at its disposal—is able to be more prescient than most other groups. But talk, as so many national proverbs phrase it, is cheap. In my experience, it is usually the government that does the talking, while it is business that does the work and takes the risks which turn talk into reality.

The government unquestionably can wield a big stick: it can tighten or relax the flow of money from its central bank to city banks, thus regulating loans made to private industry. But this, it must be noted, is only an indirect method of regulation. The government has *no direct means* to coerce private enterprises into conformity with its programs, and a number of instances leap to mind where enterprise has successfully resisted "administrative guidance" based on a pre-determined government program.

In the textile industry, for example, the government not long ago called for a voluntary cut in production by private enterprises because of what it viewed as excessive competition. Laissez-faire elements of the industry, however, mounted an effective opposition to the program, as a result of which the government was forced to reconsider its attempt to totally enforce its so-called guideline.

More recently, Japan has seen two attempts at industrial reorganization in order to cope more effectively with the kind of international competition that is expected to intensify as the scope of capital liberalization expands. One is the merger of two huge steel companies, Fuji and Yawata; the other, that of three paper mills—Oji, Jyujyo, and Honshu. In both cases, the mergers were opposed by the Fair Trade Commission on the grounds that they would tend toward monopoly and undue restraint of trade; and in

234

both cases, the Ministry of International Trade and Industry, supposedly more sensitive to the impact of capital liberalization and of foreign influence on the Japanese economy, favored the proposed mergers. With that of the paper mills, the Ministry took action too late and too ineffectively; the Commission had its own way, and the merger was not allowed. As of this writing, the fate of the steel merger is still uncertain, but here the industry seems to have been more skilful and aggressive in using the conflicting views that prevail in government, and if the merger is successful, it will be because the Ministry acted more promptly and more decisively in consort with the industry as against the perhaps narrower views of the Fair Trade Commission. It seems to me that these two instances offer a more accurate picture of the true relationship between business and government in Japan than the Westerner is likely to carry away. I should say it is a question of "checks and balances" or of "mutual dependence for convenience" rather than one of outright control by one group over the other.

Moving now to the manner by which the Japanese government imposes direct controls over foreign investment, I would like to point out first that Japan is a signatory to both the General Agreement on Trade and Tariffs (GATT) and the International Monetary Fund (IMF) treaties. Two provisions of these treaties are of special interest here: Article 8 of the IMF Treaty and Article 11 of the GATT Treaty. In agreeing to the former, the Japanese government undertakes not to restrict international payment in current transactions, and in the latter not to regulate quantitatively or otherwise the free flow of either exports of imports. These obligations are binding upon the signatory unless GATT and IMF accept reasons for reservations as essential to the protection and maintenance of the signatory's utmost national interest and security.

Then, in 1964, when Japan was admitted to the Organization for Economic Cooperation and Development (OECD), she also agreed to sign the Codes of Liberalization of Capital Movement and of Invisible Current Transactions as soon as practicable. The treaties were negotiated and signed by representatives of the executive branch of the government and later were duly ratified by the legislative branch. However, Japan's obligations under the new treaties were not self-executing by nature insofar as their domestic implementation was concerned. The government, therefore, was obliged, after ratification of the treaties, to enact new laws or amend or abolish existing laws in order to implement the country's newly-undertaken obligations. Thus, as the nature of the relationship between the Japanese economy and world economy has undergone tremendous changes during recent years, a large number of amendments were written into the Foreign Investment Law (Law No. 163 of 1950) and the Foreign Exchange and Foreign Trade Control Law (Law No. 228 of 1949), the two basic post-war statutes for the regulation of Japan's economic activities.

Here it must be remembered that the Japanese government's own interpretation of the nature and extent of its international treaty obligations insofar as liberalization is concerned does not necessarily coincide with the original intentions of the organizations themselves, GATT, IMF, and OECD, or with the way those intentions have been interpreted by the rest of the world. For example, when the government—in September, 1967, and March, 1969—announced a policy of what it called expanded liberalization, the government itself hailed these announcements as evidence of its own epochal, unfettered willingness to cooperate with the rest of the world toward a free exchange of resources and the promotion of economic welfare. The rest of the world, however, did not see these announcements in the same light; they were, in fact, severely criticized—rather as though they were invitations extended by the fox, in Aesop's fable, to the crane to sit down to dinner together.

I shall have more to say shortly about the wide disparity between the two views—that taken by the Japanese government of its own actions and that taken by non-Japanese—but first I should like to make note of two factors that further complicate an already complicated situation. When the two basic statutes of 1949 and 1950 were originally enacted, they were intended as a safeguard against the introduction of foreign capital and technology except where it could be expected to make a positive contribution to Japanese economic recovery. In those years, Japan herself was not self-supporting, and her economy was still impoverished. Both the government and the occupying authorities considered such safeguards essential to protect Japan from exploitation by foreign carpet-baggers, so to speak.

As the Japanese economy, however, pursued its near-miraculous recovery, the situation changed drastically, and it was then that a number of liberalization measures were written into the two protective laws in the form of amendments. The basic framework of the laws regulating Japan's international economic activities was nevertheless retained, and the government at present claims that the laws which formerly imposed a general prohibition should now be interpreted as providing a generalized permission, save in special cases where the government considers introduction of capital and/or technology might have a particularly adverse effect on the Japanese economy. Article 8 of the Foreign Investment Law provides for two sets of standards, one positive and one negative, by which the government may validate contracts for the introduction of foreign capital and technology. The government at present claims that it makes use solely of the negative set of standards, which are easier for foreign investors to fulfill; but what is the foreigner to say when he is confronted by two contrary sets of provisions and is told that only one is being used? His bewilderment takes an obvious form. "Why should I believe the government?" he asks; "what will happen if the situation changes and positive standards are adopted?" To which the government, in effect, replies: "You must believe what we say. It is more important for us to save face in the international economic community than to allay your apprehensions."

It is not a happy dialogue on either side, and realizing this, some government people (most particularly those in the Ministry of International Trade and Industry) have advocated the promulgation of a unified law regulating clearly and comprehensively the entire scope of Japan's economic activities. However, the Ministry of Finance, an older brother and rival of the other Ministry, has objected on the grounds that it is too soon to rewrite the laws, that we are still on the threshhold of capital liberalization, and that the situation the laws are intended to regulate remains in a continuing state of change. Thus, according to the Ministry of Finance, existing laws will have to serve until the movement toward liberalization is in the past rather than the future.

During the period following the end of the Second World War, Japan concluded several treaties of friendship, commerce, and navigation with a number of Western countries (including the United States) guaranteeing freedom of commerce across the boundaries of the signatory nations on a reciprocal basis. As between the United States and Japan, for example, Japan is permitted to regulate the influx of American capital only if it is likely to have an adverse effect on Japan's balance of payments. After Japan ratified Article 8 of the International Monetary Fund Treaty and became a member of the Organization for Economic Cooperation and Development, the United States contended that, from the international point of view, Japan no longer had a balance-of-payment problem and that she therefore no longer had the right to limit the inflow and recovery of American capital. From the Japanese point of view, however, there is obviously a tremendous gap in competitive power between Japan and the United States. The Japanese government, therefore, as well as Japanese business, wants to continue present limitations on the introduction of American capital lest it become so great as to "disrupt harmony" and thus have a disastrous effect on the Japanese economy.

Many American economists fail to see the validity of this argument. They ask why the United States should permit Japan to establish subsidiaries to sell and service more than two hundred thousand automobiles a year in the United States while American manufacturers although able to export under restrictive tariffs are not permitted to make and sell their cars directly in Japan. In reply, the Japanese say that if they liberalized to the extent that the Americans demand, the Japanese automobile industry (which they believe to be strategically important) would very likely be dominated by the "big three" of the United States, Ford, Chrysler, and General Motors. My own feeling is that this problem, like most problems involving international relations, is not a black-and-white one: it cannot be answered with either an absolute "yes" or an absolute "no." Every country has domestic problems to solve as well as international relations to be maintained as constructively as possible. The question, then, becomes one of determining to what extent there is room for reasonable compromise between the participants. And, for the compromise, Japan needs to abandon its conviction that it is a "poor" country, as compared with "rich" Western countries.

Returning now to the foreign investor in Japan, I have already pointed out that he will be much perplexed by the way Japan interprets her obligations under international treaties of which she is a signatory. His perplexity will be further aggravated by the fact that laws regulating Japan's role in international commerce, difficult and sometimes contradictory as they are, are rendered even more mysterious for the foreigner by the network of established "administrative practices" that surround them. In fact, the way that Japan implements her treaty obligations is determined not by the express provisions of the law but rather by the unexpressed practices of officials of the Ministries of Finance and International Trade and Industry who screen applications for foreign-exchange validation.

Compare, for example, Article 2 of the Foreign Investment Law with the so-called Ten Commandments announced informally by the Ministry of Finance in September, 1967. Article 2 reads: "Foreign investment in Japan should be as freely recognised as possible. As the need for the validation system provided for in this Law decreases, so it should be abolished and relaxed." (Author's translation.) It would almost seem that the Ministry of Finance was ignorant of the law when it issued its "Ten Commandments for Foreign Investors," who are told that they should:

1. Invest in industries where a fifty percent equity is automatically approved rather than in industries where a hundred percent is possible;

2. Avoid industries in which goods are produced mainly by medium to small factories;

239

3. Avoid restrictive arrangements with overseas parent companies or affiliates;

4. Cooperate with Japanese producers in the same industry in order to avoid "excessive competition";

5. Contribute to the development of Japanese technology;

6. Help promote Japanese exports;

7. Ensure that in a joint venture the number of Japanese directors reflects the Japanese equity percentage;

8. Avoid layoffs and plant closures that might disrupt the Japanese labor market;

9. Cooperate in maintaining Japan's industrial harmony and help in the achievement of her economic goals; and

10. Avoid concentrating their investments in any particular industry or industries.

It is hardly to be wondered at, then, that foreign investors, perplexed by Japan's xenophobic insularity and ignorant of her language, try frantically, but with only doubtful success, to find the key that will open the door to Japanese business. One of the ways they have hit upon—as suggested earlier in this book—is to ask a top Japanese business friend to speak on their behalf to some strategically placed top government official. Before giving my own opinion as to whether or not this is a useful procedure, I should like to enlarge briefly on the educational and social environment in Japan that has produced a relationship between businessmen and government officials which is perhaps unique in the world.

The co-author of this book has already described some of the factors that led to the Meiji restoration, and he has pointed out that once it was over, the men who led it realized the importance of tempering traditional Japanese education with Western ideas. It was the only way to bridge what might be called the "civilization gap" that resulted from Japan's long years of isolation.

As the new nation developed, more and more universities were founded, and the steadily increasing number of graduates made possible the establishment of an educational meritocracy. Most of the new universities were government-sponsored and so relatively inexpensive. Thus a boy, though his family might have been neither

well-to-do nor influential, could, once he passed a highly competitive examination, enter a "good" high school with the expectation that he would eventually be admitted to one of the more
prestigious universities. His career from then on was more or less
guaranteed: it was unlikely that he would fail to reach one of the
upper levels in business or government.

Here I should like to quote some observations made by an
American friend who has had a long and brilliant career as Far
Eastern manager of a great American corporation. "Everybody
worth knowing in Japan," he said, "seems to come from one of a
very few universities, like Tokyo or Kyoto, Hitotsubashi or Kobe,
or Keio or Waseda. On graduation from Tokyo University for
example, the top-ranking students join the most distinguished
government office available to them, the Ministry of Finance, the
Bank of Japan, the Ministry of International Trade and Industry,
or the Foreign Office. Their goal is eventually to become a cabinet
member, or perhaps even prime minister. Other gifted graduates
return to their alma mater, where they use their privileged position
to advocate theories that may be subversive of all existing institutions—including their own government. The great majority of
other students go into industry with the firm intention of becoming
president of the company. Sooner or later, however, they realize
that however firm the intention, only a very few will be able to
realize it. Disillusioned, they may let their ambition divert them
into trade unionism, where moderate success may elevate them to
positions of power in the Socialist Party. They are then in opposition to the ruling, and perhaps more conservative, Liberal-Democratic Party.

"But it must be remembered that the leaders of both parties, as
well as of business, are all graduates of the same handful of
universities. Thus, the Japanese establishment is monolithic. It is
like a spoked wheel. A leader of the Socialist Party may express
opinions that appear to be absolutely contrary to the opinions of a
Liberal-Democratic leader—but we must not be misled by the
apparent lack of agreement. The fact is that each man, when he
speaks, has taken a position on the rim of the wheel, and what he

says is determined by what spoke leads to the particular point on the wheel where he is standing. The man standing opposite him may express opposite opinions—but both men, we soon find, are bound to the axle from which all the spokes radiate. Unlike Japan, my own country is a heterogeneous society: no man is necessarily bound to a particular spoke on a rather small social wheel."

An over-simplification? Perhaps, for Japanese society is highly complex; and yet I believe there is a great deal of truth in these observations, the kind of truth that may escape a Japanese observer of the same scene. Vertical movement within the establishment was, and is, supplied by our educational meritocracy, and I believe that horizontal movement was accelerated—at least at the top—by the fact that leaders of both business and government often wore the same old-school tie. Foreign observers seem to believe generally that there is little or no freedom for horizontal movement in Japanese society, that men are bound by custom to their first chosen work-place by the system of seniority and life-employment.

I believe this is only partially true. Let us look for a moment at the government bureaucracy. When an elite official reaches his fifties, he finds that no matter how good his record or how high his intelligence, there are not many positions left for him to fill. Whatever the ministry, the minister himself, being a cabinet member, is a political appointee; the highest position a bureaucrat can aim at is administrative vice-minister. Now, suppose Mr. Tanaka joined the particular ministry he is in along with ten of his classmates, of whom only three, including Mr. Tanaka, have survived the severe competition within the ministry and become directors of bureaus. It is from these three that the vice-minister will be chosen. If Mr. Tanaka is successful, well and good; if he is not, he and the other unsuccessful bureau director will, according to custom, retire from the ministry. They will not await their own turn to be vice-minister but will leave that to the colleagues who joined the ministry the year after they did.

Now, many of these officials who are bound by custom to retire are still comparatively young and vigorous; both their intelligence and ability have been proven by the fact that they reached the second highest position available to them; their value to private industry is obvious—and, as has already been pointed out earlier in this book, that is usually the direction they take. They know intimately the ministry where they spent so many years of their lives, and industry presumes that when they go to the ministry they have left to speak on behalf of the corporation they are now serving, they are likely to get a better hearing from men who were once their juniors than complete strangers. Thus, a number of former high officials of the Ministries of Finance and of International Trade and Industry are invited to join private corporations after their retirement.

If a foreign businessman, then, has to secure some sort of approval from the government, would he not be well-advised to make friends with top business leaders who had once been government officials? On the surface the answer would appear to be an unqualified "yes"; but if we analyze the matter more closely, we find so many uncertain factors, both human and organizational, that a generalized answer must almost necessarily be false. One of the most uncertain—and determining—factors is the continued loyalty of the junior in the ministry to the retired senior now in business.

The foreigner may wonder why—in a society so seniority-minded as that of Japan—there should be any uncertainty at all on this point. The answer lies in the structure and function of the Japanese ministerial bureaucracy—which, at the risk of further oversimplification, I would say consists of three distinct layers, staffed by two different kinds of officials, career and clerical.

On the lowest, *jimukan* level, the career officials consist of graduates of elite schools who have just begun their upward climb (which they hope will end in the vice-minister's office), while members of the clerical staff consist of graduates from less distinguished schools who most probably foresee no likelihood of ever achieving a top managerial post. When the representative of a business visits the Ministry of Finance or the Ministry of International Trade and Industry to apply for validation of a contract or approval of a project, the people who receive the application, hear the plea, and give informal advice—of the kind usually called "window guidance"—are mostly non-career clerks on this lowest level of the hierarchy. Young career officials are generally more concerned with receiving their training, in the form of interdepartmental rotation, or engaging in specialized research and study, which they hope will help prepare them for promotion to a higher echelon; customarily they play little part in the giving of "window guidance" unless it concerns a basic issue which is likely to affect, or be affected by, the overall policy of the ministry.

Businessmen who have had to deal with "window-guidance" officials frequently complain that they are incapable of appreciating the broader aspects of the particular request for validation that is in question and that they like to create problems merely for the sake of creating problems. In my opinion, however, a rigid, trouble-shooting point of view on the part of a public servant entrusted with the enforcement of rules and regulations is certainly more desirable than a flexible attitude that may be tainted with the possibility of personal gain.

Let us now examine in somewhat more detail the mechanics of the relationship between the businessman and the government official to whom he has applied for validation of a contract. As I have already pointed out, it is usually the Japanese partner to a joint venture who conducts the negotiations with the government, and he usually adopts an attitude of passivity and acceptance even when confronted with what may appear to be unnecessarily rigid guide-lines. This is due in part, as I have suggested, to the vestiges of feudalism in Japanese society, in part to the strategic role played by the government in the Meiji industrialization, in part to the stringency of government controls before and during the war and under the occupation, and also in part to the general scarcity of raw materials with which Japanese industry has had to contend and which has frequently resulted in their allocation by government decree. "You might as well try to reason with a crying child," say the Japanese, "as hope to fight the authorities," and indeed a businessman who attempts to resist the government's "suggestions" invites the possibility of direct or indirect retaliation. A ministry, for example, may refuse to renew a license for the allocation of necessary materials, a refusal that will prove far more costly to the business than the initial gains it might have won as a result of its original resistance to the guidance proffered by the government.

Often a foreign investor has wanted to know why his Japanese partner failed to bring a writ of mandamus or an administrative suit against the government when their joint application for validation of capital investment seemed to be unnecessarily delayed in the screening process or when the government's strongly worded "informal advice" was altogether contrary to the original intention of the contracting parties. And the Japanese partner has had to reply, as I did above, that the business, by becoming a conspicuous target for government attack, may be greatly hindered later on and that most businesses in Japan prosper by maintaining a conciliatory attitude toward government and exhibiting a willingness to compromise.

I do not mean to imply that all Japanese businessmen are sheeplike in their dealings with government bureaucrats. I know of many cases in which repeated visits to government offices and heated discussions about the nature of the "advice" being given have resulted in major concessions by the government; in these cases, the contract that was finally validated was far nearer to the original intention of the applicants than it would otherwise have been. Sometimes there have been unfortunate consequences later on, and most times the Japanese partner's efforts have been inadequately appreciated by the foreign partner. This has often been caused by the mountainous language barrier that separates East from West.

As I pointed out earlier, when the government official says to the Japanese representative of the joint venture, "I would suggest that you delete this or that provision from the contract," or "This provision might be amended," he gives his so-called advice orally. He is usually, as I have said, on the lowest rung of the hierarchy; only a department head would have the authority to draft a written memorandum and place a department seal on it. The businessman may argue a bit, but he knows that he must accept most of the advice that has been offered. When he returns to his office, he writes a letter to the effect that "Thanks to your advice, we agree to delete this . . . and amend that . . . . " This document will then be submitted to the "window guidance" official, who will either accept it and accelerate the validating process (which must finally be completed by his superior, as I shall explain later) or else he returns the document to the business representative for further amendment. During all these negotiations, the Japanese partner generally tries to keep his foreign partner informed of the nature of the suggested and agreed-upon changes, but all too often he will do so with merely a straightforward translation, or even an inaccurate one, and without any explanation, because there is no one in the firm with the ability to explain the matter in detail in English or French or German or whatever the mother-tongue of the foreign partner may be. The latter, as a result, grows highly suspicious of his Japanese partner and accuses him of "double talk" or even of collusion with government authorities.

Much of this unfortunate lack of trust could be avoided if the Japanese partner (1) adopted a somewhat less propitiatory attitude toward the governmental bureaucrat, realizing that the adverse reaction of his foreign partner may be more disadvantageous to the business than the adverse reaction of the government official; and (2) kept his foreign partner advised to the fullest possible extent of the nature of the negotiations between him and the ministry. It would be immeasurably helpful also, of course, if the government official would keep in mind that in dealing with a Japanese representative he is also dealing with a foreign partner and that the latter has little or no acquaintance with the custom of "window guidance." Thus, the government official, in attempting to protect the economic interest of his country, may actually be harming them when he continues to insist that his advice be followed. At the same time, the foreign partner ought to bear in mind that he is hoping to do business in a foreign country that has its own customs and that, merely because those customs are not ones he is familiar with, they are not necessarily ridiculous or harmful.

246

The second, or middle, level of the government bureaucracy is occupied by career officials, generally in their forties, who have completed their basic training and preparation on the *jimukan* level. They can now participate in the basic formulation of national policy and so feel that they are the elite members of their ministry.

Insofar as foreign investment is concerned, officials on this level of the hierarchy take part in the activities and decisions of the Preparatory Committee to the Foreign Investment Council, which virtually determines the fate of all applications for validation, since the Foreign Investment Council in itself is a superior organ presided over by the Minister of Finance and almost invariably accepts or rejects applications on the basis of recommendations made by the Preparatory Committee. Influential members of this Committee are section chiefs of the Ministry of Finance, the Ministry of International Trade and Industry, the Foreign Office, the Science and Technology Bureau, the Economic Planning Agency, and the Fair Trade Commission, all of whom are responsible for foreign investment control in their respective agencies. Depending on the field of industry into which the introduction of foreign capital and technology is contemplated, section chiefs of other ministries may also sit on the Committee; for example, should the joint venture intend to deal in pharmaceuticals, section chiefs from the Ministry of Public Health and Welfare will very likely have a strong voice in the final decision.

Many officials working on this level come to feel that they are now defenders of the national interest. Being members of the elite, they are incapable of taking advice from more experienced people, and as defenders of Japan, they are prone to a xenophobia that may actually be harmful to the best interests of the country. For example, it is well known that a group of officials on this level are determined to defend to the death the Japanese electronics industry, which they claim to be still in an embryonic stage and which they say must be permitted to develop by itself, free from all foreign intervention. People of this sort will regard anyone with a more flexible attitude as in disagreement with them and will refuse to listen to anything he may have to say. It is generally believed that the so-called Ten Commandments that I listed earlier in this chapter were prepared by people on this level of the hierarchy in the Ministries of Finance and International Trade and Industry.

How may foreign investors best cope with officials of this type? The answer is difficult and hazardous, far more so than with "window guidance" officials on a lower level, and that for two reasons: first, the foreign investor seldom has the opportunity to talk to government officials who have reached this level of the bureaucracy; and second, decisions at the Preparatory Committee to the Foreign Investment Council are reached by the typical Japanese method of consensus-taking. That is to say, when a contract is presented to the Committee for validation, its members do not simply vote and then abide by the majority decision. If all the members are either in favor of validation or opposed to it, then the matter is simple; but if, as is usually the case, opinion is split, then no decision at all is made. It will simply be postponed until the application in question is amended sufficiently to gain unanimous approval. Then the "window guidance" officials will proffer more "advice" to the joint partners; the advice will take the form of an attempt to explain indirectly why the stalemate has occurred in the Committee and what the applicants may do to effect a compromise that will satisfy the Committee's requirements.

It is useless for the foreign investor to decry the system or to point out that that is not the way things are done in his country. It *is* the way things are done in Japan—and the only sensible solution for the foreigner who wants to do business in Japan is to accept that fact and to cope with the difficulties arising from it as best he can. He really has no choice.

As I suggested earlier, one of the chief causes for the "foreign capital phobia" that is so prevalent in Japan is the general ignorance among so many Japanese, including middle-level bureaucrats, about the true intentions of foreign investors in coming to Japan. Probably the best way for the foreign businessman to combat this ignorance, and so overcome the phobia, is a public relations campaign designed to put his intentions in a favorable

248

light. If he is unable to do this, then perhaps he ought not to complain too bitterly about the Japanese way of controlling foreign investments. Certainly he ought to attempt to find out as much as he can about the way the middle-level bureaucracy thinks and acts in the matter of foreign investment, for without such knowledge he will be quite unable to anticipate the bureaucracy's reaction to his application or work out viable means of accepting its guidance without compromising his own position too deeply.

The top level of the Japanese bureaucracy consists of bureau chiefs and some department chiefs: it is these officials of the Ministries of Finance and International Trade and Industry, headed of course by the ministers themselves, who make the major policy decisions that influence legislative action and that also determine the direction of administrative implementation in the field of Japan's economic activities. Insofar as international business is concerned, the Minister of Finance, as authorized by the Foreign Investment Law, heads the Foreign Investment Council, which consists of nine leaders of Japanese business, representing all major industries, and which acts as policy advisory committee to the government.

Though theoretically only advisory, the Council appears in reality to have the authority to determine national policy on international business at the highest level. On the last two occasions that the scope of capital liberalization was officially expanded, the Council's recommendations were accepted without modification by the government, and administrative implementation followed. The present deputy chairman of the Council, Mr. Ataru Kobayashi, president of Arabian Oil Company, appears to favor a freer exchange of international business opportunities, but in his capacity as deputy chairman he must act as a sort of referee between the conflicting demands of business, government, and—indirectly— foreign capital. Perhaps as a result of this fact, the policy recommendations of the Council have become so indefinite that its original intention has remained hidden from the government or been misunderstood by it.

Until quite recently "foreign capital phobia" was to be felt even at this top level of policy formulation. There were, of course, exceptions. One such was Mr. Taizo Ishizaka, the internationally-minded business leader who heads EXPO '70, who for a long time has been president of the Keidanren, the powerful Federation of Economic Organizations. Mr. Ishizaka is reported to have remarked, "Why should we worry about bringing in foreign capital and goods, tangible or intangible? So long as we retain management in our own hands and so long as we retain the right to utilize the important economic resources, we are safe. What we need, in fact, is more foreign capital and goods." But most business and government leaders did not agree. They united to keep the door to Japan's major industries closed to foreign operations, and were determined to protect the so-called strategic industries (including electronics and automobiles) from "foreign domination," instancing the recent plight of a number of European companies operating in similar fields.

In this connection, the government (principally the Ministry of International Trade and Industry) has greatly encouraged the reorganization of the automotive industry. This took the form of grouping a number of small manufacturers under the wings of Toyota and Nissan so as to increase their international competitive strength by increasing their size. Business and government were also in agreement on the need to protect small and medium-sized enterprises in the fields of food processing and distribution, since these are structurally too weak to withstand the storm of capital liberalization and compete successfully with large, technically advanced foreign enterprises.

Relying on this over-protective philosophy, many corporate managers were wont to take the irresponsible attitude that liberalization might have to be introduced into a neighboring industry but not yet into their own. This attitude has, however, undergone a major change in the past year and a half, during which capital liberalization took two strides forward in its five-year Program.

One factor that fostered a change in governmental thinking was the realization that protectionism does not accelerate the desired domestic rationalization; on the contrary, the protected industry seems to become ever more dependent. The government also became aware that its program for industrial reorganization aimed at "bigness" had a dangerous side-effect: marginal industries not in line for government help might have to seek foreign help in order to survive and compete with the newly-reorganized giant, thus introducing foreign capital more quickly and in larger amounts than was deemed desirable and so disrupting Japan's highly-prized "industrial harmony."

The changing trend in basic thinking and in subsequent guidelines is clearly illustrated by an official memorandum submitted by the Foreign Investment Council to the Minister of Finance on February 5th, 1969, outlining the Council's advice to the government concerning continued capital liberalization. The memorandum read, in part, as follows:

"The government is recommended particularly to take rapid action to implement the following:—

(1) Provided that there is no sudden change in the national and international situation, the government is advised to take more positive and progressive steps for the third phase of capital liberalization, which is intended to be announced one year or eighteen months from the date of this memorandum. For the above, the government is advised to make its position clearer, to promote the development of effective measures, including the necessary overall improvement of the legal system, and to guide private industry accordingly.

(2) Flexibility in the examination of individual applications for validation should be adopted as far as is practically possible so that substantial effects of liberalization are achieved.

(3) This Council is seriously concerned about capital liberalization in the automotive industry. The Government is advised to take rapid action for the appropriate liberalization of the industry and to implement the program. Rapid modernization and reorganization of distribution are necessary not only to promote capital liberalization but also to establish proper domestic consumer pricing policies. The latter in particular needs immediate action. Accordingly, the government is advised to formulate suitable policy for the rationalization and reorganization of the said industry, to implement it, and also to promote the liberalization of it more positively." (Author's translation)

The Council's policy formulation is prepared by a Committee of Experts, made up of seven members from academic and journalistic fields as well as from business. The role that this Committee is expected to play is similar to that of the Preparatory Committee to the Council. Some of their number have been trained abroad and thus are presumed to have a wider and more international point of view than government officials whose daily work is concerned with domestic affairs and one of whose primary duties is to safeguard Japanese interests against foreigners.

The government, by Cabinet Order, announced its basic plan for a Five Year Program for Capital Liberalization in September, 1967, with an explanation of Immediate Liberalization Measures. I confess I was somewhat shocked at the time by a discrepancy between what the government enunciated in principle and what it suggested as a means to implement what it had said in principle.

The Cabinet Order emphasized the fact that Japan had decided to launch a new and forward-looking program for capital liberalization. It established two categories of "liberalized industries," including fifty different kinds of industrial activities. It made clear that a foreign application for acquisition of shares (up to either 100% or 50%, depending on the category) in a newly established enterprise within one of the "liberalized industries" would be automatically approved by the government provided that it satisfied certain requirements, which were listed and explained.

This seemed, on the surface, to be a considerable advance, since the government now for the first time made explicit its standards for validation of an application and also established two categories of "liberalized industries." However, when I began to analyze the provisions, I found that they were, in fact, tighter than anything that had existed before September, 1967, though previous standards had been merely implied.

The understanding in both business and government, prior to the 1967 Order, was that direct foreign investment was subject to the guidelines set forth by the Ministry of International Trade and Industry in 1960. Many of these implied understandings were written into the 1967 Order, which contained, in addition, a number of new qualifications. They may be briefly summarized as follows:

(1)   The type of property that is the object of investment in kind by the Japanese partner [of a newly established joint venture], or property [that is] promised to be transferred from an existing company [after the establishment of a new company] must be real estate other than factories, shops and warehouses.

(2)   The enterprise, immediately after its establishment, is not to receive the transfer, lease and so on, of businesses, nor the transfer of properties for purposes of business operations, from an existing company, nor to amalgamate with an existing company.

(3)   More than one-third of the total shares of a joint venture company must be held by a Japanese company which is engaged in the same kind of industry as the joint venture, and at least one-half of the total shares including the above-mentioned one-third must be held by Japanese who are in the same line of business.

(4)   Actions taken by a joint venture must be in conformity with the provisions of the Japanese Commercial Code. The right to veto may not be given to a foreign partner in a joint venture.

(5)   If a foreign investor desires to make use of yen funds he possesses as a result of a previous operation in Japan and if the purpose for which he wishes to use them is other than that originally validated, he must apply for fresh authorization.

It was the contention of the government that these additional regulations were essential for the protection of Japanese management in a joint venture against possible take-over by the foreign partner. When I asked a friend who sits on the Expert Committee if the 1967 Order did not mean a substantive contraction rather than expansion of the scope of liberalization, I received what seemed to me a very illuminating reply. "You appear to know something about law," he said, "but you don't know enough about bureaucratic politics in the Japanese government to understand our true intention. Had we not recommended to the government that it establish these additional, detailed regulations, do you know what would have happened? Administrative officials would have been freer to interpret the basic guide lines for themselves and would have imposed their own limitations. Then you would have seen a real contraction of the scope of liberalization. No, under present conditions, the only way we can accomplish true liberalization is through controlled liberalization."

These remarks may seem almost incomprehensible to British and American readers, for in their countries the actions of administrative officials are always regulated by laws that define as precisely as possible the scope of executive action. In Japan, on the other hand, the purpose of law is to express minimum protection of national interest. Whenever the force of law diminishes, administrative action must increase. The Westerner may find this system unsatisfactory (just as the Japanese might find the Western way unsuitable), but the fact remains that if the Westerner wants to do business in Japan, he must do it the Japanese way. Only after he accepts that fact will he be able to find practical means of meeting the situation.

The foreign investor ought to bear in mind also the constant need for flexibility in dealing with officials of the Ministries of Finance and International Trade and Industry. He may enjoy meeting the uppermost echelon of the bureaucracy, he may find people at that level more sympathetic because they have had more experience with international business, but he must remember that he will also have to deal with officials on other levels who may think and act quite differently from the top-level bureaucrats. If he approaches the latter in a manner that juniors may consider high-handed or untimely, he may well find that he has created a bureaucratic antagonism in the Ministry that will be both irksome and obstructive. That is why I have emphasized the need for flexibility of approach to the various levels of the bureaucracy; the time when the approach is made and the people to whom it is made must be determined by the particular situation at the moment. It is a difficult puzzle—but I think also a very interesting one—for any businessman to solve.

Another question of paramount importance to the foreign investor in Japan is of course the future of the liberalization program.

Recently the United States and other Western countries have been putting strong pressure on the Japanese government to accelerate the program at a speed beyond that which the government deems wise from the point of view of its own domestic rationalization and reorganization program. Japan feels it essential to coordinate the two programs; foreign business naturally is interested chiefly in liberalization. If the West loses patience, or if Japan decides too much pressure is being exerted, an atmosphere of mutual suspicion may develop that will have a harmful effect on Japan's economic relations with the rest of the world, chiefly of course the United States. I should hate to see this happen, and I think the way to avoid it is to replace suspicion with understanding. Understanding is necessary on both sides of the world—an understanding not only of the economic problems involved but also of political and social factors that affect the climate of international relations.

The Security Treaty, for example, comes up for automatic renewal in 1970 unless either the United States or Japan objects to it. Strongly pacifist elements among the Japanese are growing ever more vociferous about their unwillingness to continue that type of military alliance. Readers may recall that in 1960, when the same subject came up, anti-Treaty and anti-American sentiment grew so violent that Eisenhower's visit had to be cancelled. Now socialist groups are organizing a similar campaign for 1970. A deterioration in Japanese-American friendship must inevitably affect economic relations. The Kennedy and Johnson administrations were comparatively broadminded and sympathetic in this respect; what attitude the Republican administration of President Nixon will take remains to be seen. There are already symptoms of deterioration in American resentment that Japan refuses to allow American automotive and electronics manufacturers unrestricted operation in Japan while Japanese manufacturers sell such products in the United States without obstruction. Should relations deteriorate still further and to a marked degree, should politics actually divide the two countries, one inevitable result will be an intensified economic war. The United States (at present the largest single importer of Japanese products and the largest single exporter to Japan) might even launch an economic embargo against Japan. It is what neither country desires and it would be to the interest of neither country, and yet—with a failure of understanding—it might conceivably happen. One of the aims of capital liberalization is to see that it does not happen, and here I think there is no basic difference between the philosophies of the two countries.

Of the 560 categories into which the Japanese government has classified domestic industries, it has announced that by the end of the five-year Program all but a hundred will be liberalized. (Among the hundred are integrated circuits and other products that the government considers "strategic.") So far, during the past two years, the government has "liberated" more than two hundred product categories, which would on the surface seem to be quite progressive—save for the fact that the remaining 350 categories are far more important. The government has promised at least two more stages in its liberalization program before the end of 1971. That would mean that at each stage at least 130 qualitatively important fields will have to be liberated. The Westerner, naturally, wonders which they will be and which will be retained on the unliberalized list—and realizes, presumably, how difficult the answers must be. Not only must the conflicting interests of Japanese business, Japanese government, and foreign investor be taken into account, but also the fragility of domestic politics and international relations as well as the dizzy speed at which technological innovations are made nowadays. A product that the government considers strategic today it may not tomorrow; and by the same token the unimportant may suddenly become important to national security.

In any case, I foresee that during the remaining two and a half years of the five-year Program there will be several periods of economic tension between Japan and the United States as a result of Japan's slow and egocentric approach to liberalization. However, these periods of tension will, I believe, have a beneficial effect in the long run, in that they will tend to accelerate the progress of the domestic reorganization which the government believes to be an essential concommitant to liberalization. The atmosphere of political instability which is expected to envelop Japan in 1970, with the consequent fear of economic reprisal by the United States, may also serve to speed the liberalization process. Thus, in my opinion, both the scope and the speed of liberalization will increase as the five-year Program approaches its terminal date. The Japanese, it must be remembered, have always been more effective at times of crisis and tension than in periods of peace and security.

As Japan's economic welfare continues to improve, with increasing liberalization, I believe that the country will become ever more keenly aware that its economic health in the future lies in the development of foreign markets on a global scale. Our domestic market, with its hundred million consumers, will soon be saturated —but the opportunity beyond the seas is limitless. However, in the development of such markets, reciprocal benefits are essential: unless Japan opens her own industries to foreigners, foreign countries are not going to let Japanese entrepreneurs operate freely within their borders.

Fear of reprisal, as a result of over-delayed liberalization, will combine, I believe, with increasing awareness of the tremendous advantages of a liberalized world to ensure that the government by the end of 1970 achieves the level of liberalization promised back in 1967. Beyond that, prediction becomes difficult and dangerous. However, I think I may safely say that once the government feels it has accomplished its stated objectives, it will sit back and relax for a few years before undertaking further moves toward increased liberalization. My chief hope is that, despite her slow progress in this direction, Japan will not muff her chance to become a leader in the expanding arena of international business— and my guess is that, when the right opportunity presents itself, she will not fail to grasp it.

13 Joint Ventures

The exact number of international joint venture companies presently operating in Japan is unknown. Strangely enough, there is in fact no general agreement as to what precisely constitutes a joint venture. The government *does* define what it considers to be the nature of a joint venture, but, as will be seen, the official definition is misleading.

First of all, the government classifies companies in which foreign investors make equity participation (*gaishi-kei kaisha*) into three distinct types: (1) companies one hundred percent of whose equity is held by foreign investors (*jyun gaishi kaisha*); (2) companies into which equity foreign capital is introduced (*gaishi donyu kaisha*); and (3) joint-venture companies (*goben kaisha*). The distinction between wholly foreign owned companies and companies partly owned by foreign investors is obvious, but confusion arises when one attempts to follow the government's definitions in distinguishing between *gaishi donyu kaisha* and *goben kaisha*.

The government says that if a company has been owned jointly by Japanese and foreign shareholders from the time of its incorporation, it is classified as a joint venture (*goben kaisha*). On the other hand, if foreign investors buy shares of a wholly Japanese owned company from Japanese shareholders, although the foreigners thereby make themselves participate in ownership and management, the company is not a *goben kaisha* but as a *gaishi donyu kaisha*.

This is clearly a misleading distinction. If one accepts it, then few international joint ventures launched prior to the Second World War could still be classified as joint ventures, since during the war all enemy property, including corporate equity holdings, was placed under a custodian, thus freeing Japanese companies from enemy claims. After the war, however, when many such pre-war joint ventures were revived, arrangements were made that did not involve the formation of a new joint venture. Take the case of National Cash Register, for example. When it returned to Japan after the war, a Japanese company that had been stripped of all foreign ownership increased its capital, allocated new shares to National Cash Register of the United States, and revived 70 percent equity control of American shareholders. Nevertheless, in accordance with official definitions, National Cash Register of Japan is today not a joint venture (*goben kaisha*) but only a *gaishi donyu kaisha*. It is obviously erroneous to put a company with at least 70 percent foreign capital in the same classification as a company like Toshiba, in which foreign equity participation is slightly over 10 percent and in which no direct management control is exerted by General Electric or other foreign investors on the board.

In my opinion, the distinction ought to be made on the basis of whether foreign investors, through their share-ownership, have sufficient impact on the management of a Japanese company for it to be considered a joint venture. In every case, a study would have to be made to determine the amount of impact, since business relies not only on money and management but also on diverse kinds of tangible and intangible economic resources, the ownership and control of which determine the amount of influence that can be exerted on any particular corporate management. It is my impression that the majority of companies now called *gaishi donyu kaisha* ought in reality to be considered joint ventures (*goben kaisha*).

There are further complications in the attempt to achieve substantively correct nomenclature. Government offices in charge of foreign investment control every year announce the number of validated cases of introduction of direct and indirect investment. The government distinction here is that in the former, investors have acquired the shares of a Japanese company with the hope and design of participating in its management; while in the latter, shares have been acquired on the open market without management ambition.

Thus, the government concept of direct investment would seem to correspond to my definition of a joint venture, but here too there are difficulties. Before 1963, a foreign investor could use his funds in Japan in any way he liked without applying for validation provided he did not want to remit either invested capital or profit out of the country. Under this system, called "yen base operation," a number of joint ventures were established. When the system was abolished, some of the yen base companies applied for validation and acquired "validated company" status, particularly on the occasion of their bringing in new money from abroad for capital increase. The great majority of yen base companies, however, remained in their unvalidated status, making it difficult for the Japanese government to determine their exact number.

A foreigner must apply for validation every time he introduces new money into the local market. Direct investment money is usually used for the incorporation of a new company, but it may also be used for the subscription of newly issued shares of an already validated and existing company. Thus, the number of cases of validated foreign investment announced annually does not even correspond to the number of validated joint venture companies. There is opportunity for considerable duplication.

Other factors must be considered in any evaluation of the role of joint ventures in the Japanese business community and indeed in Japanese life. The Japanese as a whole like to buy famous foreign brands just as Japanese manufacturers like to import advanced foreign technologies. At the same time, they fear foreign control or domination. What Japanese entrepreneurs seek, then, is to import the technologies they want and the brands people want to buy without any strings attached. Foreign investors, on the other hand, have no desire to make a free gift of the technologies they have developed to potential competitors within Japan. What foreign investors seek is to tie the hands of their Japanese partners. Reconciling these divergent interests is often most successfully accomplished through the establishment of an independent joint-venture company. The foreign investor grants licenses to permit the new entity to use certain technologies or brand-names, and if a joint venture company is the only way for the Japanese partner to acquire the licenses, then he regards the company as a necessary evil; and he also tends to regard the new entity as a child of the parent company—a child the Japanese parent hopes sooner or later to swallow.

A similar fear of foreign domination probably motivates the government in its preference for calling companies that are under foreign influence *gaishi donyu kaisha* rather than *goben kaisha*. The former phrase falls softer on the Japanese ear than the latter, and the government finds it easier to admit that leadership in an important field of industry is held by a *gaishi donyu kaisha* than by an outright joint venture. Thus it is not surprising that the investigator is hard put to determine the precise number of joint ventures in existence in Japan. Nor is it surprising either that partners in an international joint venture often find themselves lined up against each other in a kind of psychological war that necessarily impedes the progress of the company.

During the period between 1950 and 1968, the government validated the introduction of $7,220,311,000 in foreign investments. Of this amount, 21 percent ($1,540,583,000) was invested in the acquisition of Japanese corporate stocks, and of such acquisition some three-quarters were purchased on the stock market while the remaining quarter ($382,840,000) was invested with the hope and design of participating in the management of a joint venture. This "direct investment" represents 5.3 percent of total foreign investment. At the same time, the government validated 5,555 technological assistance and licensing arrangements. (See Table 13.)

The most recent figures from the Ministry of International Trade and Industry, showing the distribution of direct foreign investment by both nationality and industry, are given in Tables 14 and 15.

261

The United States, not surprisingly, leads with 645 validated investments (64%) amounting in all to $230,484,000 (67%). Switzerland is second, with 92 investments totalling $34,404,000, and is followed by the United Kingdom, Canada, the Netherlands, Saudi Arabia-Kuwait, and West Germany, in that order.

As may be seen in Table 15, the machinery industry received the largest number of direct foreign investments (379) and is followed closely by the commerce and service industries (350). Chemical industries account for 188 investments; metal industries, 54; and petroleum industries, 46. So far as amount of investment is concerned, the petroleum industry comes first with $94,376,000; chemical industries, second ($86,855,000); and machinery industries, third ($81,360,000). Commerce and trade and service industries account for only $14 million; thus their share of validated foreign investment is comparatively small.

Table 11, which shows the shareholding percentage in all companies in which foreigners have made equity participation (*gaishikei kaisha*), indicates that 58 companies are wholly owned by foreign investors and in 42 companies foreigners control the majority of issued capital. Joint ventures on a fifty-fifty basis number 117; and in about 300 companies (60% of the total) Japanese shareholders are in the majority.

According to a study I made in 1967, on the basis of data then available, 105 joint venture companies (27.5%) fell into the category of enterprises supported by equity capitalization of between ¥100 million and ¥500 million. The second category (22.5 %) was made up of enterprises with more than ¥10 million but less than ¥50 million; the third (21%), of less than ¥10 million; fourth (9%), between ¥50 and ¥100 million; fifth (8.5%), between ¥1 billion and ¥5 billion; sixth (7%), more than ¥500 million but less than ¥1 billion; and seventh (4.5%), more than ¥5 billion. Compared with foreign as well as Japanese parent companies (many of them the world's great industrial giants), joint ventures fall mostly into middle categories in their respective fields.

The Ministry of International Trade and Industry recently published a report on companies in which foreign investors have equity interest.[60] The report showed that in wholly foreign-owned manufacturing firms in 1966, the net profit to sales ratio went as high as 11.4% and the net profit to total asset ratio was 13.5%. Equivalent ratios in major Japanese companies averaged only 2.5% and 2.6%! However, the averages for all companies in which foreigners have made equity participation (*gaishi-kei kaisha*) were almost identical with those of major Japanese companies. The Ministry explains this apparent peculiarity by pointing out that important foreign petroleum refining companies were operating on a rather low profit margin basis and so lowered the ratios for all *gaishi-kei kaisha* taken as a whole. Except for the refineries, the ratios would have been much higher.

Wholly foreign-owned manufacturing firms also showed up well in 1966 so far as their financial structure was concerned. They had an average current ratio of 166.4%, a fixed ratio of 81.2%, and a debt/equity ratio of 48.5%. Equivalent ratios for major Japanese companies were 106.3%, 199.8%, and 23.3%, while for *gaishi-kei kaisha* as a whole they were 102.2%, 182.8%, and 25.5%.

One important factor is the heavy reliance placed by companies that are wholly or partially owned by foreign investors upon the internal fund reserve generated from their profitable operation for equipment investment. In 1966, wholly Japanese-owned companies invested ¥6,526 billion in plants and equipment, of which 72. 5% was derived from their internal fund reserve and the remaining 27.5% largely from bank-borrowed funds. By contrast, wholly or partly foreign-owned companies invested ¥120.5 billion in plants and equipment, of which 74% was supplied from the internal fund reserve, 20.5% from the issuance of new shares, and only 5.6% from bank-borrowed money.

Another factor that appears to have impressed the Ministry is the emphasis put by *gaishi-kei kaisha* on quality control and on public relations and advertising activities. The Ministry explains that many such companies are market-oriented to a higher degree than their Japanese competitors and that instead of relying on sales of low-priced products they make their appeal to consumers by conveying an image of both a high-price and a high-quality.

On the subject of foreign exploitation and domination of Japanese industry, some interesting figures are to be found in a book published in 1967 by Mr. Fujio Yoshida, a learned and distinguished officer of the Ministry of Finance.[61] The reader is referred to Table 17, which demonstrates that the weight of foreign investment to aid foreign subsidiaries and branches operating within Japan has never exceeded 0.5% of the total domestic fund supply for all wholly Japanese-owned industries. Further, although Japanese business relies heavily on loan financing, the amounts of loans secured from foreign sources have always been less than 11% of amounts borrowed from domestic banking circles. On the basis of such figures, I would say that Japan has been over-cowardly in seizing opportunities abroad to secure foreign investment that she might have used effectively in her domestic economic and social development. She is, in other words, under rather than overfinanced because of, in my opinion, her needless "foreign-investment phobia."

I should now like to consider in detail certain problems that have arisen in connection with Yamatake-Honeywell, a unique example of a joint venture company operating in Japan. (A "case history" of Yamatake-Honeywell Company Limited, which I prepared and published in 1967, is presented in condensed form at the end of this chapter.) One of the factors that makes Yamatake-Honeywell so well worth studying is the length and cordiality of the relationship between the two partners.

It goes back to the reign of Emperor Meiji, when Yamatake first began importing products manufactured by the Brown Instruments Company. Later, Yamatake and Brown formed a joint venture for domestic production of these previously imported products—a joint venture that survived not only the cataclysmic war between the two countries of origin but also the war-time amalgamation of Brown into the Minneapolis Honeywell Regulator Company. The pre-war association that had been so mutually beneficial was revived after the war, but this time on an expanded basis, with world-wide markets in view. The history of Yamatake-Honeywell is rather like a miniature history of Japanese industrialization, where the mind of the East is wedded to the skill of the West—to the mutual benefit of both.

A large part of my study is devoted to the changes that have occurred in the working relationship between the two partners in the fifteen year post-war period, for it was during this period that sweeping changes occurred in the economic environment of the two parent companies and so, inevitably, in that of their child. The questions I wanted to answer were how management of the three companies reacted to these detrimental changes, what impact the changes had on management, and what changes were required in the legal framework of the joint working-arrangements.

Another question to which I tried to suggest answers in making my study arises from one of the basic attributes of a joint venture. Unlike a corporate merger or a consolidation, a joint venture has often been compared to a marriage in which the personalities of the two partners remain distinct. Differences in management philosophy and method may continue to exist even after a happy corporate marriage. However, as with any long-standing and successful union, the contracting parties must learn to live with and respect such differences (should any exist) and also to foster a wholly new relationship in which the union may develop and grow. A relationship of this kind is difficult to establish in a short space of time, even between well-meaning partners who enter into their joint venture at the very beginning with confidence and trust. I wanted to determine precisely what occurred in the course of the long and fruitful relationship between Yamatake and Honeywell. I believe that the reader of the "case history" will find material to help him answer this all-important question.

Yamatake's corporate course of action has, it must be noted, followed the mainstream of Japanese economic life only up to a point. A large number of major companies were established during what has been called the "take-off" period of Japanese industry with the cooperation of foreign funds and technology. Among them may be mentioned Mitsubishi Petroleum, Sumitomo, Yokohama Rubber, Nihon Sheet Glass, Sumitomo Electric, Fuji Electric, Nihon Electric, Toshiba, Toyo Aluminum, Toyo Carrier,

Nihon National Cash Register, and Toyo Otis Elevators. Instrumental to the introduction of advanced Western technology to Japanese industry in its formative stage, many of these companies began operations—like Yamatake—as importers of advanced Western products and only later became domestic makers of such products. Then their relationship with their foreign partners was abruptly curtailed by the war, and as a result their reliance on overseas capital and technology after the war ended has been greatly reduced. Most of these companies went independent and self-supporting and succeeded in building up their own strength, technological and otherwise, during the post-war period.

Some, however, like Nihon Petroleum Refinery (Caltex) and Nihon Light Metal (ALCAN) as well as Yamatake, returned to their foreign partners, reviving and increasing capital and technological tie-ups, as soon as post-war conditions permitted. There were several reasons for such speedy renewal of foreign alliances One basic factor was that despite hostilities between the two governments, the former pre-war partners continued to experience mutual confidence and trust. Once the war ended, the Japanese partners were sufficiently open-minded about international cooperation and sufficiently free from the "foreign-domination phobia" to desire to resume relations with former friends. A third factor is that the Japanese partners found it difficult, if not impossible, to resume operations without foreign help. For one thing, there existed a wide gap in technology that was hard to overcome by purely domestic efforts; at the same time, the Japanese economy was desperately in need of that technology for the speedy reconstruction of major and basic industries like steel, aluminum, and petroleum. There was also the further factor that many Japanese businesses after the war were desperately in need of foreign funds and other foreign contacts in order to survive. Both the Japanese government and the American occupying authorities recognized, and acted upon, the cogency of these arguments.

Japanese partners in an international joint venture complain often that their foreign partners place too much emphasis on the details of contractual arrangements to serve as a basis for the establishment and management of a joint venture, while at the same time tending to place too little reliance on the establishment of mutual confidence and trust between the partners. It is that which the Japanese would emphasize as against the Western passion for legalistic detail. I think both parties to this controversy err when they go to extremes.

It is true that an agreement is the product of a consensus between human partners and that it must be administered by those partners in their joint business efforts; if one of them, then, becomes so obsessed by legalities that he altogether neglects the human aspect of the relationship, the agreement becomes nothing but dead letters on sheets of heavy paper. There is another side to the picture, however. As the responsible manager of an enterprise in a continuously changing environment, the negotiator and administrator of the agreement must have some concrete terms upon which he can rely to protect the interests of the company he represents. A contractual arrangement offers such terms. By means of it, the manager may gauge whether the joint venture is developing in the direction originally envisioned by the corporate parents. If the venture appears to be going in the wrong direction, he must have the means at hand by which to change its course. If he is too late, if things have already gone wrong, he must be able to minimize the damage to the parent company whose representative he is.

It is extremely difficult, however, to draw up a written contract in which parties to a joint venture agree expressly to provide for all foreseeable contingencies of the kind I have mentioned; and the difficulty of finding an effective and workable solution to urgent problems becomes even greater, of course, at a time of corporate crisis. However careful or prudent the negotiator may be, he is, after all, only human: his ability to foresee large-scale environmental changes and to provide for ways of coping with them is limited. Right after the war neither Yamatake nor Honeywell could have foreseen the problem that faces them today: how they may best cooperate in a division of labor in world-wide business operations. Thus, although the formality and rigidity of the original contract may serve the immediate needs of the partners, unless they permit and encourage a warm human feeling of confidence to develop between them and unless they provide for a flexible and friendly mechanism to adjust the contract to meet unforeseeable contingencies, the contract itself becomes a hindrance rather than a help to the implementation of its provisions.

With Yamatake-Honeywell, the initial agreement for the establishment of a joint venture and the granting of technological licenses (originally rather strict and formal) has been amended several times. Each change has reflected the changing requirements between the partners in meeting challenges resulting from the growth of the joint venture and from alterations in environmental conditions in both the United States and Japan. It should be borne in mind that Yamatake-Honeywell has been able to effect contractual revisions and to implement them smoothly and easily because of a long relationship characterized by mutual trust.

It was in 1964 that the working arrangement between Honeywell and Yamatake was drastically amended to permit development on a broader horizon and with a wider perspective. As a result, a basic scheme for division of labor in the exploration of business opportunities on a world-wide scale had to be established. Such a readjustment is symptomatic of the changing environment that has influenced many internationally cooperative enterprises in Japan.

On the one hand, a number of foreign parent companies of local joint ventures (including Honeywell) have begun moving toward world-wide status, while on the other a number of Japanese enterprises have been developing an unprecedented skill and strength which makes them far more useful to foreign world enterprises. To continue with our "classic" example, Yamatake-Honeywell took advantage not only of the phenomenal growth of the national economy but also of its own internal growth, managerial and otherwise, and of the strong bonds of mutual confidence between the two partners, to successfully meet the challenge posed by the question of a division of labor on a world-wide scale.

This present trend toward internationalization perplexes many

Japanese in both business and government who had always regarded the joint venture as an instrument for the acquisition of foreign technology and established brand names. Their chief motive, in other words, in establishing foreign relations was to strengthen their own position in the domestic market. An example is the many costly hours of skilled labor they have expended in converting blueprint measurements from inches to centimeters. Now, with the trend toward exportation, in cooperation with foreign partners, to overseas markets, instead of mere importation for domestic markets, blueprints have to be reconverted from centimeters to inches. This, in turn, requires conversion of plant measurement systems—which can be an extremely costly affair. When Mitsubishi entered upon a new division of labor with the Caterpillar Tractor Company on the world market, it had to pay over ¥10 billion (50 percent of shares) to build new plants and construct new equipment. Their initial investment being so large, it took more than five years before Caterpillar-Mitsubishi began to show a profit. Japanese business tends to dismiss the Caterpillar-Mitsubishi experience as being unsuitable for smaller enterprises that can afford neither so tremendous an initial investment nor so long a wait before showing profit, but it seems to me that with the present trend toward internationalization, Mitsubishi has set a highly commendable example which I hope more Japanese enterprises will follow.

There is a hitch, however. A Japanese entrepreneur can, if he has sufficient money available, effect necessary changes in measurement and production facilities, but there is one thing he cannot buy—the international posture and (if I may use the phrase) the international-mindedness of the foreign businessman. His long isolation makes for provincialism: he is all too prone to neglect the tremendous opportunities now offered by the world market. That is why Yamatake and Mitsubishi constitute so hopeful an example for other Japanese enterprises: they have succeeded in reorienting the mental pattern of their employees so as to take advantage of the ever-growing opportunities that await beyond the borders of our small islands.

YAMATAKE-HONEYWELL CO., LTD.

A Case-Study of a Japanese American Joint Venture

INTRODUCTORY NOTE: The study that follows was prepared by the author in 1966 for use in business and law school class discussions; it could not, of course, have been made without the help and understanding of the company management. A study of this kind is not intended to indicate either correct or incorrect handling of administrative problems; the history of Yamatake-Honeywell, however, has points of considerable interest for anyone who has attempted, or who hopes to attempt, to achieve cooperation between international partners in a business venture. The study was originally published in the author's *Nihon-no Goben-Kaisha* ("Joint Ventures in Japan"), and he takes this opportunity to express his thanks to the original publishers, Toyo Keizai, who have very kindly granted him permission to translate the material that follows.

1. BACKGROUND

Yamatake Shokai (a trading company) was founded in Tokyo in 1906 by the late Takehiko Yamaguchi to import machine tools, ball-bearings, and oxyacetylene welding machines. Later the company began to produce domestically some of the hitherto imported machine tools. Then, during the First World War, Mr. Yamaguchi went to the United States, where he obtained exclusive rights to import the high-quality instruments manufactured by the Brown Instruments Company. After the war was over, responding in part to a governmental drive for the rationalization of industry, Yamatake Shokai began to shift its domestic production from machine tools to industrial instruments. At the same time, the company changed its status from a private proprietorship to a stock corporation.

In 1933, Yamatake Shokai opened a new factory to assemble parts imported from Brown and later concluded a licensing contract with Brown to manufacture and sell the latter's products in Japan, establishing a royalty rate of 15% on sales of the licensed products. In 1939, Yamatake Shokai, having determined to make its instrument division independent, founded a new firm for the purpose called the Nihon Brown Instruments Company. The son of the founder of Yamatake Shokai, Mr. Toshihiko Yamaguchi, became president of the new company. (Mr. Yamaguchi is today president of Yamatake-Honeywell.) In 1941, with the imminent threat of war, Nihon Brown changed its name to Yamatake Kogyo, at the same time incorporating the sales division into a separate company.

During the war, Yamatake continued to utilize technology licensed by Brown but was of course unable to make payment for it. "Because of our belief," says Mr. Yamaguchi, "that there was never a war between our two partner companies, we kept the balance of our accounts straight. Throughout the war, we maintained an account in our balance sheets that credited Brown for their account-receivable royalties."

During the war, Brown was amalgamated into Minneapolis Honeywell Regulator Company, which had been founded in 1885 as a Delaware corporation.

270

After the war ended, a vice-president of Honeywell visited Japan to investigate the market for industrial instrument products. It was at this time that he met the founder of Yamatake (then still alive) and his son, with whom he reached the basic understanding that Honeywell would conclude a business agreement with Yamatake, taking up the partnership formerly held by Brown.

In 1949, Yamatake Kogyo, which had suffered great damage through enemy bombing, was dissolved under the provisions of the Enterprise Reconstruction and Reorganization Law, and the liquidated assets of the old company were reorganized into a new company, Yamatake Instruments. The equity capital of the new company was ¥4 million, which meant a 90% capital reduction. That same year, the United States Steel Industry Delegation was sent to Japan to assist in the reconstruction of the Japanese economy. As a result, innovative technologies for automatic production control were introduced into industry and the demand for process control equipment was greatly expanded. Further, Japanese oil refineries on the Pacific coast were reopened with the cooperation of such Western companies as Standard Vacuum Oil and Shell; this also accelerated the demand for automatic process control equipment. In this early post-war period, Yamatake, supplying Honeywell products, captured nearly a third of the Japanese market.

After the conclusion of the San Francisco Peace Treaty in 1951, a new feeling of confidence and equality grew up between Japanese and American businessmen. Mr. Yamaguchi, accordingly, went to the United States to open negotiations with Honeywell, his intention being to establish with them the kind of relationship his company had previously maintained with Brown and as a result to become the leader of the Japanese process control equipment industry.

Honeywell Inc. (the name the Minneapolis Honeywell Regulator Company adopted in 1964) employs some fifty thousand people and in 1964 ranked eighty-ninth on *Fortune*'s list of the five hundred largest American firms. It is at present the world's foremost manufacturer of automatic process-control instruments, with a diversified line that includes industrial process-control products and systems, regulators, air conditioning products and systems, micro-switches, electronics and EDP products and systems, automatic aviation instruments, and even photographic products. The number of major products that it manufactures totals more than thirteen thousand. It has seven regional headquarters, subsidiaries and affiliated companies in 19 countries, distributors in 64 countries, 183 sales and service centers, and more than a dozen factories throughout the world.

Inasmuch as its basic policy is to go into overseas markets with wholly-owned subsidiaries, the arrangements it has concluded with Yamatake (as well as with other Japanese companies) are exceptional. When Mr. Yamaguchi opened negotiations with Honeywell, he met with no basic objections to his proposals, although there were minor difficulties to be ironed out. Honeywell, for instance, preferred participation in Yamatake's equity to simple extension of technological assistance, feeling that through equity ownership it could more effectively influence management. Honeywell also expressed uncertainty about the future of the Japanese market and about the future of Yamatake as well should the Yamaguchi family withdraw from management, for it was the family that had won the company's trust. Insofar as equity ownership was concerned, Mr. Yamaguchi strongly advocated a fifty-fifty division in the belief that the two contracting parties should share equal responsibility. Negotiations were concluded on April 30, 1952. (Yamatake adopted the name Yamatake-Honeywell in 1956.)

Mr. E.W. Spencer has overall responsibility for Honeywell's world-wide operations as head of its International Division, and Mr. C. B. Meech represents the company's interests in the Far East. He is a vice-president of Honeywell and also of Yamatake-Honeywell, and he is in charge of Honeywell's relations with Japanese firms other than Yamatake-Honeywell. It has licensing arrangements, for example, with Nihon Electric for EDP products and systems, with an aviation instrument maker for automatic piloting-control products and systems, and with a camera maker for photographic products. All such arrangements were made with the prior consent of Honeywell's primary contractor in Japan, Yamatake-Honeywell.

2. ORIGINAL CONDITIONS FOR THE JOINT VENTURE AND LATER MODIFICATIONS
A) The agreement for technological assistance and business cooperation that was concluded between Yamatake and Honeywell in April, 1952, contained the following provisions:

1. *Operational Plan.* In the beginning, Yamatake would concern itself primarily with importing and selling Honeywell's finished products and also with assembling and selling imported parts. Yamatake was also to be prepared to produce licensed products as soon as practicable.

2. *Scope of Licensed Products and Technologies.* These were to include all technological information necessary to the manufacture, assembly, and sale of instruments for industrial process control and valves which was then possessed by Honeywell or which might be developed during the term of the agreement by either Honeywell itself or companies under its control. The parties agreed that discussions would be held to negotiate and determine which new Honeywell items should be added to the product lines licensed to Yamatake. Technological information concerning former Brown products would also be made available by Honeywell to Yamatake on a continuing basis.

3. *Technological Assistance.* In granting Yamatake a license to manufacture and sell the agreed products in Japan, Honeywell also undertook to furnish Yamatake with the necessary technological and operational information and to offer suggestions relative to the various phases of the operation from design to sale. Yamatake was also granted a non-exclusive right to use trademarks that were then possessed by Honeywell or that might be acquired during the term of the agreement (including those of Brown).

4. *Payment for Imported Products and Parts.* Price of parts was to be the ex-plant cost (determined by Honeywell) plus an amount to be calculated by the application of a certain fixed rate; price of finished products was to be Honeywell's state-side list price minus an amount to be calculated by the application of a certain fixed rate. All payments were to be made in dollars within sixty days of receipt of order by Honeywell.

5. *Payment of Technological Assistance Fee.* Honeywell had hoped for a continuation of the 15% rate that had been established before the War with Brown, but to this proposal Yamatake offered a number of objections, including its own limited financial resources and governmental objections to remitting yen deposits in dollars. The final agreement provided for:
   a) Royalty rate: 12%;
   b) Basis of Calculation: Sales price of licensed products manufactured and sold by Yamatake minus prices paid for imported products and parts and expenses of maintenance, repair, and service;
   c) Payback: For the purpose of extending assistance to Yamatake, Honeywell agreed to pay back 3/12 of royalties accrued during the first six-month period, 2/12 during the second, and 1/12 during the third six months after the coming into force of the contract;
   d) Settlement of Accounts Payable: Should remittance of dollars be found to

be impossible, an equivalent amount in yen was to be deposited to Honeywell's account in the Tokyo branch of the First National City Bank.

6. *Honeywell's Equity and Management Participation.* Yamatake was to double the size of its paid-up capital from ¥12 million to ¥24 million, and the right to subscribe for all the new shares(240,000 shares of common stock at a ¥50 par value) was granted to Honeywell. Yamatake's existing shareholders waived all rights to these shares. The fifty-fifty ratio was fixed for the future by a provision in the Technological Assistance Agreement that President Yamaguchi must give his consent to any change in share-holding percentages and also by a provision in Yamatake's Articles of Incorporation that existing shareholders would be entitled to subscribe for new shares in future capital increases in proportion to number of shares held at the time of the increase. (After five capital increases, the present equity capital of Yamatake-Honeywell is ¥1,260 million. The largest single stock-holder is Honeywell, which holds one half of all existing shares; of 4911 Japanese stockholders, Mr. Yamaguchi holds the largest single part—5.3% representing 1,338,300 shares.) In connection with its capital investment, Honeywell requested that two directors to represent its interests be appointed to the Yamatake board; Yamatake consented to this proposal. (At present there are sixteen members of the Yamatake-Honeywell, including the president, two vice-presidents, the managing director, ten directors—of whom six are full-time and four are non-working, a statutory auditor, and an auditor. Honeywell's representatives are three: the vice-president, Mr. Meech; the head of the International Division, Mr. Spencer; and a vice-president of the First National City Bank. The latter two are non-working directors.)

7. *Other Yamatake Obligations.* Yamatake also undertook to:

a) Maintain an embargo on export of licensed products to Communist countries, as prescribed by the United States Department of State;

b) Do its best to build and maintain equipment and facilities adequate for the production, sales, maintenance, repair, service, testing, coordination, and advertisement of the licensed products;

c) Keep accurate sales records and prepare financial reports subject to inspection by Honeywell;

d) Cooperate with Honeywell in inspections of factories, assets, and records;

e) Refrain from disclosing information relative to licensed products;

f) Engage with Honeywell in a mutual obligation to notify the other should either party discover an infringement of rights, under the terms of the contract, by a third party; and

g) Refrain from reassigning any rights or interests under the agreement.

8. *Exchange of Information.* Both parties agreed to exchange information on all matters concerning the licensed products. Should Yamatake make improvements on any of the products, it undertook to apply for local patents and to grant a non-exclusive license to Honeywell in connection therewith. This right was to remain valid for the life of the patent, regardless of the expiration of the technological assistance agreement. Honeywell was also to enjoy a non-exclusive right to use trademarks developed by Yamatake and registered in Japan in connection with the licensed products.

9. *Term of Contract.* It was agreed that the term of the technological assistance should be six years, from April 1, 1952, to March 1, 1958. It was further agreed that on expiration of the agreement, it could be renewed every other year by mutual consent. Honeywell had the right to revoke the agreement without prior notice in the event that Yamatake violated contractual obligations, defaulted in payment,

or became bankrupt or insolvent. Should the agreement be revoked, all rights conferred on Yamatake reverted to Honeywell.

10. *Applicable Law.* In the settlement of any disputes between the parties to the contract, laws of the State of Minnesota were to be applied.

B) After recommendations by the Japanese government, the original agreement was modified in a second contract dated December 2, 1952, which was validated on December 18. The two parties agreed that the contract became effective retroactively as of April 1, 1952. The changes concerned the rate of royalty and the dates of payment. It was agreed that a 9 % royalty rate should be adopted for the first six-month period, to be followed by a rate of 10 %. Value of imported products and parts and taxes to be paid by Honeywell to the Japanese government were to be deducted from royalty calculations. Due dates for royalty payments were set slightly back. In the original agreement, for example, royalties for the period between January and March were due to be paid on June 1. This was now changed to July. (On March 31, 1960, in view of the tightness of working capital, Yamatake asked Honeywell for a further extension of the period for remission. With Honeywell's consent, January-to-March royalties were now not due to be paid until October, and the other three-month periods were granted comparable delays. This revision was validated by the Japanese government on June 2, 1960.)

C) On March 1, 1956, before the expiration of the original agreement as revised, the two parties signed a third version of the Technological Assistance Agreement and further expanded the scope of their cooperation. With this new contract (officially validated on August 15, 1957) the two agreed to the following revisions:

1. *Enlargement of Scope of Licensed Products and Technology.* Eleven new items in the industrial process control field, five in the air-conditioning field, and five in the micro-switch field were added to the list of licensed products. (Yamatake was reluctant to go into air-conditioning, as Yamatake-Honeywell had had no experience in that field, and in fact at the time little was known about it in Japan, but Honeywell was very insistent, and Yamatake finally agreed.)

2. *Reduction of Royalty Rate.* As volume of sales, and consequent royalty, increased, Honeywell agreed to a reduction from 10 % to 8 % and also to further delays in payment dates.

3. *Extension of Contract Term.* Yamatake and Honeywell agreed on an extension of the contract term to March 1, 1966, but the Japanese government suggested March 31, 1964, which latter date was adopted.

3. DEVELOPMENT OF A JOINT WORKING RELATIONSHIP

A) During the depression of 1962/3, Yamatake-Honeywell suffered reverses along with other Japanese firms. At the March, 1963, accounting period, sales dropped ¥560 million as compared with the previous six months' period. The profit-and-loss statement showed a loss of ¥55 million, and payment of dividends was suspended. Mr. E. W. Spencer, then serving in Japan as a vice-president of Yamatake-Honeywell, largely in an advisory capacity, now offered concrete proposals for a reorganization of the company. With the approval of the president and the other directors, he assumed full responsibility for carrying out these reforms, which the rank-and-file of the company considered over-drastic. However, they were effective. The profit-and-loss statement of September, 1963, showed a net profit of ¥33 million; and that of March, 1965, one of ¥224 million. Dividends of 8 % were paid out for the period ending March, 1964, and were increased to 10 % the following year.

B) In January, 1964, on the eve of the expiration of the existing agreement between Honeywell and Yamatake, the two parties drew up a revised contract, called "The Know-how and Industrial Property Licensing Agreement," the basic principles of

which may be summarized as follows:
1. Royalty rate was further reduced to 5%.
2. The new agreement was to remain in effect until March 31, 1974.
3. To increase the range of licensed products and technologies, a more general and comprehensive definition was adopted. The fairly restrictive definition previously in use provided that unless the particular items were listed in the defining provision of the contract, the license thereto was considered non-existent. The new contract provided that licensed products would include the following categories of Honeywell products:

a) All industrial process control products and systems; scientific measurement apparatus manufactured and sold at the time of the contract revision by the industrial products group division and their affiliated companies;

b) Air-conditioning systems, control systems, fire alarm systems, etc., manufactured and sold by the controls group divisions of Honeywell and their affiliated companies;

c) Micro-switch products manufactured and sold by the micro-switch division of Honeywell and affiliated companies;

d) Photographic products manufactured and sold by the Denvor Division of Honeywell and affiliated companies;

e) Improvements, applications, modifications, or replacements of licensed products which might be manufactured and sold by Honeywell, Honeywell's affiliates, or Yamatake during the term of the agreement; and

f) Other products that might be added to the list of licensed products by future revisions of the agreement.

4. Obsolete products and parts, manufacture and sale of which had been suspended by Honeywell and its affiliates before April 1, 1964, were dropped from the list of licensed products.
5. To facilitate exchange of information on new products even while in a developmental stage and to avoid duplication of effort in research and development, a joint committee was established.
6. Should Yamatake-Honeywell develop new technologies independent of licensed products, the company was now obliged to inform Honeywell of such developments and to grant Honeywell a non-exclusive license, if requested, for the commercial production thereof. However, the two parties agreed to negotiate conditions should such an exchange of information become necessary. Further, it was agreed that Honeywell might subcontract Yamatake to design and develop certain Honeywell products on a paid basis.
7. Provisions in previous agreements now considered obsolete were to be deleted, such as:

a) Yamatake's obligation to assure Honeywell that it would make reasonable efforts to guarantee sale, manufacture, repair, and service of licensed products;

b) The obligation to build and maintain satisfactory production facilities;

c) The guaranty of Honeywell's share-ownership in Yamatake; and

d) The guaranty that directors representing Honeywell's interests would be appointed to the Yamatake board.

8. Yamatake-Honeywell, rather than Honeywell, would now be responsible for the training of Yamatake personnel.

Discussions with government authorities resulted in two amendments that were agreed to by the contracting parties in August, 1964:

a) The term of the contract was shortened from ten to five years.

b) The provision recognizing Honeywell's right to utilize Yamatake's improvements even after expiration of the agreement between the two parties was deleted. Government validation of the amended revision was granted on August 20, 1964. The parties agreed that the contract should take effect retroactively as of April 1, 1964.

C) Some of the problems facing Yamatake-Honeywell at present may be briefly summarized as follows:

1. In the field of process controls, the company is far ahead of its domestic competitors, but in such areas as industrial instruments, valves, and micro-switches, it is facing tough competition from Yokokawa Electric-Foxborough, Hokushin Electric-Fisher and Porter, and Takeishi Electric. Further, new marketing approaches to unexplored fields, such as foods, pharmaceuticals and government and public works, are under serious consideration and study.

2. As a result of its experience during the depression, the company felt the need for increased stability of management by product diversification. Yamatake-Honeywell's reliance for the expansion of its product lines upon the introduction of new products and technologies by Honeywell has been severely criticized by some of the younger engineers as showing a lack of independence. They have expressed the hope that the company will channel its research and development toward independent technologies. The recent production of the "VSI series" has somewhat allayed criticism of this sort. At the same time, much is still hoped for from the proposed coordination scheme between Honeywell and Yamatake-Honeywell to avoid duplication of effort in research and development and to achieve an effective international division of labor.

3. Volume of export remains small. Including indirect export through outside trading companies, percentage of export to total sales is not more than 20%. Yamatake-Honeywell believes that, for the time being at least, it is more economical and efficient to utilize the already existing world-wide sales network of Honeywell than to try to develop new self-owned and independent distribution systems abroad.

4. Corporate development has been so rapid that the present management organization is, according to some of the company's managers, no longer satisfactory. In the course of re-examining existing set-ups, they have laid particular emphasis on the following needs:

a) That for more direct communication among the various divisions of the two companies in their desire for a more effective exchange of technological information;

b) That for more efficient administration of salesmen and service engineers, who at present find themselves in a difficult position among several divisional chains of command and between the field and central authorities in a growing organization; and

c) That for increased top-level coordination of market research, public relations, manufacturing, and sales activities, which frequently are carried out in contradictory fashion on the authority of an independent division.

5. Inasmuch as the equity ownership of the company is divided among a great number of Japanese shareholders, caution is essential in selecting the proper time for increase of capital; balance must be kept between the shareholders' demand for payment of dividends and the corporate demand for the accumulation of retained earnings.

6. Yamatake-Honeywell employs a total of 2,030 people, including 1,419 office personnel and 611 factory workers. Their average monthly salary is ¥40,000; their average age is 28.4 years; and they have been with the company for an average of

6.1 years. These employees belonged to a closed shop enterprise union which is an affiliate of All Japan Metal Workers Union.

D) Production and sales figures for Yamatake-Honeywell during the period between April, 1964, and March, 1965 (the 31st and 32nd accounting periods), were (in millions of yen):

	Production	Sales
Industrial instruments	2,782	3,617
Valves	1,328	1,314
Micro-switches	569	721
Control equipment	1,471	2,832
Photographic products	—	676
TOTAL	6,149	9,159

Both Japanese and American managers of Yamatake-Honeywell are satisfied with the results of their international joint venture. Mr. Meech concludes: "In short, the success of our business depends upon the superiority of our technology as compared with our Japanese and American competitors. I am confident in this because I think that both Honeywell and Yamatake-Honeywell have a great future technical-growth potentiality."

14 Management Differences

That there are differences between American and Japanese ways of managing business no one in either country would deny. It is precisely what accounts for those differences that is not quite so obvious. Some economists feel that the basic cause is a kind of managerial gap resulting from the continuing backwardness of Japanese management. If that is true, bridging the gap is a comparatively easy task: all that Japanese management has to do is imitate American management, profiting by the experience of people who have achieved a higher degree of managerial progress.

But not all economists are agreed that the basic cause is quite so simple. Some are convinced that differences in managerial practices result from environmental differences that have compelled businessmen in the two countries to adopt special, and sometimes apparently incompatible, ways of thinking and acting. If these economists are right, then the problem is a far more complicated one. It is possible to bridge a gap; it is not possible to change history.

For one thing, measurements commonly used to evaluate managerial efficiency, such as the two ratios of net profit to sales and net profit to total assets, represent only those aspects of corporate output that can be translated into tangible monetary values. But business, in my opinion, is more than that. It is a kind of combustion engine, into which we put men and materials, funds and technologies, and out of which we want to ensure that we get the maximum amount of energy. Thus, certain aspects of the engine's output—such as loyalty of the company's employees—are not measurable by monetary standards but only by the subjective value judgment of those who determine the corporate will. A man whose sole interest is the optimization of profit will find that such subjective judgments may coincide with the objective ones that are measurable in terms of money. However, an opinion survey made by the Committee for Economic Development in 1964[62] suggests a different conclusion. In fact, the great majority of top managers in Japan who attempt to evaluate thoughtfully the results of managerial decision are of the opinion that their corporate activities should contribute first to the satisfaction of their employees and second to the "social and economic betterment of the greater company of Japan." If top managers act on this belief, it is evident that traditional methods of measuring results must fail to evaluate the real amount of energy output.

In the second place, if management thinking is preconditioned by environmental factors, domestic as well as foreign, and if corporate output, both tangible and intangible, is to be evaluated in its entirety, then more attention must obviously be paid to the relationship between the enterprise and the environment in which it exists and also to the effect that that relationship exerts on corporate operations and achievements.

Third, a study in depth must be made—both in Japan and the United States—of the actual intentions and motivations of managers and also of the interrelations between business and environment in Japan and in the United States and their effect on respective management.

Only after we have completed such investigations will we be in a position to compare total managerial efficiency in Japan and the United States while taking into account differences in human values and motivation as well as in environmental reactions. Recently I was involved in just such a project. With the kind cooperation of the Japanese Committee for Economic Development, a group of young Japanese executives and I attempted to determine, in line with the points I made above, exactly how Japanese management compares in efficiency with American management. So far, in our discussions, we have made comprehensive comparisons between Japanese and American managers; we have attempted to isolate the chief characteristics of Japanese management, and we have tried to relate those characteristics to the environmental factors that created them.[63]

At the same time, also with the cooperation of the Committee for Economic Development, we undertook an awareness survey of Japanese corporate managers, asking them to answer such questions as the following:

1. To what extent do you feel you are aware of the impact of environmental change, both domestic and foreign, on your enterprise?

2. What positive steps are you taking to cope with such changes?

3. What do you feel your corporate strength to be when you are compelled to compete with gigantic foreign enterprises?

Out of 1,547 questionnaires mailed to company managers, 713 were filled out and returned to us.[64] At the moment of writing, we are still engaged in analyzing the results. However, as will be seen in the course of this chapter, some interesting points have already appeared that may contribute substantially to this question of how Japanese managers compare in efficiency with American managers. Obviously, a similar survey ought to be made in the United States; comparative results would, we feel, be extremely useful; but lacking that as yet, the survey we have conducted in Japan is not without points of particular interest.

To begin at the top, presidents of Japanese companies and chairmen of the board belong mostly to an age group that is between 62 and 66. They are about ten years older than their American counterparts, and once they assume top management positions they are likely to retain them longer than top managers in the United States: average length of service of a corporate president in Japan is 13.4 years, in the United States it is 5.7 years. Lack of a comprehensive program guaranteeing income on retirement in

Japan as compared with the United States is generally considered a highly relevant factor in the differing terms of service in the two countries. Further, the Japanese manager is paid a great deal less than his American colleague. In Japan, few top executives receive an annual salary exceeding $30,000; in America, presidents of leading enterprises are paid $150,000 a year or more.

There are a number of factors peculiar to Japanese management that may seem strange to the American. For one thing, it must be remembered that since positions on the board are often awarded to senior officers because of their long and successful service within the life-time employment system, a rounded personality tends to be more highly regarded than an aggressive one and is more likely to win out in the competition for top management positions.

Further, all corporate officers are members of the board in Japan, and the total amount of their remuneration is always pre-determined by the articles of incorporation of the company or by resolutions made at general meetings of shareholders. Thus, the amount that every board member (including the president) will receive in both salary and bonus is determined in advance, and the maintenance of corporate harmony is considered to be more important in determining these figures than the contribution that each particular individual is likely to make.

Since a directorship is seen as a kind of final reward, the size of the board in Japan tends to become very large, averaging 14.4 members among leading enterprises. Many such board members are paid salaries little larger than those received by department heads, which in the Japanese hierarchy is the rank just below that of director. According to available data, promotion to membership on the board entails only about a ten percent increase in salary. The amount received by the president is likely to be only about three times that paid to a department head without the rank of director.

It goes without saying that the larger the board the less effective it is at fulfilling its chief function: that of corporate decision-making. Therefore, in Japan, actual authority tends to be delegated to a few top executive officers, leaving the other members of the board with merely nominal functions to perform. This weakening of authority is most sharply felt in the case of the company auditor, an honorary position usually granted to a director just before his retirement. As a consequence, essential details of proper auditing have often been neglected, and corporate accounts have been mis-represented—although not wilfully—to shareholders. Because of this kind of misrepresentation, shareholders have been surprised by sudden and unexpected bankruptcies during the recent period in which the rapid pace of economic growth was temporarily halted. Such bankruptcies have alarmed government as well as business and have resulted in an increasing tendency to make corporate officers more responsible and also to make wider use of certified public accountants and similar professionals.

Top managers in Japan, as everywhere else in the world, are much influenced by the environment in which they have grown to maturity. Consider first the kind of education to which they are exposed. Of children between the ages of six and fifteen, 99.9% receive compulsory education in elementary schools and junior high schools. In 1965, 67.4% of junior high school graduates went on to study in senior high schools, and 24.5% of senior high school graduates continued on to colleges or universities. High schools offer a wide variety of vocational training which is useful to students who plan to look for work immediately after graduation, but colleges and universities generally make no attempt to offer courses of the Harvard Business School kind, aimed at the training of professional managers. Most professors believe that "education" and "professional training" are two quite different things and that the purpose of a university is to develop a rounded personality while providing the student with a general academic background. They believe that it is not their responsibility but rather that of the employer to offer graduates specialized professional training. In other words, it is the responsibility of the Japanese university to prepare the material that the future employer may then mold as he chooses.

This function of the university has satisfied Japanese business so long as it has been not only willing but eager to maintain the *status quo* in a relatively isolated environment. Competing companies were expected to know their place within the establishment, while within the companies themselves the discipline necessary to maintain orderly development was ensured by Japan's "seniority-conscious life-time employment system" and internal energy for orderly growth was supplied by the national emphasis on group loyalty. Thus, Japanese business, with its strong desire for harmony, has generally preferred the so-called amateur managers to aggressive professionals. Further, it must be borne in mind that in the long run in Japan it is what you know rather than whom you know that will determine how fast and how far your ride up the escalator will be; and at the top, relations between businessmen and bureaucrats help to vitalize a status-oriented system that might otherwise grow dangerously static. These two factors are, in a sense, "built-in mechanisms" to keep Japan's tradition-ridden and paternalistic system from stultification.

The co-author of this book has already sketched in the pre-Meiji background to the growth of Japanese business and has pointed out some of the effects that the caste system, with merchants at the bottom, had on the initial development of a capitalist economy in Japan. In my opinion, the fact that the modernization of Japanese industry was led by government bureaucrats and important financiers and industrialists meant that the lot of the merchant was not remarkably improved. He could sell only what the industrialist supplied to him, and it was the latter who was rewarded for creating something new. Indeed, in a relatively primitive society, the creation of the new is difficult; the selling of it, to eager customers, is easy. More recently, as Japan prepared for war and as she was engaged in the throes of waging it, consumer goods were necessarily reduced to the absolute minimum. Once again, it was a sellers' market, not a buyers' one. I believe that this accounts largely for the fact that even today Japanese product planning is production-oriented rather than market-oriented. The producer believes that he is the best arbiter of what the consumer wants. This production-oriented way of thinking may also—at least, to a certain extent—be responsible for the Japanese method of determining prices of products. Generally, a producer calculates the cost of manufacturing and marketing a product, adds a certain amount for general administrative expenses and of course what he considers a reasonable profit; on the basis of all this he fixes the price at which the product will be offered to the consumer. This custom will no doubt appear strange to market-oriented businessmen who first research how much end-consumers will be willing to pay for the product and who then adjust manufacturing costs in order to meet that price and at the same time make a profit.

There is, nevertheless, severe competition among Japanese enterprises to expand their market share of the particular products or services they offer. So much emphasis, in fact, is placed on ever increasing share-winning that economy of operation that ought to accompany expanded volume tends to be neglected. With the gross national product increasing at the extremely rapid rate of about ten percent a year, Japanese businessmen feel that cost-saving here and there is trivial and even uneconomical because it will likely have a restraining effect on corporate efforts to increase volume of sales, thus consigning the company to maintain its previous share of sales in an expanding market. Little attention, therefore, has been given by Japanese business to control marketing expenses.

Other factors that make up the overall picture of the Japanese market have already been treated earlier. One, of course, is the fact that until recently both individual purchasing power and volume of consumption were both very small. One needs only to compare the gross national product (which is third among the countries of the world) with per capita GNP (which is twentieth). Furthermore, in order to satisfy the relatively small but extremely divergent demands of Japanese consumers, a great number of small retail shops with limited or specialized product lines have been found necessary; and big wholesalers have had to use many sub-distributing agents if they wanted to get their merchandise to the small retailers economically. In 1964, wholesalers accounted for 15% of outlets and retailers for 85%, whereas wholesalers enjoyed 82% of the total volume of sales and retail shops only 18%. According to government statistics, the amount of merchandise traded between wholesalers of various sizes is far greater than that traded between wholesalers and retailers. Even in Japan such a system is considered wasteful, but both manufacturers and distributors feel it is unavoidable so long as consumer purchasing power remains small and buying habits continue unchanged.

Another factor stems from the closed nature of the Japanese society, where everyone is expected to be constantly aware of his relation to everyone else. Let us say that Mr. A., a wholesaler, is a friend of Mr. B., the owner of a retail shop; the friendship may well be an inherited one. Under such conditions, it would be extremely difficult for either Mr. A. or Mr. B. to terminate the relationship—even though that might be beneficial to one or both of them. Further, if either should violate the relationship through behavior considered overselfish by their friends he stands in danger of ostracism and perhaps of losing his business as well. In addition, because Mr. A. and Mr. B. are friends and because Mr. A. and Mr. D. are friends, they enjoy more favorable trade relations than those existing between Mr. A. and Mr. C.; were that not so, someone would have had to lose face—a calamity to be avoided at any cost.

Thus, many Western businessmen criticize Japanese management because it operates by the "rule of exception" rather than by a more comprehensive "general rule." In my opinion, such criticism is all too often justified. It is virtually impossible to standardize marketing procedure; manufacturers often find they cannot maintain retail prices; any sort of standard manual for sales promotion becomes difficult to arrive at if sales have to be tailored to the taste of individual consumers; and systematic training of salesmen is also rendered far more difficult. Even with public relations men and advertising agents, once a choice has been made it is seldom changed even when a change is obviously desirable. Such are some of the inconveniences about which Japanese businessmen complain, but only a few of them have been courageous enough to remove those inconveniences by breaking with tradition.

The financing of Japanese enterprises has also tended to follow a unique pattern, ever since the inception of Japanese capitalism, as has already been pointed out, in early Meiji days. More recently, in the years of economic recovery immediately following the war,

Japanese business relied heavily on debt financing. In a rapidly expanding economy, under strong inflationary pressure, this type of financial management was considered to be less risky than equity financing. The government itself encouraged large investments in plant facilities through liberal extension of city bank loans, backed up by the money-issuing central bank, the Bank of Japan. Whenever a market is capable of absorbing industrial supplies quickly, like dry soil during rain, an increase in volume of sales, with consequent expansion of market sales, has always guaranteed the success of an enterprise.

Japanese businessmen were, naturally, aware of the danger of relying too heavily on bank loans. But there were, or seemed to be, compensations. A loan of ¥100 million today might be worth only ¥50 million tomorrow, thus easing the return of the used money; at the same time, an identical increase in equity capital might simply have entailed future contraction of corporate net worth, making the actual cost of the initial investment very high. "Since everyone else is using borrowed money for business expansion," said the entrepreneurs, "why shouldn't I do the same? If I do not and as a result cannot meet the increased demands of tomorrow's market, my market share may decrease and may be very expensive to regain."

Then, between 1962 and 1965, the pace of Japanese expansion seemed to be—at least temporarily—halted, and many businesses felt a deflationary pressure. For the first time since the war, businessmen realized the importance of maintaining a sound balance of payment and began to appreciate how heavy a burden interest on bank loans can be. However, around 1966, the basic attitude of Japanese business shifted once again to positive expansion. As a result of the progress of trade and capital liberalization programs, many Japanese businesses felt the impact of gigantic overseas international enterprises. To meet this challenge, both business and government agreed that Japanese enterprises had to be increased in both size and scale and that, once again, bank-borrowing was the key. This time, however, they were far more keenly aware of the need to improve managerial efficiency.

Table 16 gives a percentage breakdown of the Japanese corporate asset structure in the ten-year period between 1956 and 1966. As will be seen, the Japanese debt/equity ratio in 1964 fell below the twenty percent level, and since then it has continued to decrease in spite of business's desire to improve the situation. The government's efforts to help, by providing special tax incentives for the maintenance of a better debt/equity ratio, have also met with but little success.

This poor showing, insofar as the debt/equity ratio is concerned, arises from the small amount of earnings Japanese businesses retain on their annual balance sheets, although the size of the equity capital itself in the average Japanese company is by no means smaller than that of a comparable American company. Many enterprises in Japan complain that the profit margin they derive from sales is too thin because of what they believe to be the "excessive price competition" that characterizes the Japanese market. Worthy of note also in this connection is the fact that smooth administration of cash flow is often obstructed by the local practice of allowing an extremely long term for the collection of accounts receivable on negotiable instruments. Depending on the relationship between debtor and creditor, payment often does not become due for a period as long as six to nine months.

However, inasmuch as accounts payable may be offset by accounts receivable, the practice has generally been considered workable within the framework of the Japanese economic society. Delay in expected payment may nevertheless cause a temporary imbalance in the corporate financing program that all too often results in a cash drain situation. The cash-hungry companies go to the banks for short-term loans to meet seasonal payments, thus increasing the percentage of short-term borrowing in their balance sheets. Salaries and dividends are often paid with bank-borrowed funds.

Thus, business expansion for the mere sake of bigness has not only slowed down the total asset turnover rate to less than once a year but it has also increased the financial burden on sales by as much as five to seven percent. This also means that the percentage

287

of financial costs in the added value structure (often as low as 20–30% in Japan because the manufacturer of the finished product tends to rely heavily on raw material processors and subcontracted makers of parts and components) rises to almost 17% in such industries as steel, chemicals, and pulp and paper.

Concomittantly, the corporate structure of many Japanese enterprises grows ever more complicated and a mechanism to control it becomes ever more necessary, making use of experts who have received professional training. The "wise old man" who has been with the firm for thirty years, assisted by his clerical staff equipped with abacuses, may no longer be adequate to the needs of the firm. But Japanese universities, as I have pointed out, prefer to offer a general education to specialized training. As a result, there is a serious shortage of professionally trained accountants and financial managers.

Corporate accounting and financing practices are often developed by "amateur" managers on the basis of their own experience. Such practices, therefore, necessarily differ from one company to another. Since there is no uniformity, the certified public accountant has difficulty to apply any uniform rules in auditing and controlling his client's books. Incidentally, the hiring of a certified public accountant from the outside is likely to create suspicion and antagonism in a company which has been trying to build "group loyalty" as an aid in meeting competition.

Although it is true that the people of Japan will probably still unite in the interests of the "national destiny," as they have so often in the past, the fact remains that a great deal of Japanese corporate energy has been generated by competition intentionally created between vertically oriented subsystems. In a corporate system, the accounting department belongs to one subsystem while the finance department belongs to another. Since these two subsystems are often staffed by "amateur" managers who share no professional training, they tend to engage in fierce competition with each other. As a result, many Japanese corporations find it extremely difficult to install and maintain a "checks and balances" situation which is so desirable between the accounting and finance departments in order to develop a proper overall financial strategy.

It is a truism to say that a professional manager does not need to be an expert himself, but he does need to know how to make use of experts in the best interests of his company. Some Japanese managers have acquired this skill in the course of years of experience. Here again, however, the lack of formal education for the systematic development of this type of manager combined with unnecessarily bitter rivalry between "amateur" managers loyal to their own subsystems tend to prevent a Japanese company from enjoying the services of an officer able to coordinate the work of both treasurer and controller and direct overall financial strategy to the best interests of the company.

The lack of experts in accounting and finance is one of which Japanese businessmen are aware, but they seem to feel that the lack can best be filled by the introduction of electronic data processing systems. Only companies, they say, that master this innovation in control technique can survive in tomorrow's business competition. Mitsubishi Heavy Industry, for example, I am told, is inaugurating an off-the-job program to train more than three thousand employees in the use of the computer during the next year. I am not, however, convinced that such programs will always be effective. Japanese management is based on a seniority-oriented, life-time employment system that lays particular emphasis on human relations and individual approaches, whereas efficient control of information and accounting can only be realized by means of a universal system that cuts across differences between divergent human subsystems. Therefore, although a Japanese company may install computers without any difficulty, they will probably not be used efficiently until the company effects a wholesale reorganization, creating a trinity of controls of information, accounting, and management. Because of the nature of Japanese society, such reorganizations will almost certaintly not be easily effected, yet unless they are, the modern electronic computer will be of little more use to the company than its old-fashioned abacus.

In evaluating the relationship between Japanese management as it is today and the various environmental factors that have produced it, one must consider first of all the type of education to which Japanese managers have been exposed. As I have indicated, the Japanese have always preferred a "humanistic" to a professional education, even in so special a field as that of business management, and such managerial candidates have filled the social requirements for orderly progress in the Japanese establishment. Business itself acquiesced in this preference for a static social world by adopting the seniority-oriented, permanent-employment system that still characterizes it. Most recently, however, pressures exerted by the enlargement of the corporate structure and the swift progress of technological innovation have given rise to new demands for professionally trained managers not only on the functional level, where expert skills are essential, but also on the top management level. These new demands are keenly felt in both the finance and accounting departments, where the introduction of MIS and EDP systems has necessitated a corresponding introduction of experts to handle them. The burden on top management increases with the expansion of the corporate scale. Younger, professionally trained managers are often welcomed to replace older "amateurs" on this level simply for reasons of physical endurance.

A second crucial factor is the sociological one. Emphasis on "the greater company of Japan" and on "group loyalties" in competition have given strength to the Japanese industrial complex in its formative stage and also, later on, in its military period. Japan's individually-oriented and relation-conscious approach has always been thought effective in the maintenance of harmony and order within divergent subsystems of the larger establishment. The working theory—the system—which is based on this is embodied and practiced in the rule of exception and in Japan's seniority-oriented, life-time tenure. However, the widening horizon that world business sees before it, in the form of mass-production and mass-marketing, would seem to demand for Japan both a more liberal and a more uniform approach.

The built-in safety mechanisms—the educational meritocracy and the top-level cross-fertilization—that vitalized Japan's static institutions have lost their magic. What Japan requires now, to replace them, is a group of aggressive, professionally trained managers of the kind familiar to the West. Here strong subsystem loyalty obstructs, rather than promotes, the adoption of a mechanical, overall system for control and coordination. What is needed is the rule of uniformity rather than exception, particularly in the fields of marketing and finance. Only then can distribution be streamlined and terms of collection for accounts receivable be shortened, at the same time accelerating the economy of corporate activities. The tendency to grant a higher status to people in production than in marketing will linger for a time, but that too will, I believe, fade away with the growth of mass-marketing of consumer products.

Still another critical factor is the role of government in the shaping of Japanese business. Here one must consider political as well as legal aspects; and whether or not business *ought* to depend on government initiative, the fact remains that the Japanese government wields tremendous power over Japanese business and can either facilitate its progress or impede it.

For one thing, it has been the Ministry of Education that has molded university systems so as to supply the type of human resources the government desired. Just as it has guided business in the past by inaugurating an educational meritocracy and by facilitating top-ranking cross-fertilization, it can exert a further profound effect on business if it decides to endorse and encourage the development of professional schools of business. This, however, will be a most unlikely event until current student unrest quietens down; any positive move in that direction could provoke an overreaction from those opposed to business-university coordination.

Further, as has already been pointed out, it was the Japanese government that determined to transform the country from a feudal to a capitalist economy and that provided business with the ability not only to see the light of day but also to grow. Except for the government, Japanese business could never have reached its current pinnacle. There have also, however, been unfortunate results: over-expanded financing, a bad debt/equity ratio, a disproportionate burden on profit, and high-powered marketing for the sake of merely increasing volume of sales and market share. So long as the Japanese economy continues to grow at anything like its current rate, the existing policy may be effective, but both government and business ought to take cognizance of the fact that in the quieter days which must inevitably come, an over-expanded economy may suffer. I believe that it is the responsibility of business, rather than of government, to anticipate when such a day is likely to come and to prepare for it.

The government may now, however, use its legislative power to pass an act or an amendment to an existing law to effect such necessary changes as the raising of salaries for executives and the tightening of controls so that corporate books and accounts are audited by experts. Furthermore, the government could make plans for the improvement of Japan's distribution system and allocate funds to implement the plans, thus offering material assistance to businessmen eager to streamline the existing distribution system in order to meet competition from abroad.

I have long argued that mere scale of business will not enable Japanese enterprises successfully to meet competition from foreign giants. I was much heartened, therefore, to read in the 1968 Economic White Paper, that the government was, for the first time, emphasizing business's need to improve "overall managerial efficiency" and was taking into consideration its interrelationship with various environmental factors.

There is something to be said on both sides of the question as to whether the Japanese market is overdeveloped or underdeveloped, but there is no doubt that the weak financial position of both channelers and consumers is largely responsible for two serious defects in the economic structure: the inefficient variety of distribution channels and the long terms allowed for payment of accounts receivable. In the production area also, the dual economic structure —with the gigantic assemblies on the one hand and on the other the minor part and component makers and the raw material supply subcontractors—has created a number of problems, one of the most serious of which is the low percentage of added value in the Japanese price structure. As the per capita gross national product rises, standards of the lower section of the dual structure may also rise. It must, however, be noted that these problems are aggravated by the government's promotion of a policy of high-powered economic growth centered around big business, and the problems are likely to remain as restraining factors for some time to come.

Thus it may be seen that many factors go toward the shaping of Japanese management and that most of these factors are inter-related. Further, in order to effect any profound change, most need to be reexamined—although not necessarily discarded. Group loyalty, for example, is a highly commendable trait, but it ought to be severed from unnecessary inter-group rivalry; life-time employment has also contributed much to the growth of the Japanese economy and may contribute more, but the seniority system should be replaced by one based on promotion by merit.

Assuming that the character of Japanese business is beginning to approach more nearly toward that of its American counterpart, one may wonder what aspects are likely to be the first to change. In my opinion, education is the place to begin. If Japan's future leaders are given a wider perspective and if, at the same time, they acquire professional skills, they can become a very effective spearhead to launch the attack in other areas. Business should take the lead in the initial reformation, as—in my opinion—it ought to begin to make positive approaches to political, economic, and legal problems that in the past it has left to the government. This may have been wise, and even practical, at times when government control was strong, but now, particularly with the expanding scope of liberalization, Japan is moving from a controlled economy to a free economy. The responsibility of the private sector must, therefore, inevitably increase.

I should like to note some current attitudes among Japanese businessmen by referring to the awareness survey of which I spoke at the beginning of this chapter. First, on the supremely important question of Japan's international competitive strength, leaders of business may be divided into three distinct groups. One expressed confidence that Japan can compete successfully against her foreign counterparts with present managerial resources and capabilities; the second, more prudently, asserted that successful competition was possible if Japan had more time in which to prepare for it; while the third group stated blankly—and pessimistically—that Japan could not possibly compete against foreign competition.

Going now into more detail, business leaders in the first category expressed their confidence in the Japanese economy in the following order: overall managerial efficiency, marketing ability, research and development ability, top management ability, capital strength, skill of employees, quality of products, percentage of indirect cost in the total cost structure, and product pricing. In the second group, the emphasis was somewhat different. First came confidence in the quality of the products; this was followed by top management ability, product pricing, skill of employees, research and development ability, marketing ability, capital structure, percentage of indirect cost, and lastly overall managerial efficiency. To me it seems illogical to list overall managerial efficiency first if you are going to put product quality and pricing at the bottom of the list. I would therefore tend to side with the second group, for I think they have shown some harder and clearer thinking.

As a result of the replies we received, we gave somewhat arbitrary names to four distinct and partly opposing types of businessmen: the strategist as against the administrator and the independent innovator as against the policy-dependent type. The administrator and policy-dependent type have answers to almost everything, and the answers sound as though they were taken from management text books. These men expressed interest in scientific approaches to administration of personnel, adoption of MIS, and problems of organization and wholesaling.

Many of those whom we placed in the "strategist-independent innovator" group expressed extremely conservative and traditional points of view. It was their belief that human beings were more important than organization; they preferred the abacus to the computer; and they felt that training of personnel should be accomplished through practical work experience rather than through formal programs.

To the question, "Do you always have available capital to invest?" it is interesting to note that the strategist-independent innovator answered "yes" while the other group answered "no." Does this mean, then, that in Japan a positive strategist type has a practical advantage over the administrator type? Is there a connection between the affirmative answers to this question and the positivist group that expressed its confidence in Japan's international competitive strength?

Japanese managers in general take a forward-looking stance toward the kinds of managerial reform that they can initiate and carry through themselves within their own enterprises. They say that they are interested in, and working toward, the establishment of MIS, the introduction of EDP systems, the expansion of intra-company training programs, the promotion by merit system, the improvement of the debt/equity ratio, an increase in investment for research and development, the development of new products, and the improvement of welfare facilities. These businessmen appear to be particularly eager to use the introduction of the EDP systems, merit promotion systems, improvement of debt/equity ratio, and the development of new products as instruments to push forward strategic operations. However, the same men take a passive attitude in dealing with such problems as the current labor shortage, labor union policies, rationalization of distribution, expansion of production facilities, strengthening of subcontractors, and the reorganization of industries. Here they say that they are content to wait either for the government to act or for the social environment to change.

Further, there was a general indication among businessmen who replied to the questionnaire that they intended to rely on government help to solve certain managerial problems of a type that the managers themselves ought to have handled within their own enterprises. These problems included rationalization of management functions, abolition of uneconomical divisions, and reduction of production schedules.

A curious dualism appeared in the answers to questions about future problem-solving. All the businessmen who replied expressed keen interest in tomorrow's problems, such as changes in the consumer structure or in employees' attitudes, shortage of social overhead capital, and government intervention in the formulation of industrial policy. The way they think about these problems, however, is nothing like the more concrete manner in which they face the importance of establishing MIS, increasing research and development investment to meet the challenge arising from the product-development race, the progress of technical innovation, and the spreading use of computers.

Much to our regret, we were unable to chart the future direction of such important and essential changes that might result from a reexamination of the executive function. One final fact that emerged from the survey is that most Japanese managers think of corporate merger as a defensive rather than an offensive operation.

An analysis of the survey reveals that some businessmen, although aware of the problems that may well confront them in the immediate future, had difficulty meeting and solving the problem within the same conceptual framework. Unless Japan consciously tries to close this gap, unless she makes a serious effort to correlate awareness with action, she will not be able to meet the severe international competition of the future.

There was serious disagreement between the strategist and the administrator type of businessman when it came to determining means of meeting competition. But an administrator cannot maintain his leadership in our dynamically changing world unless he is equipped with some positive strategy; at the same time, the strategist without a scientific approach will find it extremely difficult to control his business operations, which are—or ought to be—expanding day by day. Thus, Japan, if she is to continue growing, must find the middle road between the two extremes that is best suited to her environment and temperament.

Japanese businessmen are eager in their search for new tools and ideas of management control, and they are quick to utilize them. However, when in the course of their application of such tools to concrete situations, they are faced with practical constraints—educational, sociological, political, legal, or economic—they tend to avoid trying to solve the basic issue and merely go on looking for some use for the new tools. Such an evasive attitude could be disastrous for the Japanese businessman who hopes to live in today's dynamically changing environment, both domestic and foreign. It is particularly disheartening that the Japanese executive, when he attempts to answer the problems of tomorrow, seems to rely more and more on either governmental policy or unexpectedly beneficent changes in environment. He ought to be totally aware that since environment influences management, management by the same token can change and affect environment. The Japanese executive must free himself from his traditional ways of thought that result in excessive reliance on government policy; he must find the will and the courage to venture into the new industrial age, at the same time doing his best to change and remold the environment in which he lives and works to the best interests of his company.

NOTES

[1] Basil Hall Chamberlain, *Things Japanese* (London & Tokyo: Kegan Paul & Trench, 1890).

[2] *Asia Scene*, August, 1967.

[3] Ralph Hewins, *The Japanese Miracle Men* (London, 1967).

[4] Jean Lequiller, "Japanese History of the Twentieth Century," *Le Japon* (Paris: Editions Sirly, 1966).

[5] Roy Miller, *The Japanese Language* (1967).

[6] Daniel L. Spencer, "An External Military Presence, Technological Transfer and Structural Change," *Kyklos*, XVIII (1965), fasc. 3.

[7] Regulation for Transfer of Factories (1880).

[8] Prof. W. Kanno, *Nihon Shogyo-shi* (Tokyo, 1930).

[9] Charles David Sheldon, *The Rise of the Merchant Class in Tokugawa Japan* (Locust Valley, New York: J. J. Augustin Inc., 1958).

[10] *Ibid.*

[11] Englebert Kaempfer, *History of Japan 1690–92* (Glasgow, 1906).

[12] Jean Lequiller, *op. cit.*

[13] Ralph Hewins, *op. cit.*

[14] For a detailed account, see T. F. M. Adams, *A Financial History of Modern Japan* (Tokyo, 1965).

[15] *Asahi Evening News*, December 4, 1967.

[16] The top hundred have over four thousand affiliates, to which must be added twenty-five affiliated banks.

[17] *Management Japan*, May 15, 1967.

[18] *Asahi Evening News*, September 25, 1967.

[19] A typical clause that Japanese authorities like to insert in foreign joint-venture agreements is: "The [joint venture] New Company shall be managed with full consideration of the commercial and management customs of Japan."

[20] *Op. cit.*

[21] *Mainichi*, December 17, 1967.

[22] William Craig, *The Fall of Japan* (New York: The Dial Press, 1967).

[23] *Transactions of the Asiatic Society of Japan*, X, Third Series (Tokyo, 1968).

[24] Iwao Hoshii, *The Economic Challenge to Japan* (Tokyo, 1964).

[25] *The Japan Times*, September 7, 1968.

[26] T. F. M. Adams, "The Special Shareholder," *Investor's Chronicle* (London: June 14, 1968).

[27] *Asahi Shimbun*, January 28, 1968.

[28] *The East*, III (Tokyo: The East Publications Inc., 1967).

[29] "Consider Japan," *The Economist* (London, 1963).

[30] David and Evelyn Thompson Riesman, *Conversations in Japan* (New York: Basic Books, 1967).

[31] "Consider Japan," *op. cit.*

[32] *Shipping and Trade News*, October 28, 1967.

[33] *Japan Labor Bulletin* (The Japan Institute of Labor), VI, No. 12, December, 1967.

[34] Peter F. Drucker, *The Effective Executive* (New York: Harper & Row, 1967).

[35] *Japan Labor Bulletin* (The Japan Institute of Labor), VI, No. 10, October, 1967.

[36] *Asahi Evening News*, December 4, 1967.

[37] *Asia Scene*, November, 1967.

[38] *Mainichi Daily News*, February 26, 1969.

[39] AFOSR 533–67 (Washington, D. C.: Howard University, 1967).

[40] *Asahi Shimbun*, Advertising Dept., August, 1964.

[41] *Philosophy and Culture East and West* (Honolulu: University of Hawaii Press, 1960).

[42] *The Japan Times*, October 19, 1967.

[43] *Reader's Digest*, November, 1967.

[44] The story of Mr. Nohagi's early life is told by himself in *Okaasan* ("Mother"), (Tokyo: Jitsugyo-no-Nihonsha, 1965).

[45] *Shukan Bunshun*, No. 485, September 2, 1968.

[46] Charles David Sheldon, *op. cit.*

[47] Kota Hoketsu, *Watakushi no Rirekisho* ("Autobiography"), (Tokyo: Nihon Keizai Shimbun, 1968).

[48] Accurate figures are difficult to arrive at because many merchant vessels are registered under flags of convenience.

[49] A list of professional consulting firms is available at the American Chamber of Commerce in Tokyo.

[50] Report to the Federation of British Industries in 1961, quoted in *Consider Japan, op. cit.*

[51] Marshall E. Dimock, *The Japanese Technocracy* (New York and Tokyo: Walker/Weatherhill, 1968).

[52] *Ibid.*

[53] *Asia Scene*, August, 1967.

[54] Handel Evans, article in *Marketing* (the official journal of the British Institute of Marketing), March, 1966.

[55] *Mainichi Daily News*, March 2, 1969.

[56] The source of the statistics on Japan is the Japan Publishers' and Editors' Association; for those of other countries, the Statistics Yearbook of the United Nations, 1966. (For the purpose of this table, a daily newspaper is

defined as a publication containing general news and appearing at least four times a week.)

[57] *The Book of Changes* has been published as *The Man of Many Qualities— A Legacy of the I Ching*, (Cambridge, Mass.: Massachusetts Institute of Technology Press, 1968).

[58] *Consider Japan, op. cit.*

[59] Citations are from Norman Macrae, "The Risen Sun," *The Economist*, May 27, 1967, pp. 23–24.

[60] Noritake Kobayashi, *Nihon no Goben Kaisha* ("Joint Ventures in Japan") (Tokyo: Toyo Keizai, 1967), pp. 35–50.

[61] *Gaishi-kei Kigyo ni Kansuru Chosa-hokoku-sho* ("Report on Companies with Foreign Capital"), Ministry of Trade and Industry, September 20, 1968, tables 3–1 and 3–2.

[62] Fujio Yoshida, *Shihon Jiyuka to Gaishi Ho* ("Capital Liberalization and the Foreign Investment Law"), Tokyo: Zaisei Keizai Kohosha, 1967. Of particular interest is the table on p. 331.

[63] *Keiei Rinen to Kigyo Katsudo* ("Management Activities and Corporate Activities"), (CED: 1964).

[64] *Kokusai Keiei Hikaku o Tsujite Mita Keiei Koritsuka no Shomondai* ("Problems concerning the improvement of Management Efficiency based on an International Comparative Study of Management") (Overall Managerial Efficiency Study Group: An Interim Report, 1968).

[65] *Waga Kuni Keieisha no Ishikozo to Keiei Koritsu* ("Structure of Management Awareness and Management Efficiency") (CED: An Interim Report, 1969).

SOURCES FOR TABLES

Table 1: Japanese Economic Planning Agency, Economics Statistics Monthly

Table 2: Fuji Bank Bulletin, January 1969

Table 3: Japanese Economic Planning Agency, Economics Statistics Monthly

Tables 4, 5: From *The Year 2000* by Herman Kahn and Anthony J. Wiener, The Macmillan Company, New York, 1967. Copyright by the Hudson Institute, Inc.

Table 6: Fuji Bank Bulletin, 1969

Table 7: Japanese Economic Planning Agency

Table 8: Japanese Ministry of International Trade and Industry

Table 9: Japanese Economic Planning Agency

Table 10: Estimate as of June 1, 1964, by the Population Research Institute of the Ministry of Welfare

Table 12: Japanese Ministry of International Trade and Industry

Table 11, 13–17: Prepared by N. Kobayashi using MITI and Bank of Japan data.

300

TABLE 1
Gross National Expenditure

(In billions of yen)

Fiscal year	Personal consumption expenditure	Gross private domestic capital formation				Surplus of the nation on current account	Government purchases of goods and services		Total gross national expenditure
		Subtotal	Private residential construction	Producers' durable equipment	Increase in business inventories		Subtotal	Capital formation	
1952........	4,009.7	1,089.4	175.2	697.8	216.4	△ 1.5	1,139.1	459.5	6,236.8
1953........	4,759.4	1,299.7	217.8	865.3	216.6	△ 122.1	1,406.8	589.6	7,343.7
1954........	5,167.8	1,196.8	249.3	790.0	157.5	29.9	1,440.2	583.5	7,834.7
1955........	5,553.0	1,526.0	258.4	944.1	323.6	89.7	1,616.3	713.7	8,785.0
1956........	6,006.1	2,380.4	318.4	1,486.2	575.8	△ 125.0	1,630.9	685.5	9,892.4
1957........	6,569.1	2,874.4	370.2	1,904.5	599.7	△ 91.1	1,854.0	813.0	11,206.5
1958........	7,023.8	2,273.0	402.9	1,709.5	160.6	166.6	2,054.7	944.4	11,518.2
1959........	7,759.8	3,204.1	500.5	2,220.9	482.7	93.6	2,319.7	1,110.0	13,377.2
1960........	8,774.0	4,548.7	613.8	3,231.5	703.4	11.3	2,712.9	1,315.4	16,046.9
1961........	10,199.6	6,122.0	822.0	4,231.7	1,068.3	△ 356.6	3,342.5	1,716.9	19,307.7
1962........	11,776.6	5,289.9	952.1	4,105.3	232.5	6.9	4,116.3	2,185.1	21,189.7
1963........	13,615.0	6,708.9	1,225.8	4,388.7	1,094.4	△ 365.9	4,768.1	2,447.8	24,726.2
1964........	15,510.3	7,557.9	1,544.8	5,122.9	890.2	39.9	5,477.6	2,792.9	28,585.7
1965........	17,539.4	6,992.1	1,858.2	4,804.6	329.3	411.8	6,406.0	3,319.9	31,349.2
1966........	19,790.3	9,050.0	2,148.2	5,646.6	1,255.2	415.5	7,405.6	3,896.0	36,661.4
1967........	22,568.4	12,125.5	2,847.7	7,486.1	1,791.7	648.2	8,617.8	4,618.9	43,263.7

TABLE 2
National Accounts

	Fiscal 1967 actual ¥ billion	Fiscal 1968 estimate ¥ billion	Fiscal 1969 forecast ¥ billion	Percentage change on preceding year		
				Fiscal 1967	Fiscal 1968	Fiscal 1969
Personal consumption expenditure	22,568.4	26,050.0	30,000.0	14.0	15.4	15.2
Private capital formation.............	12,127.7	14,050.0	16,950.0	34.0	15.9	20.6
Residential construction	2,847.7	3,650.0	4,600.0	32.6	28.2	26.0
Producers' durable equipment	7,486.1	8,900.0	10,400.0	32.6	18.9	16.8
Change in inventories	1,793.9	1,500.0	1,950.0	42.7	—16.4	30.0
Government expenditure	8,617.8	9,830.0	11,200.0	16.4	14.1	13.9
Current expenditure	3,998.9	4,620.0	5,300.0	13.9	15.5	14.7
Capital expenditure	4,618.9	5,210.0	5,900.0	18.6	12.8	13.2
Surplus on current account	—48.4	450.0	288.0			
Exports & income from overseas ...	4,616.7	5,637.7	6,390.0	8.7	22.1	13.3
Imports & payments to overseas	4,665.1	5,187.6	6,102.0	21.8	11.2	17.6
Gross national product.............	43,265.5	50,380.0	58,438.0	18.0	16.4	16.0
Real rate of growth				13.2	11.6	11.4
Price changes						
Rate of increase in consumer prices (cities)				4.1	6.0	5.0
Rate of increase in wholesale prices				1.5	0.8	1.5
Rate of increase in mining & manufacturing production				18.7	16.5	16.5

TABLE 3
Personal Income and Distribution

(In billions of yen)

Fiscal year	Personal income				Personal expenditure		
	Compensation of employees	Proprietors' income	Personal property income	Total	Taxes & public charges	Personal consumption expenditure	Personal savings
1952	2,432.1	2,129.4	222.0	4,968.3	320.4	4,009.7	455.9
1953	2,909.3	2,175.2	307.5	5,604.9	349.2	4,759.4	283.7
1954	3,201.3	2,365.1	365.1	6,272.5	348.6	5,167.8	511.3
1955	3,505.9	2,723.0	477.9	7,061.4	367.1	5,553.0	866.7
1956	4,017.2	2,738.9	551.9	7,672.7	401.9	6,006.1	948.8
1957	4,487.4	2,882.7	666.1	8,429.5	356.8	6,569.1	1,134.1
1958	4,936.6	2,833.4	784.9	8,992.8	367.1	7,023.8	1,197.4
1959	5,524.1	3,026.0	986.6	10,046.2	391.9	7,759.8	1,431.5
1960	6,483.0	3,467.8	1,207.2	11,739.4	519.5	8,774.0	1,877.0
1961	7,793.6	3,920.6	1,475.2	13,876.8	661.0	10,199.6	2,306.7
1962	9,155.5	4,259.5	1,737.5	15,950.4	830.5	11,776.6	2,492.3
1963	10,697.5	4,857.6	2,028.8	18,552.4	1,000.7	13,615.0	2,907.7
1964	12,407.5	5,395.0	2,373.9	21,325.1	1,192.2	15,510.3	3,387.8
1965	14,284.7	5,805.1	2,737.4	24,190.0	1,411.2	17,539.4	3,693.2
1966	16,413.6	6,518.7	3,154.6	27,667.8	1,582.9	19,790.3	4,473.5
1967	19,064.7	7,702.1	3,651.0	32,236.6	1,869.8	22,568.4	5,720.2

TABLE 4
GNP, Ten Major Countries
(Billion 1965 U.S. Dollars)

	GROWTH RATES	1965	1975	GNP 1985	2000	2020
United States.............	2.0	692.3[2]	844	1,028	1,384	2,060
	4.5		1,075	1,669	3,231	7,790
	5.5		1,183	2,020	4,510	13,200
U.S.S.R.	2.0	297.0	362	441	594	883
	5.0		484	788	1,640	4,350
	7.0		584	1,150	3,170	12,300
West Germany	3.0	112.4	151	203	316	571
(including	4.5		175	271	525	1,260
W. Berlin)	5.5		192	328	732	2,140
United Kingdom	2.0	98.5[2]	120	146	197	293
	4.0		146	216	389	852
	5.0		160	261	543	1,440
France	3.0	94.1	126	170	265	480
	4.5		146	227	439	1,060
	5.5		161	275	613	1,790
Japan	5.0	84.0	137	223	463	1,230
	7.5		173	356	1,056	4,480
	9.0 & 7.5[1]		199	471	1,393	5,920
China	3.0	60.0	83	113	169	305
	5.0	74.0	121	196	408	1,080
	7.0	90.0	177	348	961	3,720
Italy	3.0	56.8	77	103	160	290
	4.5		88	137	265	639
	5.5		97	166	370	1,808
Canada	3.0	48.3	65	87	136	245
	5.0		79	128	266	707
	6.0		86	155	371	1,190
India	2.0	48.3	59	72	97	134
	5.0		79	128	266	707
	6.0		86	155	371	1,190

[1]Declining population growth rate after 1985 should cause a reduction in maximum GNP growth rate from 9.0 (for 1965–85) to 7.5 per cent.

[2]United Nations definition—see source note below.

NOTE: The 1975 and 1985 lower forecasts for U.K., China, and India have been adjusted to provide a constant rate of change in GNP per capita.

TABLE 5
GNP Per Capita, Ten Major Countries
(1965 U.S. Dollars)

	1965	1975	1985	2000	2020
United States	3,557	3,860	4,180	4,760	5,560
		4,850	6,510	10,160	18,600
		5,140	7,380	12,480	26,300
Canada	2,464	2,800	3,240	4,040	5,330
		3,360	4,550	7,070	12,600
		3,550	5,160	8,670	17,500
France	1,924	2,380	3,050	4,480	7,470
		2,710	3,920	6,830	14,300
		2,950	4,660	9,070	22,100
West Germany	1,905	2,510	3,310	5,150	9,360
(including		2,850	4,230	7,790	17,600
W. Berlin)		3,100	5,030	10,410	27,400
United Kingdom	1,804	2,180	2,650	3,570	5,320
		2,580	3,750	6,530	13,500
		2,790	4,380	8,440	20,300
U.S.S.R.	1,288	1,410	1,560	1,880	2,450
		1,850	2,660	4,650	9,660
		2,130	3,590	7,890	22,700
Italy	1,101	1,450	1,920	2,940	5,070
		1,620	2,440	4,450	9,830
		1,770	2,910	5,930	15,400
Japan	857	1,310	2,010	3,990	10,200
		1,620	3,080	8,590	33,200
		1,810	3,820	10,000	35,900
India	99	95	91	86	79
		128	169	270	552
		143	216	406	1,020
China	75	82	91	106	127
	98	134	186	321	681
	129	223	399	969	3,210

SOURCE: Low GNP was divided by low population, high GNP by high population, except for China and India where low was divided by high and high by low. For these two less-developed countries it was assumed that the magnitude of their population worked against economic growth rather than in favor of economic growth, as in the case of the developed nations. The low forecasts for the U.K., China, and India in 1975 and 1985 were adjusted to make a constant rate of growth in per capita GNP.

TABLE 6
Gross National Product

(Unit: ¥1 tril., 1960 value)

	fiscal 1965	fiscal 1966 est.	fiscal 1971 est.	av. growth rate	
				'71/'66	'71/'65
Gross National Product	24.66	27.05	40.20	8.2	8.5
Personal consumptive spending	13.38	14.43	20.13	6.9	7.0
Gov't purchase of goods, services	1.91	1.98	2.49	4.7	4.6
Private equipment investment	4.51	4.89	7.77	9.7	9.5
Private housing investment	1.26	1.38	2.47	12.3	11.8
Gov't fixed capital formation	2.51	2.81	4.67	10.7	10.9
Exports, other revenue from abroad	3.80	4.37	7.20	10.5	11.2
(deduction) Imports, other payments abroad	3.22	3.72	5.77	9.2	10.2

TABLE 7
Ownership of Durable Consumer Goods in Japan
(By individual household, in percentage)

	Urban areas		Rural areas	
ITEM	1966	1967	1966	1967
Sewing machines	80.1	82.1	65.2	80.8
Cameras	59.7	63.9	31.1	38.7
Television sets	94.6	96.7	94.1	94.9
Electric washing machines	77.7	81.3	68.6	75.7
Refrigerators	69.4	76.9	36.6	49.3
Vacuum cleaners.......................	49.2	56.1	15.6	21.9
Electric fans	73.3	75.5	41.8	50.6

TABLE 8

Estimated Shipments by Industry

Unit: ¥1 billion

	1965	% share	1975	% share	1985	% share	Rate of growth 1965–1975	Rate of growth 1975–1985
Total	29,497.1	(100.0)	80,000	(100.0)	160,000	(100.0)	10.5%	7.2%
Food	3,697.8	(12.3)	9,050	(11.3)	16,460	(10.3)	9.4	6.2
Fibers	2,602.3	(8.8)	4,320	(5.4)	6,110	(3.8)	5.2	3.6
Textile products	441.0	(1.5)	1,150	(1.4)	2,290	(1.4)	10.1	7.1
Lumber & wooden products	1,057.2	(3.6)	2,420	(3.0)	3,900	(2.4)	8.6	4.8
Furniture & fixtures	402.1	(1.4)	1,300	(1.6)	3,020	(1.9)	12.5	8.8
Pulp, paper & paper products	1,117.8	(3.8)	2,880	(3.6)	5,530	(3.5)	10.0	6.7
Publishing, printing	915.4	(3.1)	2,480	(3.1)	4,720	(3.0)	10.5	6.6
Chemicals	2,800.6	(9.5)	8,560	(10.7)	19,250	(12.0)	11.8	8.4
Petroleum & coal products	826.5	(2.8)	2,160	(2.7)	4,120	(2.6)	10.1	6.7
Rubber products	376.8	(1.3)	960	(1.2)	1,940	(1.2)	9.8	7.3
Leather & leather products	175.2	(0.6)	480	(0.6)	1,150	(0.7)	10.0	9.2
Stone, clay & glass	1,047.5	(3.6)	3,720	(3.4)	5,220	(3.3)	10.0	6.7
Iron & steel	2,691.1	(9.1)	6,640	(8.3)	11,120	(7.0)	9.5	5.3
Non-ferrous metals	1,162.5	(3.9)	2,960	(3.7)	5,950	(3.7)	9.8	7.2
Machinery	7,829.1	(26.6)	22,640	(28.3)	48,770	(30.4)	11.2	8.1
Other mfg. ind.	975.5	(3.3)	3,680	(4.6)	8,180	(5.1)	14.2	8.3
Metal products	1,373.1	(4.7)	5,600	(7.0)	12,270	(7.7)	15.1	8.2

TABLE 9

Economic Projection by Area

Unit: Population–1,000
Income from production–¥1 billion

Area	1965 Population	1965 Income from production	1985 (a) Population	1985 (a) Income from production	1985 (b) Population	1985 (b) Income from production
Hokkaido......	5,170	1,134	4,700	4,400	6,300	5,800
Tohoku	11,510	2,236	9,700	7,700	11,000	9,600
Tokyo Metropolitan area	26,960	8,002	40,500	50,000	38,500	42,800
Chubu	16,490	4,002	22,500	23,000	20,500	22,000
Kinki	18,040	5,282	26,000	28,500	24,500	26,600
Chugoku & Shikoku	10,850	2,423	9,800	8,300	11,000	10,800
Kyushu	12,370	2,382	11,000	8,000	12,000	10,900

NOTES: 1. (a) Calculations based on the assumption that the trend toward concentration prevailing in the period from 1955 to 1965 will continue.

(b) Calculations based on the assumption that the new National Development Plan will effect a decentralization of growth.

2. At 1965 prices

3. Tohoku: Aomori, Iwate, Miyagi, Akita, Yamagata and Fukushima prefectures.

Tokyo Metropolitan area: Tokyo, Kanagawa, Chiba, Saitama, Tochigi, Ibaragi and Gunma prefectures.

Chubu: Niigata, Toyama, Ishikawa, Fukui, Yamanashi, Nagano, Gifu, Shizuoka and Aichi prefectures.

Kinki: Mie, Shiga, Kyoto, Osaka, Hyogo, Nara and Wakayama prefectures.

Chugoku and Shikoku: Tottori, Shimane, Okayama, Hiroshima, Yamaguchi, Tokushima, Kagawa, Ehime and Kochi prefectures.

TABLE 10

Estimated Population Trend

Unit: 1,000

	Total	0–14	15–59	60 up
1955 (census) ...	89,276	29,798	52,233	7,244
1960 (census) ...	93,884	28,012	57,582	8,290
1965 (census) ...	98,275	25,166	63,583	9,525
1970	103,327	23,810	68,424	11,092
1975	108,635	24,620	71,039	12,976
1980	113,265	25,087	73,502	14,676
1985	116,458	24,335	75,379	16,744
1990	118,619	22,722	76,342	19,555
1995	120,225	21,545	76,210	22,470
2000	121,353	21,362	75,025	24,966
2005	121,698	21,481	72,615	27,602
2010	120,817	21,124	68,867	30,826
2015	119,015	20,226	67,118	31,671

Note: Estimate as of June 1, 1964, by the Population Research Institute of the Ministry of Welfare.

TABLE 11

Foreign Stock Acquisition: Shareholding Percentage

	Number of Companies	Share Holding Percentage of Foreign Investors					
		$x = 100\%$	$100\% \rangle x \rangle 50\%$	$x = 50\%$	$50\% \rangle x \rangle 30\%$	$30\% \rangle x \rangle 15\%$	$15\% \rangle x$
1950~1953	70	4	17	15	8	8	18
1954	6	1		1	2	1	1
1955	2				1		1
1956	5		1		1	2	1
1957	7			1	2	2	2
1958	1					1	
1959	10		1	1	3	3	2
1960	12	1		3	6	2	
1961	19			3	13	3	
1962	22			1	15	3	3
1963	53	2		10	33	7	1
1964	77	8	3	18	39	9	
1965	69	14	3	18	29	3	2
1966	78	12	8	23	28	6	1
1967	93	16	9	23	29	10	6
Total	524	58	42	117	209	60	38

TABLE 12
Number of Validations of Joint Ventures

Fiscal year	Manufacturing					Non-Manufacturing					Total				
	Total	Foreign share				Total	Foreign share				Total	Foreign share			
		under 25%	under 50%	50%	over 50%		under 25%	under 50%	50%	over 50%		under 25%	under 50%	50%	over 50%
1950–1963....	170 (54)	34 (30)	96 (15)	29 (6)	11 (3)	27 (9)	4 (4)	8 (2)	2 (–)	13 (3)	197 (63)	38 (34)	104 (17)	31 (6)	24 (6)
1964..........	38 (13)	2 (1)	28 (9)	8 (3)	– (–)	26 (9)	1 (1)	12 (6)	6 (2)	7 (3)	64 (24)	3 (2)	40 (14)	14 (5)	7 (3)
1965..........	34 (13)	4 (4)	21 (7)	8 (1)	1 (1)	24 (4)	– (–)	6 (5)	8 (1)	10 (3)	58 (17)	4 (4)	27 (10)	16 (2)	11 (3)
1966..........	41 (12)	3 (3)	20 (7)	17 (1)	1 (1)	30 (5)	3 (3)	9 (3)	6 (1)	12 (–)	71 (17)	6 (6)	29 (8)	23 (2)	13 (1)
1950–1966.....	283 (92)	43 (38)	165 (38)	62 (11)	13 (5)	107 (29)	8 (8)	35 (11)	22 (3)	42 (7)	390 (121)	51 (46)	200 (49)	84 (14)	55 (12)

Note: Figures in parentheses indicate acquisition of shares of existing enterprises.

310

TABLE 13

Induction of Foreign Capital

Induction of Foreign Capital (Unit: $1,000)

Fiscal Year	Technological Assistance: Number of Contracts	Participation in Management	Acquisition of Shares of Stock: Acquired on Market	Other	Sub-total	Corporate Debentures	Beneficiary Certificates	Loans	Foreign Bonds	Total	Number of Joint Ventures Formed[3]
1950...	27	2,572	—	578	3,150	—	—	—	—	8,150	22
1951...	101	11,646	1,560	119	13,326	—	—	4,026	—	17,352	23
1952...	133	7,166	2,106	851	10,123	25	146	34,457	—	44,751	16
1953...	103	2,687	1,205	1,110	5,002	—	562	49,362	—	54,926	9
1954...	82	2,467	1,268	235	3,970	—	58	15,279	—	19,307	6
1955...	72	2,309	1,527	1,265	5,101	7	52	47,054	—	52,214	2
1956...	144	5,360	3,155	1,005	9,520	15	115	93,652	—	103,302	5
1957...	118	7,282	3,297	911	11,490	—	128	123,979	—	135,597	7
1958...	90	3,698	5,133	2,519	11,350	28	116	231,473	30,000	272,967	1
1959...	153	14,561	9,550	2,920	27,031	30	214	127,615	—	154,890	10
1960...	327	31,593	21,960	20,598	74,151	20	555	127,132	9,800	211,658	12
1961...	320	40,170	55,848	20,124	116,192	77	1,280	387,605	72,425	577,529	19
1962...	328	22,618	91,850	50,200	164,668	86	650	358,419	155,000	678,824	22
1963...	564	42,656	91,185	51,420	185,262	247	798	503,954	194,050	884,302	53(10)[2]
1964...	500	30,644	42,635	11,566	84,846	851	1,828	650,760	174,500	912,785	77(13)[2]
1965...	472	44,643	33,347	5,341	83,331	2,726	398	379,551	62,500	528,506	69(11)[2]
1966...	601	39,812	68,901	18,021	126,735	261	390	329,711	—	457,097	78(10)[2]
1967...	638	29,777	126,981	3,163	159,834	123	284	637,544	50,000	847,785	87(12)[4]
1968...	782	41,178	396,165	7,810	445,553	31	159	673,648	143,980	1,263,371	?
TOTAL	5,555	382,840	957,585	199,758	1,540,583	4,526	7,591	4,775,212	892,255	7,220,311	518(56)[2]
1/1	5.3(25.2)[1]	13(61.9)[1]	2.8(13.3)[1]		21(100)[1]	0.06	0.1	66.1	12.4	100	

[1] Figures represent percentages to total share acquisition.

[2] Number of new share issues by Yen base companies.

[3] Numbers include not only companies newly established but also companies which recently issued shares or where existing shares are acquired by foreign investors.

[4] Includes cases where foreign investors acquired shares with Yen funds.

TABLE 14 *Direct Investment: Distribution by Country*

	1949~1961		1962		1963		
	Number	Amount	Number	Amount	Number	Amount	Number
U.S.A.	211	92,713	27	13,011	59	32,611	90
Canada	7	6,629	—	—	1	14	3
U.K.	34	8,287	4	7,313	2	2,361	7
West Germany	11	2,335	1	189	2	364	3
France	5	939	2	72	1	22	—
Switzerland	3	386	4	844	24	4,811	17
Netherlands	5	1,777	1	833	1	1,875	—
Denmark	1	17	—	—	—	—	—
Belgium	—	—	1	56	—	—	—
Hong Kong	4	255	—	—	—	—	—
Panama	9	3,448	—	—	1	590	—
Venezuela	5	701	3	301	—	—	1
Saudi Arabia ...	1	6,945	—	—	—	—	—
Kuwait	1	6,945	—	—	—	—	—
Rep. of China	1	75	—	—	—	—	—
India	4	7	—	—	—	—	—
Thailand	—	—	—	—	—	—	1
Australia	—	—	—	—	—	—	2
Others	1	55	—	—	1	7	1
Japan	—	—	—	—	—	—	—
Total	303	131,511	43	22,618	92	42,656	125

TABLE 15 *Direct Investment: Distribution by Industries*

	1950–1961		1962		1963		
	No. of validations	Validated Amount	Number	Investments	Number	Investments	Number
Machinery	118	23,200	23	6,512	34	7,621	4
Metal	13	11,715	1	56	5	1,277	
Chemical	57	32,424	13	8,473	14	11,137	2
Textile .	9	896	1	229	13	103	
Petroleum	26	45,855	1	5,555	3	18,236	
Rubber and Leather	16	11,376	4	1,794	1	667	
Construction	6	297	—	—	1	22	—
Glass & Cement	10	3,168	—			—	
Transportation and Communication	15	451	—	—	—	—	—
Warehouse	1	6	—	—	—	—	—
Commerce & Foreign Trade ...	24	.. 1,727	—	—	8	150	2
Service Industries	4	250	—	—	1	14	
Others	4	152	—	—	12	3,429	1
TOTAL	303	131,511	43	22,618	92	42,656	12

[1]1967 figures include direct investment by yen funds. Other figures represent on
[2]Data on amounts by industries are not available
[3]Categories of validated industries are not known
[4]+indicates necessary adjustment by adding figures for 1967.

unt	1965		1966		1967		Total	
	Number	Amount	Number	Amount	Number	Amount	Number	Amount
49	70	30,363	77	20,718	111	20,036	645	230,484
64	3	690	5	4,073	3	411	22	12,081
95	6	212	6	580	7	558	66	22,307
24	3	53	3	858	18	2,384	51	6,501
—	2	49	1	104	6	1,174	17	2,360
52	10	12,477	23	9,813	11	495	92	34,404
—	—	—	1	1,042	1	4,167	9	9,695
—	—	—	—	—	1	16	2	33
—	1	100	1	37	—	—	3	193
—	1	15	4	627	4	66	13	963
—	1	34	2	592	3	362	16	5,025
59	1	39	—	—	—	—	10	1,110
—	—	—	—	—	—	—	1	6,945
—	—	—	—	—	—	—	1	6,945
—	1	3	—	—	—	—	2	78
—	—	—	—	—	3	37	7	44
7	—	—	—	—	—	—	1	7
1	—	—	2	6	1	1	5	218
57	7	610	6	1,359	9	230	25	2,428
—	—	—	1	1	22	2,250	23	2,251
44	106	44,643	142	39,812	200	32,187	1,011	344,073

est-ts	1965		1966		1967[1]		1968		Total	
	Number	Investments	Number	Investments	Number	Investments	Number	Investments[2]	Number	Investments
35	35	12,148	41	7,798	57	12,102	30		379	81,360[4]
04	5	1,798	6	4,956	17	1,949	2		54	23,453[4]
83	21	8,447	23	9,838	27	9,301	12		188	86,855[4]
91	1	50	1	136	7	774	2		36	2,388[4]
52	4	74,854	2	2,530	6	2,785	—	—	46	94,376
36	1	23	2	1,278	—	—			25	15,275[4]
—	1	139	—	—	—	—	7		8	458[4]
3	2	1,803	5	1,379	4	414			22	+7[8] 6,768[4]
—	4	30	—	—	1	125			20	607[4]
—	—	—	—	—	65	—			1	6
74	14	3,063	36	5,802	3	1,439	40		215	13,354[4]
24	7	159	13	240	13	41			33	828
24	11	2,129	13	5,854	200	3,257	8		78	18,345[4]
44	106	44,643	142	39,812		32,187	101	41,178	1,112	385,251

investments on validated basis.

TABLE 16 *Transition in the Ratios of Capital Composition (in percentages)*

Year	External Capital						Owned capital				Increase-decrease rate of total capital against that of preceding year
	Book debt (including notes payable)	Short-term loans from financial institutions	Long-term loans from financial institutions	Debentures	Others	Total	Capital	Capital surplus	Profit surplus	Total	
1956	27.7	16.8	9.6	2.0	16.6	72.7	10.5	9.7	7.1	27.3	19.6
1957	27.0	18.1	10.0	1.9	17.7	74.7	10.7	6.8	7.8	25.3	30.6
1958	25.5	19.3	11.3	2.0	16.4	74.5	11.5	6.1	7.9	25.5	11.0
1959	26.6	18.2	11.9	2.2	17.3	76.2	10.9	4.9	8.0	23.8	16.7
Fiscal 1960	28.5	17.4	11.9	3.0	16.6	77.4	10.9	3.6	8.1	22.6	36.0
" 1961	28.8	17.0	12.3	3.0	16.6	77.7	11.5	3.1	7.7	22.3	22.2
" 1962	28.4	18.0	12.7	2.8	16.1	78.0	12.1	2.6	7.3	22.0	16.5
" 1963	28.5	17.3	12.8	2.7	18.2 (16.6)	79.5 (77.9)	11.9	2.3	7.3 (7.9)	20.5 (22.1)	16.7
" 1964	29.1	17.6	12.5	2.5	18.6 (17.1)	80.3 (78.8)	11.7	1.9	6.3 (7.9)	19.7 (21.2)	15.8
" 1965	28.2	18.3	13.4	2.5	18.6 (17.2)	81.0 (79.6)	11.3	1.6	6.1 (7.6)	19.0 (20.4)	12.0
" 1966	30.0	17.8	12.9	2.3	18.6 (16.5)	81.6 (81.0)	10.5	1.5	6.4 (7.9)	18.4 (19.9)	14.8

Notes: 1. Percentages for "Profit surplus" after Fiscal 1963 are those after allocations had been made for corporate taxes, etc. Percentages for those before allocations had been made for corporate taxes, etc., are indicated within parentheses.

2. Percentages in "Debentures" are those for fixed liabilities. Percentages in "Others" are those for liquid liabilities to be redeemed within a year.

3. Source: Hojin Kigyo Tokei (Statistics on Corporate Enterprises)

TABLE 17

Weight of Foreign Investment

	Direct Investment (1,000 U.S. dollars)						Foreign Loans (1,000 U.S. dollars)		
	Subsidiaries		Receipt by Branch	Total	Domestic Fund Supply to Industry	A/B	Loans	Increase of Domestic Bank Loans[1]	A/B
	Direct Investment	Loans		(A)	(B)		(A)	(B)	
1951...	11,649			11,649				4,026 (14)[2]	5,231	0.27
1952...	7,166			7,166				34,459 (124)	6,102	2.03
1953...	2,687			2,687				49,362 (178)	5,433	3.28
1954...	2,467			2,467				15,279 (55)	2,406	2.28
1955...	2,309	data unavailable		2,309 (8)[2]	8,437	0.09	47,054 (169)	2,839	6.95
1956...	5,360			5,360 (15)	18,047	0.11	93,652 (337)	8,704	3.89
1957...	7,282			7,282 (26)	16,124	0.16	123,979 (446)	8,474	5.26
1958...	3,698			3,698 (13)	17,297	0.08	231,473 (833)	8,320	10.01
1959...	14,561			14,561 (52)	24,182	0.22	127,615 (459)	10,477	4.38
1960...	31,593			31,593 (114)	36,314	0.31	127,132 (457)	15,288	2.98
1961...	40,170	11,665		51,835 (189)	42,361	0.44	387,605 (1,395)	14,833	9.40
1962...	22,619	40,570		63,189 (227)	50,862	0.45	358,419 (1,290)	23,474	5.49
1963...	42,657	16,775	2,000	61,432 (221)	58,262	0.38	503,945 (1,814)	26,205	6.92
1964...	30,644	17,986	5,193	53,823 (194)	52,555	0.37	650,960 (2,346)	22,635	10.36
1965...	44,643	15,639	9,363	69,645 (251)	51,468	0.49	379,551 (1,365)	23,775	5.75
1966...	39,812	7,081	5,169	52,662 (190)	48,383	0.39	329,711 (1,188)	30,222	3.96

[1] Figures in this column represent 100 million yen
[2] Figures in brackets represent 100 million yen

INDEX/GLOSSARY

Fukuzawa, Yukichi, 117, 122
funds:
    corporate, 184–185
    political; see political
Furukawa (group), 54, 58
futon ("bedding")

gaishi donyu kaisha ("company with inducted foreign capital equity"), 258–259, 261
gaishi-kei kaisha ("company with foreign equity participation"), 258, 262, 263
geisha, 84, 132–133
General Agreement on Trade and Tariffs (GATT), 235, 236
General Electric, 59, 220, 259
General Federation of Trade Unions, 183
General Foods, 194
General Motors Corporation, 238
gift-giving, 208
giri ("duties," "obligations," "responsibilities")
goben kaisha (joint venture"), 258–259, 261;
    see also joint venture
go-between, 73–75, 133, 146
Goto, Keita, 127
government control, 40, 47, 49–50, 55 111–112, 120, 176ff, 216
    over foreign investment, 229ff
    of money flow, 234
government enterprises, 33–34, 39, 54;
    see also public corporations
government protection, 40, 216
    of consumers, 200
    of Oi Securities Co., 66–67
    of oil industry, 169–170
    of Sanyo Special Steel Co., 67
    of small businesses, 195, 197, 217, 250
    of Yamaichi Securities Co., 63ff, 77
gross national product, 161–162, 164, 168, 209, 215–216, 220, 284
group:
    vs. individual, 24, 48, 50, 56, 70, 80, 101, 104, 111, 232, 283, 288, 290, 293

grouping:
    corporate, 53–54, 58–60, 68

harakiri; see seppuku
Harris, Townsend, 29
Hattori, K., & Co., 135
Hayashi, Yuteki, 117
Hector Whaling Company, 137
heimin ("ordinary people"), 37
Heinz, H. J., 194–195
Hitachi, Ltd., 58, 87–88, 106, 135
Hoan-kai ("Peace Preservation Association"), 184
Hoketsu, Kota, 136ff
Honda Motor Co., 56–57
Honda, Soichiro, 45, 120, 127
Honshu Paper Mfg. Co., 234
Hori, Shigeru, 182
Hoshii, Iwao, 72–73, 127, 177
hosho-nin ("responsible person"), 73, 102
household expenditure, 165, 200–201
household income, 96, 200
Hughes Aircraft, 219

Ichimura, K., 112
Idemitsu Kosan K.K., 55, 56–57, 101, 135
Idemitsu, Sazo, 57, 101, 132
identification:
    with one's company, 104, 108, 134–135
Ihara, T., 215
Ikeda, Hayato, 161
Ikeda, Masanosuke, 186
Iketani, Ryohei, 131
Iketani Seisaku-sho K.K., 131
Ikuseikai, 183, 184
Immediate Liberalization Measures, 252
Imperial Army, 33, 37, 45, 72, 119, 139, 232
Imperial Navy, 140
Imperial Palace, 181
Imperial Rescript, 71, 139–140
Imperial University, 137, 179
import:
    amount of, 14, 162
    of raw materials, 168, 170, 172

320

mezurashii ("strange")
middlemen, 189, 191, 197
Miki, T., 184
Million Card Service, 203
Minami, K., 50
Minami, Shunji, 142
Ministry of Agriculture, 136, 217
Ministry of Construction, 181
Ministry of Education, 136, 291
Ministry of Finance, 44, 47, 49, 50,
    66–67, 79, 112, 136, 177, 216,
    217, 218, 237–238, 239, 241,
    243, 247, 248, 249, 254
    Minister of Finance, 64, 69, 142,
        247, 249, 251
Ministry of Home Affairs, 112, 183,
    184
Ministry of International Trade and
    Industry (MITI), 112, 136,
    169, 177, 186–187, 190, 202,
    212, 217, 235, 237, 239, 241,
    243, 247, 248, 249, 250, 252,
    254, 261, 262–263
Ministry of Justice, 78
Ministry of Munitions, 54
Ministry of Public Health and Welfare,
    247
Ministry of Transportation, 112
Minneapolis-Honeywell Regulator
    Company, 264
Minobe, Ryokichi, Governor, 181
MIS system, 290, 294, 295, 296
Mitsubishi (group), 34–35, 36–37, 48,
    55, 58, 59–60, 68, 135, 182
    Caterpillar-Mitsubishi, 269
    Mitsubishi Bank, 47, 64, 67, 182,
        201–202
    Mitsubishi Electric, 219
    Mitsubishi Estate Co., 35, 182,
        199
    Mitsubishi-ga-hara (field), 35, 182
    Mitsubishi Heavy Industry, 289
    Mitsubishi Kinyo-kai, 56
    Mitsubishi Petroleum, 265
    Mitsubishi Shoji, 135, 197, 215
    Mitsubishi Shokai, 34
    Mitsubishi Trust and Banking Co.,
        64
Mitsui (group), 38, 43, 46, 48, 58, 59
    68–69, 108, 134, 135
    Mitsui and Company, 54–55, 68,

    135, 197, 215
Mitsui Bank, 47, 56, 68
Mitsui Chemical Industry Com-
    pany, 69
Mitsui Club, 123
Mitsui Getsuyo-kai, 56
Mitsui Miike Machinery, 69
Mitsui Petrochemical Co., 69
Mitsui Real Estate Company, 68
Mitsui Shipbuilding and Engineer-
    ing Co., 69
Mitsui Trust and Banking Co.,
    66–67
Sewa-nin-kai, 56
Mitsukoshi:
    Mitsukoshi Aigo Kai, 53
    Mitsukoshi Clinic, 53
    Mitsukoshi Department Store, 53,
        209
Mitsumi Denki K.K., 88
mobility:
    in the salaryman class, 104
money:
    printing of, 36
    foreign, 230, 260
monopoly, 62, 234
    monopolistic products, 193
Morinaga caramel package, 199

nakodo ("go-between"), 73, 133
National Bank Regulations, 46
National Cash Register, 259, 266
national income:
    per capita, 164–165, 168, 209, 284,
        293
    "Plan for Doubling National In-
        come," 161, 163
National Tax Administration Agency,
    186
National Tax Bureau, 186
nationalism, 28, 109, 118, 120, 125,
    172, 175, 176, 232
neo-colonialism, 170, 172
Nestlé, 194, 205
newspapers:
    circulation of, 207
Nichiro Fisheries Company, 194–195
Nichiro-Heinz K.K., 194–195
Nielsen, A.C., Company, 200
Nihon Light Metal (ALCAN), 266

323

purge, 140, 144, 179

rate of growth, 161, 164, 215–216
raw materials:
    lack of, 168, 210
    sources of, 168ff, 212
recession, 46, 61, 77, 286
recreation, 163, 165
research and development, 219
responsibility, 45, 60, 68, 70ff, 77, 80,
    85, 105, 115, 119
retailers, 189, 190, 191, 193, 284–285
retirement:
    age, 105–107, 112–113, 114
    allowance, 73, 94, 106, 113, 114,
    136
    job after retirement, 94, 105–107,
    112–113, 114
    of government officials, 135–136,
    186, 242–243
Ricoh, Ltd., 112
ringisho, 80, 81–82, 85–86, 119, 120
Rotary Club, 133

saboru ("sabotage")
Safeway Stores, 195–196
salaryman, 57–58, 86, 88–89, 91ff, 119,
    223
    average age, 201
    placement, 93
    profile, 95ff
salesmen, 39, 121
samurai, 29, 33, 37–40, 42, 46–47, 83,
    117, 191
Sanshu no Jingi ("The Three Sacred
    Treasures")
Sanwa Bank, 38, 66, 201–202
Sanyo Electric Co., 106
Sanyo Special Steel Co., 51, 63, 67, 77,
    78
Sapporo beer can, 199
Sato, Prime Minister, 181–182, 183,
    184
Satsuma Rebellion, 33, 38, 113
savings, 99–100, 104, 200
    clubs, 201
Scenic Beauty Ordinance, 181
School for Foreign Studies, 42
Science and Technology Bureau, 247

Sea and Ski, 205
section chiefs, 87, 88–89, 119
securities companies, 63, 64–65, 66,
    76–77, 79
Seikei Kenkyu-kai, 184
Seisaku Kondan-kai, 184
sekininsha ("responsible person"), 73,
    75
Self-Defense Agency, 185
seniority, 88, 103, 115, 126, 242, 243,
    283, 289–290, 293
seppuku ("self-disembowelment")
shareholders, 49, 53–54, 55, 78, 82ff,
    185, 258, 259, 262, 281, 282
Shibaura Sugar Mfg. Co., 69
Shibusawa, Eiichi, 35–36, 46, 48, 117
Shigemitsu, Aoi, 139
Shinko (group), 58
Shiseido Co., Ltd., 191–192
    Shiseido Hambai Gaisha, 192
    Shiseido Hanatsubaki-kai, 192
    Shiseido Trading Company, 192
    Shiseido wholesale chain, 192
shizoku ("samurai"), 37
Shoda, Heigoro, 35
shogunate, 28–29, 30–31, 32, 38, 40
    Hideyoshi, 122
    Ieyasu, 122
    Yoshinobu, 35
Showa Aircraft Industry, 69
Showa Denko K.K., 185
Showa men, 116, 120–121, 176
Siberia:
    development of, 221–222
Sogo, Shinji, 72
Sohyo, 183
Soka-Gakkai, 183
sokaiya ("shareholders' general meet-
    ing man"), 78, 82ff
Sonno Joi ("Revere the Emperor and
    expel the barbarians"), 31
Sony Corporation, 56–57, 107
Soviet Union:
    trade with, 215, 221–222
stamp system, 192
standard of living, 162, 166, 168, 209
    White Book on the, 96
status, 76–77, 95, 107
stock market, 51, 63
Sumitomo (group), 38, 47, 58, 135
    Sumitomo Bank, 66, 201–202

Sumitomo Credit Service Company, 202
Sumitomo Electric, 265
Sumitomo Hakusui-kai, 56
Sumitomo Trading Co., 195, 197
supermarkets, 195ff, 204

taian ("lucky day"), 25, 26
Taisho men, 116, 118–120, 121, 176
Taisho Pharmaceutical Company, 194
Taito Co., Ltd., 69
Takashimaya Department Store, 209
talent bank, 106–107
Tanaka, Kakuei, 184
taxation, 223
technology:
  military, 120
tegata; *see* deferred payment notes
Teijin Limited, 88
telecommunications:
  cosmic, 219
Tenno, Tenno Heika ("Emperor"), 116
terakoya ("temple school"), 41
textile industry, 234
Thompson, J. Walter, 199
thought processes, 15, 16, 17, 26, 50, 176
Tokai Bank, 66
Tokai Power Station, 220
Tokio Marine and Fire Insurance Co., 126, 180–182
tokushu kabunushi ("special shareholder")
Tokyo Club, 123
Tokyo District Court, 185
Tokyo District Public Prosecutor's Office, 186
Tokyo Higher Court, 185
Tokyo Metropolitan Government, 114, 181, 182
Tokyo Shibaura Electric Co. (Toshiba), 59, 87, 106, 122, 135, 259, 265
Tokyo Stock Exchange, 49, 53, 66, 79
Tokyu, 58, 127
  Tokyu Department Store, 89
tonya ("wholesaler"), 191, 196–197
Toyama medicines, 193, 207–208
Toyo Aluminum, 265
Toyo Boseki K.K. (Toyo Spinning Co.), 36

Toyo Carrier, 265
Toyo Koatsu Industries, 69
Toyo Otis Elevators, 266
Toyo Rayon, 56, 68, 87, 106
Toyota, 58
  Toyota Motor Company, 69, 122, 250
trading companies, 51, 54, 62, 135, 170, 197, 215, 219
traditionalism, 120, 211
training:
  employee training, 86, 87–88, 93, 117–118
  foreign training, 42, 108–109
  language training; *see* language
  vocational training, 282
  of foreign representatives, 156–157
  of Japanese technicians, 220
treaties:
  Japan-U.S. Security Treaty, 71, 175, 214, 222, 223, 255
  Treaty of Portsmouth, 20, 44
  Washington Naval Treaty, 20;
    see GATT *and* IMF
Tsukigase K.K., 131
Tsukumo Trading Company, 34
Tsuruga Power Station, 220

Ultra High Frequency communications, 219
United Nations, 219
university, 240–241, 291
  autonomy, 222
  function, 282, 288
  strife, 222
U.S. Steel Co., 180

values, 23, 50, 165
Victor stereo-phonograph, 122, 124

wa ("harmony")
war:
  China Incident, 20
  First World War, 44
  Korean War, 45
  Manchurian Incident, 138
  Pacific War, 14, 70, 119, 120, 139